Oxford Practice Grammar

Basic

Norman Coe
Mark Harrison
Ken Paterson

OXFORD
UNIVERSITY PRESS

OXFORD
UNIVERSITY PRESS

Great Clarendon Street, Oxford OX2 6DP

Oxford University Press is a department of the University of Oxford.
It furthers the University's objective of excellence in research, scholarship,
and education by publishing worldwide in

Oxford New York

Auckland Cape Town Dar es Salaam Hong Kong Karachi
Kuala Lumpur Madrid Melbourne Mexico City Nairobi
New Delhi Shanghai Taipei Toronto

With offices in

Argentina Austria Brazil Chile Czech Republic France Greece
Guatemala Hungary Italy Japan Poland Portugal Singapore
South Korea Switzerland Thailand Turkey Ukraine Vietnam

OXFORD and OXFORD ENGLISH are registered trade marks of
Oxford University Press in the UK and in certain other countries

First published 2006

2010 2009 2008 2007 2006
10 9 8 7 6 5 4 3 2 1

ISBN-13: 978 0 19 431023 9
ISBN-10: 0 19 431023 X

Illustrated by Ann Johns, Belinda Evans, and Neil Gower
Cover illustration by Joanna Usherwood
Index by Sue Lightfoot

Printed in China

Oxford Practice Grammar
Basic

Contents

		page
	Introduction	IX
	Key to symbols	IX

Tenses: present

1	**Be:** Present Simple (1)	2
2	**Be:** Present Simple (2)	4
3	Present Simple (1)	6
4	Present Simple (2)	8
5	Present Continuous (1)	10
6	Present Continuous (2)	12
7	Present Simple or Present Continuous	14
8	Imperative	16
	Test A	18

Tenses: past

9	**Be:** Past Simple	20
10	Past Simple	22
11	Past Continuous	24
12	Past Simple or Past Continuous	26
13	Present Perfect (1)	28
14	Present Perfect (2)	30
15	Present Perfect (3)	32
16	Past Simple or Present Perfect	34
17	Present Perfect Continuous	36
18	Present Perfect Simple or Continuous	38
19	Past Perfect	40
20	**Used to**	42
	Test B	44

Tenses: future

21	**Be going to**	46
22	**Will** and **shall**	48
23	**Will** or **be going to**	50
24	Present Continuous for the future	52
25	Present tense: **when, before, after, until,** etc.	54
26	Future	56
	Test C	58

Sentences and questions

27	Nouns, verbs, adjectives, etc.	60
28	Word order: subject, verb, object	62
29	'Yes/no' questions	64
30	**Where, when, why, how**	66

31	Who, what, which	68
32	How long/far/often …?	70
33	What … like?	72
34	Who and what: subject and object	74
35	Whose is this? ~ It's John's.	76
36	Question tags	78
37	Short answers	80
38	So am I, I am too, Neither am I, etc.	82
	Test D	84

Modal verbs

39	Ability: can, can't, could, couldn't	86
40	Can/Could I? May I? Can/Could you?	88
41	Must, mustn't	90
42	Have to	92
43	Must/have to, mustn't/don't have to	94
44	Must, can't, may, might, could	96
45	Should, shouldn't	98
46	Should, ought to, had better	100
47	Need, needn't, needn't have	102
48	Had to do/go, should have done/gone	104
	Test E	106

Articles, nouns, pronouns, etc.

49	Articles (1): a, an or the	108
50	Articles (2): a/an, the or no article	110
51	Plural nouns; one and ones	112
52	This, that, these, those	114
53	Countable and uncountable nouns	116
54	A, some, any, no	118
55	I and me (subject and object pronouns)	120
56	There or it/they	122
57	My, your; mine, yours	124
58	Myself, yourself, etc.; each other	126
59	Direct and indirect objects	128
60	Much, many; how much/many; more	130
61	A lot of, lots of, a little, a few	132
62	Something, anybody, nothing, etc.	134
63	Every/each; one/another/other/others	136
64	All, most, some, none	138
	Test F	140

Adjectives and adverbs

65	Adjectives (order)	142
66	Adjectives: -ed or -ing	144
67	Cardinal and ordinal numbers	146
68	Comparison: (not) as ... as	148
69	Too and enough	150
70	So and such	152
71	Comparative adjectives	154
72	Superlative adjectives	156
73	Adverbs (1): adjectives and adverbs	158
74	Adverbs (2): adverbs of frequency	160
75	Adverbs (3): place, direction, sequence	162
76	Adverb + adjective; noun + noun; etc.	164
77	Position of adverbs in a sentence	166
	Test G	168

Prepositions

78	Prepositions of place and movement	170
79	Prepositions of time	172
80	As/like; as if/as though	174
81	In; with; preposition + -ing	176
82	Other uses of prepositions	178
83	Verb + preposition	180
84	Adjective + preposition	182
	Test H	184

Verbs

85	Have and have got	186
86	Make, do, have, get	188
87	Phrasal verbs (1): meanings and types	190
88	Phrasal verbs (2): separability	192
89	Passive sentences (1)	194
90	Passive sentences (2)	196
91	Have something done	198
92	Infinitive with/without to	200
93	Verb + -ing; like and would like	202
94	Verb + to or verb + -ing	204
95	Purpose: for ...ing	206
96	Verb + object (+ to) + infinitive	208
	Test I	210

Conditionals and reported speech

97	Zero Conditional and First Conditional	212
98	Second Conditional	214
99	Third Conditional	216
100	Reported speech (1)	218
101	Reported speech (2)	220
102	Reported questions	222

Test J	224

Building sentences

103	And, but, so, both … and, either, etc.	226
104	Because, in case, so, so that	228
105	Since, as, for	230
106	Although, while, however, despite, etc.	232
107	Relative clauses (1)	234
108	Relative clauses (2)	236
109	Relative clauses (3)	238

Test K	240

Appendices

1	Nouns	242
2	Regular verbs	243
3	Irregular verbs	244
4	Adjectives and adverbs	245

Exit test

Exit test	247

Index

Index	255

Introduction

The *Oxford Practice Grammar* is a series of three books, each written at the right level for you at each stage in your study of English. The series is intended for your use either in a classroom or when working independently in your own time.

The books are divided into units, each of which covers an important grammar topic. Each unit starts with an explanation of the grammar and this is followed by a set of practice exercises. Tests at the end of each unit or section of units give the opportunity for more practice and enable you to assess how much you have learned.

You may want to choose the order in which you study the grammar topics, perhaps going first to those giving you problems. (Topics are listed in the Contents page at the front of each book and in the Index at the back.) Alternatively you may choose to start at the beginning of each book and work through to the end.

Exam practice

The first level in the series is *Oxford Practice Grammar – Basic*. This is suitable for elementary to pre-intermediate learners, and those working for the PET exam. The second is *Oxford Practice Grammar – Intermediate*, for students who are no longer beginners but are not yet advanced in their use of English. It is suitable for those studying for the Cambridge FCE. *Oxford Practice Grammar – Advanced* is for those who have progressed beyond the intermediate level and who wish to increase their knowledge of English grammar and become more confident when using it. It helps students prepare for CAE, CPE, TOEFL, IELTS, and other advanced-level exams.

The Oxford Practice Grammar – Basic is written for elementary to pre-intermediate students of English.

Grammar topics are explained simply and clearly and you are given lots of opportunity to practise.

Each new topic is presented on a left-hand page and the practice section follows on the same page or the facing page. You can therefore look across to the explanation while you are working through the exercises.

Appendices at the back of the book summarize how to form plurals of nouns, verb endings, comparative forms of adjectives, and adverbs. They also include a table of irregular verbs.

An exit test provides an opportunity for more practice, and prepares you for *Oxford Practice Grammar – Intermediate*.

There is an interactive *Oxford Practice Grammar* website at www.oup.com/elt/practicegrammar.

Key to symbols

The symbol / (oblique stroke) between two words means that either word is possible. *We put **does** before he/she/it* means that *We put **does** before he*, *We put **does** before she* and *We put **does** before it* are all possible. In exercise questions this symbol is also used to separate words or phrases which are possible answers.

Brackets ( ) around a word or phrase in the middle of a sentence mean that it can be left out. *She said (that) she lived in a small flat* means that there are two possible sentences: *She said that she lived in a small flat* and *She said she lived in a small flat*.

The symbol ~ means that there is a change of speaker. In the example *When did Jane go to India? ~ In June*, the question and answer are spoken by different people.

The symbol ▶ in an exercise indicates that a sample answer is given.

1 Be: Present Simple (1)

1 Here are some examples of **be** in the Present Simple:

*This **is** my brother. He's ten years old.*
*I'm a student. These **are** my books.*
*They **aren't** at home. They're at the theatre.*

2 We form the Present Simple of **be** like this:

POSITIVE

	FULL FORM	SHORT FORM
Singular	I am	I'm
	you are	you're
	he/she/it is	he's/she's/it's
Plural	we are	we're
	you are	you're
	they are	they're

NEGATIVE

	FULL FORM	SHORT FORM
Singular	I am not	I'm not
	you are not	you aren't
	he/she/it is not	he/she/it isn't
Plural	we are not	we aren't
	you are not	you aren't
	they are not	they aren't

3 In speech, we usually use the short forms:

She's my sister.   *He's my brother.*
I'm from Italy.   *They're German.*

4 We use **be**:
- ▶ to say who we are:
  *I'm Steve and this **is** my friend Bill. We're from Scotland.*
  *I'm Janet and these **are** my sisters. This **is** Sandra and this **is** Patricia. Sandra and Patricia **are** doctors.*

- ▶ to talk about the weather:
  It's cold today.
  It's a beautiful day.
  It's usually hot here
  *It **isn't** very warm today.*

- ▶ to talk about the time:
  It's ten o'clock.
  It's half past four.
  You're late!

- ▶ to talk about places:
  *Milan **is** in the north of Italy.*
  *John and Mary **are** in Yorkshire.*

- ▶ to talk about people's ages:
  *My sister **is** six years old.*

Practice

A **Maria is from Brazil. She is writing about herself and her family. Put full forms of *be* in the gaps.**

- ▶ I *am* a student from Brazil.
- ▶ My parents *are not* (not) rich.
- 1 My father .... a teacher.
- 2 My mother .... (not) Brazilian.
- 3 She .... from America.
- 4 I .... twenty years old.
- 5 My little brother .... two.
- 6 My older brothers .... (not) students.
- 7 They .... in the army.
- 8 It .... often very hot in Brazil.

B Now fill these gaps. This time, use short forms of *be*, as in the examples.

▶ I'm............. a doctor. ▶ I'm not....... (not) a bank manager.

1 She .... (not) a teacher.
2 He .... a student.
3 They .... at home.
4 They .... (not) in the park.
5 It .... (not) cold today.

6 It .... eight o'clock.
7 We .... from Paris.
8 We .... (not) from Bordeaux.
9 You .... (not) twenty-one.
10 I .... twenty-four.

C Choose words from the box to put in the gaps.

He's	She's	~~They're~~	It's (x2)	are	is	We	isn't

▶ My parents live in Scotland. They're........ teachers.
1 New York .... in England. .... in America.
2 Paul .... from Germany. .... German.
3 My sister is a doctor. .... thirty years old.
4 .... six o'clock! .... are late.
5 Look at the time! Chris and Mary .... late.

D Look at these pictures. These people are saying who they are. Write sentences, choosing the correct jobs from the box, as in the example.

a pop star	a farmer	a bank manager	~~a footballer~~	a dentist	a doctor
~~a policeman~~	an artist	a teacher	a film star	a scientist	a photographer

▶ Italy — Paolo, Federico
names: I'm Paolo and this is Federico.
nationality: We're from Italy.
jobs: I'm a policeman and Federico is a footballer.

1 Sweden — Bjorn, Liv
names: ....
nationality ....
jobs: ....

2 Mexico — Maria, Pedro
names: ....
nationality: ....
jobs: ....

3 Australia — Jim, Mary
names: ....
nationality: ....
jobs: ....

4 Japan — Tomoko, Akira
names: ....
nationality: ....
jobs: ....

5 India — Rajiv, Vikram
names: ....
nationality: ....
jobs: ....

2 Be: Present Simple (2)

1 We use **be**:
  ▶ to talk about how we feel:
    I'm happy.   *They're sad.*
    They're bored. *She's tired.*
    We're hungry.   *I'm thirsty.*
    He isn't afraid. *They're cold.*

  ▶ to greet people:
    Bill: *Hello. How are you?*
    Jane: *I'm fine thanks. How are you?*

  ▶ to apologize:
    I'm sorry I'm late.

  ▶ to describe things:
    It isn't expensive. It's cheap.
    It's an old film. It isn't very good.
    These photos are bad!
  (For other uses of **be**, see Unit 1.)

2 We use **there + be** to talk about the existence of something. **There + be** can be used to talk about where things are:

  SINGULAR: ***There's** a supermarket in this street.*
            ***There is** a telephone in the flat.*

  PLURAL : ***There are** some good cafes in the centre of the town.*

We also use **there + be** to talk about when things happen:

  ***There is** a bus to London at six o'clock.*
  ***There are** taxis, but **there aren't** any buses on Sunday.*
  ***There isn't** another train to Manchester today.*

3 We form questions with **be** in the Present Simple like this:

  QUESTIONS
  Singular **Am** I
              Are you   } late?
              Is he/she/it
  Plural   **Are** we
              Are you   } late?
              Are they

Here are some examples of questions using all the forms of **be**:
  ***Am I** late for the film?*
  ***Are you** twenty years old?*
  ***Is he** at home now?*
  ***Is she** French or Italian?*
  ***Is it** time to go home?*
  ***Are we** ready to leave?*
  ***Are you** both at university?*
  ***Are they** in London today?*

Practice

A Make sentences about the pictures using the words in the box. Use *He/She/They* and the Present Simple of *be*.

| tired | sad | ~~thirsty~~ | happy |
| hungry | bored | afraid | cold |

▶ *She's thirsty*   1 He ....   2 They ....   3 ....

4 ....   5 ....   6 ....   7 ....

B Use *there* + the correct form of *be* to say what we can and cannot find in the town of Smallwood.

▶ (a cinema: ✓)   There's a cinema.
▶ (a river) There isn't.......... a river.
▶ (restaurants: 10) There are.......... ten restaurants.
1 (a castle: ✓) .... a castle.
2 (baker's shops: 2) .... two baker's shops.
3 (a zoo: ✓) .... a zoo.
4 (banks: 6) .... six banks.
5 (a luxury hotel: ✓) .... a luxury hotel.
6 (a theatre) .... a theatre.
7 (newsagents: 6) .... six newsagents.
8 (many tourists) .... many tourists.

C Write questions by putting the words in brackets ( ) in the correct order.

▶ (thirsty – you – are)   Are you thirsty?..........................
1 (a teacher – you – are)   ....
2 (they – bored – are)   ....
3 (is – afraid – he)   ....
4 (she – tired – is)   ....
5 (are – you – how)   ....
6 (cold today – it – is)   ....
7 (she – Spanish – is)   ....
8 (they – from London – are)   ....

D Put forms of *be* in these conversations.

Steve: This (▶) is.............. Joan, my sister.
Tom: Hello, Joan. (1)................ you a student?
Joan: No, I (2)................ a dentist. I work in Brighton.
Mike: How are you, Sally?
Sally: I (3)................ fine, thanks.
Mike: (4)................ you hungry?
Sally: Yes. (5)................ there a good restaurant near here?
Mike: Yes. There (6)................ a good, and cheap, restaurant in Wellington Street.

E Write questions using the words in brackets ( ) and a form of *be*.

QUESTIONS

▶ (you/Spanish)? Are you Spanish..........................? ~ No, I'm French.
1 (you/hungry)? ....? ~ No, I'm thirsty.
2 (she/your sister)? ....? ~ No, she's my mother.
3 (I/late)? ....? ~ No, you're on time.
4 (they/from America)? ....? ~ No, they're from Canada.
5 (he/a tennis player)? ....? ~ No, he's a footballer.
6 (you/happy)? ....? ~ No, I'm sad.
7 (she/at home)? ....? ~ No, she's at work.
8 (he/twenty)? ....? ~ No, he's eighteen years old.

3 Present Simple (1)

1 We form the Present Simple like this:

POSITIVE	
Singular	I **know**
	you **know**
	he/she/it **knows**
Plural	we **know**
	you **know**
	they **know**

*I **know** the answer.*
*She **starts** work at 9.30.*

We add -s after **he/she/it**:

I start → he starts   I live → she lives

If a verb ends in -ch, -o, -sh or -ss, we add
-es after **he/she/it**:

I watch → he watches   you do → he does
they go → it goes   we wash → she washes

If a verb ends in a consonant (**b**, **c**, etc.) + **y**
(e.g. **study**), we use -**ies** after **he/she/it**:

I study → he studies   I fly → it flies

(For more examples, see Appendix 2, page
243.)

2 Now look at these examples of the negative:
*I **don't like** that music.*
*He **doesn't listen** to his teacher.*

NEGATIVE	
FULL FORM	SHORT FORM
I **do not** know.	I **don't** know.
You **do not** know.	You **don't** know.
He/She/It **does not** know.	He **doesn't** know.
We **do not** know.	We **don't** know.
You **do not** know.	You **don't** know.
They **do not** know.	They **don't** know.

Note that we say:
He does not know. (NOT ~~He does not knows.~~)

3 We use the Present Simple:
▶ to talk about things
   that happen regularly:
   *He **plays** golf every day.*

▶ to talk about facts:
   *She **comes** from France.*
   (= She is French.)
   *Greengrocers **sell** vegetables.*
   *I **don't speak** Chinese.*

Practice

A Add -s or -es to the verbs in the sentences if it is necessary. If it is not necessary, put a tick (✓) in the gap.

▶ He work s...... in a bank.
▶ They live ✓...... in France.
1 I watch .... TV every day.
2 She go .... to work by car.
3 The film finish .... at ten o'clock.
4 We play .... tennis every weekend.
5 They go .... on holiday in August.
6 He speak .... Italian and French.
7 She do .... her homework every night.
8 We start .... work at half past eight.

B Now finish these sentences using a verb from the box. Use each verb once. Remember to add -s or -es if necessary.

fly	study	finish	~~eat~~	sell	smoke	drink	live

▶ He *eats*.......... toast for breakfast.
1 I .... coffee three times a day.
2 My father .... a new language every year.
3 She .... to New York once a month.
4 He .... ten cigarettes a day.
5 They .... in Ireland.
6 He .... work at six o'clock.
7 I .... fruit in a shop.

C Write these sentences, using the negative form of the Present Simple.

▶ (He/not/live/in Mexico) *He doesn't live in Mexico.*...
1 (She/not/work/in a bank) ....
2 (I/not/play/golf) ....
3 (Paul/not/listen/to the radio) ....
4 (We/not/speak/French) ....
5 (You/not/listen/to me!) ....
6 (My car/not/work) ....
7 (I/not/drink/tea) ....
8 (Sheila/not/eat/meat) ....
9 (I/not/understand/you) ....

D Put in the verbs from the box, in the Present Simple. Use each verb once.

leave	start	arrive	~~get~~	watch	work	brush
eat	have	like	drink	go	stop	

Interviewer: How do you start the day, Jim?
Jim: Well, I (▶) *get*............ up at six o'clock. I get washed and dressed, and I
(1)................ breakfast at seven o'clock. After breakfast, I (2)................
my teeth. I (3)................ to work at eight.
Interviewer: When do you get to work?
Jim: I usually (4)................ at my office at about half past eight. First, I
(5)................ a cup of coffee, and then I (6)................ work at 8.45 a.m.
Interviewer: Where do you work?
Jim: I (7)................ in a bank. I am a computer operator. I (8)................ my job.
It's very interesting.
Interviewer: When do you eat lunch?
Jim: I (9)................ work and I have lunch at one o'clock. I (10)................ a cup
of tea at half past three.
Interviewer: When do you finish work?
Jim: I (11)................ the office at six o'clock. I eat dinner when I get home. Then I
(12)................ TV for an hour or two.

E Use the table to write facts about Joan. A tick (✓) means that something is true. A
cross (✗) means that something is not true. Use the verbs in brackets ( ).

▶	1	2	3	4
from Scotland ✓	in a bank ✗	in a flat ✓	French ✓	new films ✗
from England ✗	in a shop ✓	in a house ✗	Italian ✗	old films ✓

▶ (come) *She comes from Scotland.*   ▶   *She doesn't come from England.*
1 (work) She .... in a bank.   She .... in a shop.
2 (live) She ....   She ....
3 (speak) ....
4 (like) ....

4 Present Simple (2)

1 We use the Present Simple:
  ▶ to talk about feelings and opinions:

> *I **like** pop music. I **don't like** classical music.*
> *She **loves** football!*
> *Philip **wants** a new car.*
> *I **don't want** a cup of tea, thanks.*
> *He **feels** sick.*

  ▶ to talk about thoughts:

> *I **don't think** she likes her new job.*
> *I **don't know** the answer.*
> *He **doesn't understand** me.*

For other uses of the Present Simple, see Unit 3.

2 We form Present Simple questions like this:

QUESTIONS			
Singular	**Do**	I/you	} know?
	Does	he/she/it	
Plural	**Do**	we	
	Do	you	} know?
	Do	they	

Note that we put **do** before **I/you/we/they**:
> ***Do** you **speak** Spanish?*
> ***Do** you **work** in the town centre?*
> ***Do** they **know** the answer?*

We put **does** before **he/she/it**:
> ***Does** he **walk** to work?*
> ***Does** Steve **enjoy** his job?*
> ***Does** she **play** the piano?*

Note that we say:
> *Does he walk?* (NOT ~~Does he walks?~~)

Practice

A Put in the words from the box in the correct form. Use the Present Simple. Use each verb once.

like	not	know	~~love~~	feel	think	not like	want	not understand

▶ She thinks that films are fantastic! She _loves_......... films.
1 I .... sick. Can I have a glass of water please?
2 I don't know the answer because I .... the question.
3 I .... he's tired. He works too hard.
4 We .... that new painting. We think it's terrible!
5 I want to telephone Jane, but I .... her phone number.
6 They're thirsty. They .... something to drink.
7 I .... your new car. It's very nice. Was it expensive?

B Write sentences about Peter. (✓ = like, ✓✓ = love, ✗ = not like, ✗✗ = hate)

▶ (tennis ✗)   _He doesn't like tennis._...
▶ (music ✓✓)   _He loves music._..
1 (coffee ✓)   He ....
2 (films ✗)   He ....
3 (his job ✓✓) ....
4 (fish ✗✗)   ....
5 (holidays ✓✓) ....
6 (golf ✗)   ....

C This is an interview with Mary Woods about herself and her husband, John. Write the questions, using the ideas from the box.

like films	read books	listen to the radio	play golf
watch TV	play a musical instrument	smoke	go to the theatre
drive a car	like pop music	drink coffee	live in London
like dogs	speak any foreign languages		

QUESTIONS

▶ Do you live in London .... ?
▶ Does John play golf .... ?
1 .... ?
2 .... ?
3 .... ?
4 .... ?
5 .... ?
6 .... ?
7 .... ?
8 .... ?
9 .... ?
10 .... ?
11 .... ?
12 .... ?

ANSWERS

~ Yes, I live in north London.
~ No, but he plays tennis.
~ Yes, I speak French.
~ Yes, I like all the programmes on TV.
~ Yes, he listens to the radio in the morning.
~ No, but he loves cats.
~ No, I don't like films.
~ Yes, he has two cups in the morning.
~ No, but I have a bicycle.
~ Yes, he plays the piano.
~ No, I prefer classical music.
~ Yes, I love musicals.
~ Yes, I read one book every week.
~ No, he doesn't like cigarettes.

D You are on holiday, and you are in a Tourist Information Centre. Ask questions using the table below.

A	B	C
Do	you	stop at the railway station?
Does	the sports centre	finish before eleven p.m.?
	all the banks	start here?
	the number 38 bus	sell maps of the city?
	the restaurants	change tourists' money into pounds?
	the concert	sell souvenirs?
	the sightseeing tour	have a swimming pool?
	the museum	serve typical English food?

▶ Do you sell maps of the city? ....
1 .... the sports centre ....
2 ....
3 ....
4 ....
5 ....
6 ....
7 ....

5 Present Continuous (1)

1 We form the Present Continuous like this:

> **be + -ing form**
> *I am eating.*

Here are the forms of the Present
Continuous:

POSITIVE

FULL FORM	SHORT FORM
I **am** eating.	I'**m** eating.
You **are** eating.	You'**re** eating.
He/She/It **is** eating.	He'**s** eating.
We **are** eating.	We'**re** eating.
You **are** eating.	You'**re** eating.
They **are** eating.	They'**re** eating.

NEGATIVE

FULL FORM	SHORT FORM
I **am not** eating.	I'**m not** eating.
You **are not** eating.	You **aren't** eating.
He/She/It **is not** eating.	He **isn't** eating.
We **are not** eating.	We **aren't** eating.
You **are not** eating.	You **aren't** eating.
They **are not** eating.	They **aren't** eating.

2 To make the **-ing** form, we add **-ing** to the
verb:

listen → listening	play → playing
work → working	read → reading

3 But notice these irregular spellings:

win → winning	get → getting
shop → shopping	sit → sitting
swim → swimming	travel → travelling
dance → dancing	write → writing
shine → shining	

(For more details on the spelling of the **-ing**
form, see Appendix 2, page 243.)

4 We use the Present Continuous:
- ▶ to talk about actions and situations in
  progress now:

- ▶ to talk about actions and situations in
  progress around now, but not exactly at
  the moment we speak:

Practice

A Look at these pictures.

**Decide what is happening (✓) and what isn't happening (✗) in each picture, and then
write positive or negative sentences.**

▶ (George/eat/breakfast)	✗	*George isn't eating breakfast.*
(George/sleep)	✓	*George is sleeping.*
1 (They/work)	....	....
(They/sit/in the garden)	....	....
2 (I/study/music)	....	....
(I/learn/Japanese)	....	....

3 (He/play/tennis) ....
  (She/win) ....
4 (We/spend/a day at the seaside) ....
  (The sun/shine) ....

B **Finish the postcard using the words in brackets ( ) in the Present Continuous. Use full forms (e.g. *is sitting*).**

Dear Peter,

Jenny and I (▶) *are staying* .... (stay) here for a week.
The sun (1)........................ (shine) and it's very hot.
We (2)........................ (sit) on the beach and I
(3)........................ (drink) an orange juice.
We (4)........................ (not/swim) because we're
both tired. We (5)........................ (watch) the boats on
the sea at the moment. They (6)........................ (travel) fast,
but I can see fifteen or sixteen. Jenny (7)........................ (read)
her book, and I (8)........................ (write) all the postcards!

Jim and Jenny

C **Match the two halves of the sentences. Then put in the correct form of the verb in brackets ( ).**

▶ My aunt *is staying* .... (stay)
  with us this week

1 I .... (go) to work by
  bike this week

2 My father .... (take)
  some medicine

3 Anna is not in the office this week

4 Pauline needs some exercise

5 We .... (eat) in a
  restaurant this week

6 Jill doesn't feel well

7 Tom .... (study)
  more now

a so he can't drink beer at the moment.

b because she .... (work)
  at home.

c so she .... (stay) at
  home today.

d so I *am sleeping* .... (sleep) in the
  living room.

e because our oven is broken.

f because he wants to get a good mark.

g because I haven't got money for petrol.

h so she .... (walk) to
  school this week.

▶ *d* ...... 1 .... 2 .... 3 .... 4 .... 5 .... 6 .... 7 ....

6 Present Continuous (2)

1 Look at these questions:
 *Are you **enjoying** that drink, Ann?*
 *Is he **watching** TV at the moment?*
 *Are they **working** hard?*

2 We form Present Continuous questions like this:

QUESTIONS		
Singular	Am I	
	Are you	} winning?
	Is she/he/it	
Plural	Are we	
	Are you	} winning?
	Are they	

3 Here are three common Present Continuous questions. They all mean 'How are you?':
 *How's it **going**?*
 *How are you **getting on**?*
 *How are you **doing**?*

4 We do not usually use the Present Continuous to talk about opinions or thoughts:
 *I **like** tennis. I **know** your sister.* (NOT ~~I'm liking tennis. I'm knowing your sister.~~)

We do not usually use these verbs in the Present Continuous:

like	know	hate
love	understand	believe
mean	remember	want

5 **think** and **have**:
 ▶ we cannot use **think** in the Present Continuous to express opinions:
 *I **think** he's nice.* (NOT ~~I'm thinking he's nice.~~)

 ▶ we can use **think** in the Present Continuous to talk about an action:
 *She's **thinking** about the film.*

 ▶ we cannot use **have** in the Present Continuous to talk about possessions:
 *I **have** a ticket.* (NOT ~~I am having a ticket.~~)

 ▶ we can use it to talk about actions:
 *I'm **having** breakfast. He's **having** fun.*

Practice

A **Make questions by putting the words in brackets ( ) in the right order.**

 ▶ (enjoying – your work – you – are – ?)   Are you enjoying your work?
 1 (she – having lunch – is – ?)   ....
 2 (playing football – are – they – ?)   ....
 3 (the cat – sleeping – is – ?)   ....
 4 (the sun – is – shining – ?)   ....
 5 (you – are – coming – to the cinema – ?)   ....
 6 (listening – are – they – ?)   ....
 7 (eating – at the moment – she – is – ?)   ....
 8 (it – raining hard – is – ?)   ....
 9 (I – getting better – at tennis – am – ?)   ....
 10 (are – winning the match – we – ?)   ....

B Make questions and answers. Use the Present Continuous.

QUESTIONS

ANSWERS

▶ (she/work/in Peru this year?)
   Is she working in Peru this year?

~ (No, she/study/in Mexico)
~ No, she's studying in Mexico.

1 (you/study/English at the moment?)
   ....

~
~ .... (Yes, I/work/hard)

2 (they/listen/to the radio?)
   ....

~
~ .... (No, they/play/CDs)

3 (Peter/wash/now?)
   ....

~
~ .... (Yes, he/have/a bath)

4 (they/live/in Madrid at the moment?)
   ....

~
~ .... (Yes, they/learn/Spanish)

5 (David/sing/in a group this year?)
   ....

~
~ .... (No, he/work/in a restaurant)

C Put a tick (✓) next to a correct sentence, and a cross (✗) next to a wrong sentence.

▶ She's liking pop music. ✗
▶ He's learning French. ✓
1 They're enjoying the film.
2 We're loving ice-cream.
3 She's believing he's right.
4 John's thinking about my idea.
5 He's having lunch at the moment.

6 She's eating a banana.
7 He thinks it's a good idea.
8 'Huge' is meaning 'very big'.
9 Mick is knowing Jane.
10 She's hating classical music.

D Complete this conversation. Use the verbs in brackets ( ) in the Present Continuous.

Paul: Hi Steve! What are you doing?
Steve: (▶) I'm going .... (I/go) to the bank. What are you doing?
Paul: (1)...................... (I/shop). (2)........................ (I/look) for a new tennis
        racquet. (3)........................ (I/play) a lot of tennis at the moment, and I need a
        new racquet.
Steve: Where is Jackie? Do you know?
Paul: Yes. She isn't in England at the moment. (4)........................ (She/work) in France
        for a month.
Steve: What (5)........................ (she/do) in France?
Paul: (6)........................ (She/sing) in a night-club.
Steve: Really? What about Fred and Sue? What (7)........................ (they/do)?
Paul: (8)........................ (They/study) for an exam. They're always in the library at the
        moment.
Steve: How is your sister? Is she all right?
Paul: Yes, she's fine, but she's tired. (9)........................ (We/paint) the living-room. It's
        hard work.
Steve: Can I help you?
Paul: No, it's OK. My father (10)........................ (help).
Steve: Well, I hope you find a good racquet.

7 Present Simple or Present Continuous

Compare the Present Simple and the Present Continuous:

1 We use the Present Simple to talk about facts (things which are true at any time):

*Anna **speaks** good Spanish.*
*Journalists **write** newspaper articles.*
*I **come** from Norway. (= I am Norwegian).*

We use the Present Continuous to talk about actions in progress at the time of speaking:

*Anna's busy. She's **speaking** on the phone.*
*What **are you writing**? ~ A letter to Jane.*
*Look! The bus **is coming**.*

2 We use the Present Simple for situations that exist over a long time, and for actions that are repeated (e.g. people's habits, or events on a timetable):

*Mike **works** for an advertising company.*
*He **lives** in Paris. (= His home is in Paris.)*

*He **lives** in Paris.*

*Jane **travels** a lot in her job.*
*I **do** a lot of sport.*

We can use words like **usually**, **often**, **every**:
*We **usually go** out to dinner at weekends.*
*I **often go** to football matches on Sundays.*
*The buses **leave every** hour.*

We use the Present Continuous for things that continue for a limited period of time around now (e.g. holidays, visits, temporary jobs, school or university courses):

*John **is working** in the USA for six months.*
*He's **living** in New York.*

*He's **living** in New York.*

*Jane's **travelling** around Europe for a month.*
*I'm **doing** a one-year course in tourism.*
*We're **painting** the flat.*

3 We use the Present Simple with thinking and feeling verbs (e.g. **know, forget, notice, understand, recognise, remember, like, love, hate, want, prefer, need**):

*I **don't know** which train to catch.*

We do not usually use the Present Continuous with thinking and feeling verbs:

NOT *I'm knowing someone who lives in Venice.*

4 We use **have** in the Present Simple to talk about possession:

*I **have** a new car.*

We use **think** in the Present Simple to express opinions:

*I **think** she's interesting.*

We use **have** and **think** in the Present Continuous to talk about actions:

*I'm **having** fun.*
*He can't come, he's **having** dinner at the moment.*
*I am **thinking** about my work.*

Practice

A **Complete the sentences with the Present Simple (*I do*) or the Present Continuous (*I am doing*).**

▶ I _leave_ (leave) home at 7 o'clock every morning.

1 She usually .... (work) in the Sales Department in London, but at the moment she .... (do) a training course in Bristol.

2 Linda .... (wash) her hair every day.

3 He .... (try) very hard in every game that he .... (play).

4 Excuse me. I think that you .... (sit) in my seat.

5 .... (you/listen) to the radio very often?

6 Don't talk to me now. I .... (write) an important letter.

7 Why .... (they/drive) on the left in Britain?

8 It .... (not/get) dark at this time of year until about 10 o'clock.

9 It usually .... (rain) here a lot, but it .... (not/rain) now.

10 A: What are you doing?

    B: I .... (bake) a cake. Why .... (you/smile)?

    .... (I/do) something wrong?

B This is Anna's first letter in English to David. There are some mistakes in it. Cross out the incorrect forms and write in the correct form. Put a tick (✓) if the form of the verb is correct.

Dear David,

    I **live** (►) ✓............. in a large flat in Rome. I'm having (►) have.......... two sisters. They are called Rosa and Maria. We **are getting up** (1)............... at seven o'clock every morning, and we **have** (2)............... coffee and a small breakfast. I **leave** (3)............... the flat at eight and walk to the university. I **am finishing** (4)............... classes at five every day, and I **arrive** (5)............... home at six. This month I **work** (6)............... very hard for my first exams.

At the moment, I **eat** (7)............... breakfast in the kitchen of our flat: my mother **drinks** (8)............... coffee, and my sisters **are reading** (9)............... magazines.

    On Saturday afternoons **I am playing** (10)............... tennis with my friends, or I **go** (11)............... to the cinema. Today, I'm going to see a new English film! Sometimes I **am watching** (12)............... American films on TV, but I'm **not understanding** (13)............... the words! **Are you liking** (14)............... films?

    With best wishes,
    Anna

C Write the sentences using the Present Simple or the Present Continuous.

  ► (Usually she/work/at the office, but this week she/work/at home)
    Usually she works at the office, but this week she's working at home.

1 (You/not/eat/very much at the moment. Are you ill?)

    ....

2 (She/know/three words in Italian!)

    ....

3 (I/take/the bus to work this week, but usually I/walk.)

    ....

4 (I/study/Japanese this year. It's very difficult.)

    ....

5 (you/watch/the television at the moment?)

    ....

6 (I/not/remember/the name of the hotel.)

    ....

7 (She/speak/three languages.)

    ....

8 (The sun/shine/. It's a beautiful day!)

    ....

8 Imperative

1 These are imperatives:
   Go. Help. Come. Wait.

We use the imperative like this:
   Come *in!* **Have** *a cup of tea.*
   Turn *left at the post office.*
   Don't touch! *It's hot.*

Note that sometimes the imperative is one word, but often we give more information:
   Help!
   Help *me!*
   Help *me with my suitcase.*

We can say **please** after an imperative to be more polite:
   Help *me with my suitcase, please.*
   Hurry *up, please. We're late.*
   Come *here, please.*
   Listen *to me, please.*

2 We form the negative like this:
   Don't be *late.*
   Don't forget *your books!*
   Don't wait *for me.*

We normally use the short form **Don't**.

3 We use the imperative:

► to give instructions:
   Turn *right at the corner.*
   Don't forget *your passport.*

► to give warnings:
   Look *out! There's a car coming.*
   Be *careful! That box is very heavy.*

► to give advice:
   Have *a rest. You look tired.*
   Take *a coat. It's cold today.*
   Don't see *that film. It's terrible!*

► to ask people to do things:
   Come *in please, and* **sit** *down.*
   Listen *to this song. It's wonderful.*
   Pass *the butter, please.*

► to make offers:
   Have *another orange juice.*
   Make *yourself a cup of coffee.*

► to 'wish' things:
   Have *a good trip!*
   Have *a nice holiday!*

Practice

A **Make complete sentences by filling the gaps with phrases from the box. Use each phrase once.**

Turn left	Come in	~~Don't wait~~	Don't forget	Stop the car!	Help me!	Have
Don't listen	Pass	Don't be late!	Open	Come	Catch	Take

► *Don't wait* .... for me. I'm not coming tonight.
1 .... an umbrella with you. It's raining.
2 .... a rest. You look tired.
3 .... at the end of the road.
4 .... I can't swim!
5 .... to take your passport.
6 .... There's a cat in the road.
7 .... to my party, please.
8 .... your books at page 84.
9 .... the salt, please.
10 .... to that record. It's terrible.
11 .... The bus leaves at 9 o'clock.
12 .... and have a glass of lemonade.
13 .... the first train in the morning.

B Steven is writing a letter to a friend. Put the verbs in the box into the gaps.

open	forget	~~come~~	be	bring	have	turn	wait	make

20, Sea Parade
Brighton

Dear Paul,

(►) _Come_......... and see me next weekend. I'm staying in a house by the sea. Don't
(1)............... to bring your swimming costume with you! It isn't difficult to find the house.
When you get to the crossroads in the town, (2)............... right and drive to the end of
the road. (3)............... careful because it is a dangerous road! (4)............... some
warm clothes with you because it is cold in the evenings here. If I am not at home when you
arrive, don't (5)............... for me. The key to the house is under the big white stone in the
garden. (6)............... the front door and (7)............... yourself a cup of tea in the
kitchen! (8)............... a good journey!

Best wishes,
Steven

C What are these people saying? Look at the pictures and match the words in the box
to make imperatives.

Come	right.
Have	out!
Pass	~~me!~~
Turn	an orange juice.
~~Help~~	your umbrella.
Don't	in.
Don't forget	to me!
Listen	the milk, please.
Look	touch it!

► _Help me!_...
1 ....
2 ....
3 ....
4 ....
5 ....
6 ....
7 ....
8 ....

Test A: Tenses – present

A Katy and Sandra are talking about their daily lives. Write the correct forms of the Present Simple. Use short forms if you can.

Katy: (▶) *Do you get up*............. (you/get/up) early?

Sandra: No, not really. (1)................................ (My sister/go) to the bathroom first at about eight o'clock. (2)................................ (not/get up) until about eight thirty. What about you?

Katy: Well, (3)................................ (Mike/try) to get me up at about seven, but (4)................................ (he/not/usually/succeed)!

Sandra: (5)................................ (I/be/not) very hungry in the morning. What about you? (6)................................ (you/eat) much for breakfast?

Katy: (7)................................ (I/not/usually/like) to eat much, but (8)................................ (Mike/study) for an hour before breakfast, so (9)................................ (he/eat) quite a lot.

Sandra: (10)................................ (he/have) a big lunch as well?

Katy: (11)................................ (I/not/know). (12)................................ (He/not/tell) me!

Sandra: (13)................................ (you/drive) to work?

Katy: Yes. (14)................................ (there/not/be) any buses. What about you?

Sandra: Well, (15)................................ (my sister/want) to buy a new car, but at the moment, (16)................................ (we/both/walk).

B Felix is on holiday in Portugal with his wife, Jilly, and their children, Tom and Sally. He's emailing their oldest child, Simon, who is at home in England. If the Present Continuous form is correct, put a tick (✓). If it's wrong, either change the spelling or change it to the Present Simple as necessary.

'How are you geting (▶) *getting*............... on, Simon? We're thinking (▶) *We think*............... it's great here. Everyone is having (▶) ✓...................... a good time. I'm siting (1)...................... in the hotel Business Centre. Tom is swiming (2)...................... in the pool. Sally is lying (3)...................... on the beach, and Jilly is shoping! (4)....................... We're liking (5)...................... Portugal. We're all relaxing. (6)...................... What are you doing? Are you working hard (7)...................... at the moment? I'm knowing (8)...................... your exams start tomorrow. Good luck! Is it raining (9)...................... in England? The sun is shineing (10)...................... here, of course! I'm learning (11)...................... a bit of Portuguese, but not very much. I'm understanding (12)...................... some of the things that people say, but only if the words are similar to English. Hope to hear from you soon!'

C Hazel and Jeremy are on the phone. Complete their conversation using either the Present Simple or Present Continuous. Use short forms if you can.

Jeremy: (▶) <u>Are you working?</u> ... (you/work?)

Hazel: Yes. (1)........................ (I/finish) a piece of homework for tomorrow. Why? What are you doing?

Jeremy: Well, (2)........................ (I/think) about my homework, but I'm afraid (3)........................ (I/not/actually/do) it at the moment. I'm tired and bored. (4)........................ (you/want) to go out?

Hazel: No. Look at the weather. (5)........................ (it/rain). (6)........................ (I/never/go out) in the rain. By the way, (7)........................ (you/know) the new girl in our class, the one with glasses? (8)........................ (I/think) (9)........................ (she/come) from Venezuela. Anyway, (10)........................ (she/stay) with Peter's family this month.

Jeremy: Yes, I know. (11)........................ (she/do/well) at school, isn't she? Peter says (12)........................ (she/speak) three languages: Spanish, English and French. (13)........................ (I/not/speak/any languages)!

Hazel: Tired, bored and stupid! Why would I want to go out with you, anyway?

D This is the opening part of a book. One unnecessary word has been crossed out already as an example. Find twenty-one more, and cross them out.

Today is the 1 June 1964. The sun ~~shines~~ is shining and the birds sing are singing. What is does everyone doing do? Well, Mrs Green is reads reading a newspaper. She is reads reading a newspaper every day before breakfast. Her husband, Mr Green, is danceing dancing in the garden. He likes is liking dancing in the morning.
    'Have you another cup of coffee, darling', says Mr Green.
    'But I'm still drink drinking my first cup, dear', replies Mrs Green, 'and anyway, where's our daughter today? She is usually bringing brings me my coffee.'
    'Mary,' says Mr Green (but he doesn't stop dance dancing), 'she's she works working in London this week. Don't you remember?'
    'Stopping Stop dancing and listening listen to me. I never forget forgetting anything. I was just giving you a little test. Anyway, it's time for work.'
    'Alright, darling, but don't forget not your briefcase.'
    'Thank you, dear. Don't dancing dance too hard!'

E Use the words in the box to complete the list for new students.

~~Leave~~ (✗)   show (✓)   smoke (✗)   ~~work~~ (✓)   check (✓)   give (✗)   copy (✗)

▶ <u>Work</u> .... hard, but take a break now and again!
▶ <u>Don't leave</u> .... your bags or coats in the lecture hall.
1 .... that you know all the examination dates.
2 .... your computer password to another student.
3 .... your ID card when you enter the building.
4 .... in the lecture halls or classrooms.
5 .... your essays from the Internet!

9 Be: Past Simple

Tenses: past

1 We form the Past Simple of **be** like this:

POSITIVE

Singular	I **was**
	you **were**
	he/she/it **was**
Plural	We/you/they **were**

NEGATIVE

	FULL FORM	SHORT FORM
Singular	I **was not**	I **wasn't**
	you **were not**	you **weren't**
	he/she/it **was not**	he/she/it **wasn't**
Plural	we/you/they **were not**	we/you/they **weren't**

QUESTIONS

Singular	**Was** I	
	Were you	} right?
	Was he/she/it	
Plural	**Were** we/you/they	right?

Here are some examples with **was** and **were**:

*I **was** in New York last week.*
*We **were** at home yesterday evening.*
*They **weren't** late this morning.*
***Was** it a good film?*

2 Look at these examples of how we use the Past Simple of **be**:

▶ **was/were** + facts about the past:
*John F. Kennedy **was** an American president.*
*Our first house **was** in the centre of town.*
A: ***Were** your answers correct?*
B: *No, they **were** all wrong!*
*Paula **wasn't** at the party.*

▶ **was/were** + place and time:

	+ PLACE	+ TIME
*We **were***	*in Spain*	*in June.*
*She **wasn't***	*at home*	*last night.*

*George and Joanna **weren't** in London at the weekend. They **were** in Brighton.*
*Steve and Mary **were** here at six o'clock.*

▶ **was/were** + adjective (e.g. **cold**, **tired**):
*It **was** cold yesterday.*
*They **were** tired after the journey.*
*The train **was** late again this morning.*
A: ***Were** your exams easy?*
B: *The first exam **was** easy, but the second one **wasn't**.*

Practice

A Complete the sentences using *was* or *were*.

▶ Today I am happy but yesterday I *was* sad.

1 Now Jane is at home but last week she .... on holiday.

2 Today it's raining but yesterday it .... sunny.

3 This year there is a jazz festival here and last year there .... a pop festival.

4 Today Mr Brown is at work but yesterday he .... ill.

5 These days there are houses here but a hundred years ago there .... trees.

6 Today I feel fine but yesterday I .... in bed all day.

7 My mother is a manageress now but she .... just a shop assistant last year.

8 Today is Saturday and we are at home, but yesterday we .... at school.

9 This summer we are staying at home but last summer we .... in Greece.

10 Today Tina and Jack are tired because yesterday they .... at the gym.

B Mary spent last weekend in Madrid. Ask her some questions using *was* or *were*.

► (your hotel/good?)   Was your hotel good?

1 (your room/comfortable?)   ....

2 (the weather/nice?)   ....

3 (the streets/full of people?) ....

4 (the shops/expensive?)   ....

5 (the city/exciting at night?) ....

6 (the museums/interesting?) ....

7 (the people/friendly?)   ....

8 (your flight/OK?)   ....

C George and Sally have been married for fifty years. They are talking about their first house. Use *wasn't* or *weren't* with George's word and *was* or *were* with one word from the box to complete their conversation.

new	Italian	big	green	cheap	~~cold~~	bad

► George: The house was warm.
   Sally: No, it wasn't warm, it was cold. ....

1 George: The garden was small.
   Sally: No, it ....

2 Sally: The neighbours were French.
   George: No, they ....

3 George: The living-room was red.
   Sally: No, it ....

4 Sally: Our first chairs were expensive.
   George: No, they ....

5 George: The kitchen was old.
   Sally: No, it ....

6 George: The local shops were good.
   Sally: No, they ....

D Put *was*, *wasn't*, *were* or *weren't* in the gaps in these conversations.

Peter: (►) Was .... Paul at work today?
Julie: No, he (1)............... in the office. I think he's sick.

Henry: (2)............... you in South America last year?
Steve: Yes. I (3)............... in Bolivia on business, and then my wife and I (4)...............
        in Brazil for a holiday.

Paula: Philip and I (5)............... at home in London last week. We (6)............... at
        Mike's house in Cornwall. It was lovely there. Do you know Mike?
Jane: Yes, I (7)............... at Mike's party in Oxford in the summer. (8)............... you
        there?
Paula: No, we weren't there. Philip and I (9)............... in Portugal in the summer.

10 Past Simple

1 We form the Past Simple of regular verbs by adding -**ed** to the verb:

walk → walked	watch → watched
open → opened	ask → asked

There are some exceptions:

▶ verbs ending with -**e**:

+ -**d**:	live → lived	like → liked

▶ verbs ending with a consonant and -**y**:

-**y** → -**ied**:	apply → applied
	try → tried

▶ most verbs ending with one vowel and one consonant:

-**p** → -**pped**:	stop → stopped
	plan → planned

(For more details on the form of the Past Simple, see Appendix 2 on page 243.)

2 Many verbs have an irregular Past Simple form:

do → did	have → had
take → took	buy → bought
come → came	stand → stood
find → found	ring → rang
go → went	say → aid

(For more details, see Appendix 3, page 244.)

3 We form the negative with **didn't** and the infinitive (e.g. **do, take, understand**):
> I **didn't understand.** (NOT ~~didn't understood~~)

We form questions with **did** and the infinitive (e.g. **watch**):
> **Did** you **watch** the film?

4 We use the Past Simple to talk about an action or situation in the past which is finished. We often say when it happened (e.g. **yesterday, last night**):
> Chris **phoned** me **yesterday.** He **wanted** to ask me something.
> **Did** you **enjoy** the concert **last night?**

5 We can use the Past Simple with **for** to talk about something that continued for a period of time, and ended in the past:
> I **lived** in Rome **for two years.** Then I went to work in Japan.

Practice

A Put a tick (✓) next to the correct forms of the Past Simple, and cross out those which are incorrect. You can look at Appendix 3, page 244, before you do the exercise.

walked ✓	drinked	went	played	writed	swam
taked	wrote	cooked	gived	spent	finded
drank	asked	flew	made	sended	buyed
gave	meeted	took	left	found	winned
met	passed	stoped	followed	sent	eated
won	cryed	comed	drove	bought	brought
leaved	swimmed	cried	stopped	ate	crossed

B Complete the sentences using the Past Simple form and the words in brackets ( ).

▶ We _went_ .... (go) on holiday to Scotland last year.

1 I .... (take) a taxi from the airport to the city centre.

2 We .... (walk) to the park and then we .... (play) tennis.

3 The man in the shop .... (say) something to the woman, but she .... (not/hear) him.

4 I .... (ring) the doorbell and a woman .... (open) the door.

5 I .... (write) a letter to a friend, and then I .... (post) it.

6 A: .... (you/understand) the film?
   B: No. I .... (try) to understand it, but the actors .... (speak) very quickly.

7 A: .... (you/buy) some clothes at the market?
   B: Yes, I .... (buy) a pair of trousers and a shirt.

8 A: .... (you/enjoy) the festival?
   B: Yes. It .... (not/rain) and we .... (listen) to some good music.

C Make sentences using the correct form of the Past Simple.

▶ (When/you/leave/the party?) _When did you leave the party?_ ....

1 (When/you/finish/your exams?)
   ....

2 (I/wait/for an hour, but he/not/phone.)
   ....

3 (you/watch/the news on TV last night?)
   ....

4 (Mark/stop/smoking last month, and he/start/playing tennis again last week.)
   ....

5 (He/ask/me a question, but I/not/know/the answer.)
   ....

6 (I/live/there for a few years, but I/not/like/the place.)
   ....

D It's the beginning of a new term at university. Two students, Nick and Eric, are talking about the summer holidays. Complete their conversation using the correct Past Simple form of the words in brackets ( ).

Nick: What (▶) _did you do_ .... (you/do) in the summer?

Eric: I (1)..................... (take) a trip around Europe by train.

Nick: (2)..................... (you/go) on your own, or with some friends?

Eric: A couple of friends (3)..................... (come) with me.

Nick: How many countries (4)..................... (you/visit)?

Eric: I (5)..................... (go) to six or seven countries. I (6)..................... (have) a great time, and I really (7)..................... (love) all of them.

Nick: Which one (8)..................... (you/like) most?

Eric: Sweden, I think. I (9)..................... (enjoy) exploring the marvellous countryside and I (10)..................... (take) lots of photographs.

Nick: When (11)..................... (you/arrive) back home?

Eric: Last week. I'm still rather tired.

11 Past Continuous

1 We form the Past Continuous like this:

POSITIVE
I/He/She/It   **was**
You/We/They **were** } **waiting.**

NEGATIVE

	FULL FORM	SHORT FORM	
I/He/She/It	**was not**	**wasn't**	**waiting.**
You/We/They	**were not**	**weren't**	**waiting.**

QUESTIONS
Was I/he/she/it
Were you/we/they } **waiting?**

(For rules on the spelling of **-ing** forms (e.g. **waiting**), see Appendix 2 on page 243.)

2 Look at this example:
A: *What **were** you **doing** at seven o'clock last night?*
B: *I **was driving** home from work.*

Driving		
6.30	7.00	7.15

*I **was living** in Japan in 2001. (I lived there from 1999 to 2003.)*

We use the Past Continuous for an action or situation that was in progress at a particular time in the past (e.g. at seven p.m., in 2001).

3 Now look at this:
*When I **walked** into the room, Ann **was writing** postcards and Keith **was reading**.*

Ann   Keith

We use the Past Simple (**walked**) for a completed action. We use the Past Continuous (**was writing**) for an action in progress in the past.

4 We can use **when** or **while** before the Past Continuous:
*I met her **when/while** we **were working** for the same company. (**when** = during the time)*

We can only use **when** (NOT ~~while~~) before the Past Simple:
*When I **met** her, we **were working** for the same company. (**when** = at the time)*

Practice

A **Complete the sentences by putting the verbs in brackets ( ) into the Past Continuous.**

▶ It <u>was snowing</u>........ (snow) when I left home this morning.

1 I tried to explain my problem to her, but she .... (not/listen).

2 He .... (talk) on the phone when I arrived.

3 A lot of people .... (wait) for the 7.30 bus last night.

4 I .... (live) in London when I met them.

5 I nearly had an accident this morning. A car .... (come) towards me, but I moved quickly out of the way.

6 At the end of the first half of the game, they .... (win).

7 It was a sunny afternoon and people .... (sit) on the grass in the park. Then it suddenly started to rain.

8 Which hotel .... (you/stay) in when you lost your passport?

9 Fortunately, I .... (not/drive) too fast when the child walked into the road in front of me.

10 I looked out of the window, and I saw that it .... (not/rain) any more.

11 What .... (you/do) at three o'clock yesterday afternoon?

B Describe what the people in the picture were doing when Rick came into the room. Use the correct verb from the box in the Past Continuous.

brush	watch	read
listen	write	eat
paint	sit	play

▶ George was reading .... a newspaper.

1 Julie .... a sandwich.

2 Sue and Liz .... table tennis.

3 Frank .... television.

4 Caroline .... on the floor.

5 Barbara .... a letter.

6 Rita .... her hair.

7 Alison .... to some music.

8 Ann .... a picture.

C Look at this information about Shirley and Kevin and complete the sentences about them, using the Past Continuous (*I was doing*) or the Past Simple (*I did*).

SHIRLEY		KEVIN	
1980–86	lived in New York	1982–90	lived in Washington
1983–86	studied at university	1983–85	did a course in Computing
1986	left university	1985–1990	worked as a computer operator
1986–90	worked as a translator	1989	met Shirley
1989	met Kevin	1990–1995	ran his own company
1992	married Kevin	1992	married Shirley

▶ In 1982 Shirley was living .... in New York.

1 In 1984 Kevin .... in Washington.

2 In 1984 Shirley .... at university.

3 In 1984 Kevin .... a course in computing.

4 When Shirley .... university in 1986, Kevin .... as a computer operator.

5 When Kevin .... Shirley, she .... as a translator.

6 While Shirley .... as a translator, she .... Kevin.

7 In 1992 Kevin .... his own company.

8 While he .... his own company, Kevin .... Shirley.

12 Past Simple or Past Continuous

1 Compare the Past Simple and the Past Continuous:

PAST SIMPLE	PAST CONTINUOUS
He *talked* to her last week.	He *was talking* to her when I saw him.
I *didn't talk* to her yesterday.	I *wasn't talking* to anyone, I was watching the TV.
Did you *talk* to your sister?	*Were* you *talking* to her before I came?

2 We use the Past Simple to talk about a complete event in the past:

> Last Saturday morning, Paul **played** football in the park.

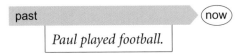

Here are some more examples:
> On Sunday I **made** a cake.
> It **rained** a lot on Saturday morning.

We use the Past Continuous to talk about an action that was in progress, when something else happened:

> Last Saturday, Paul was playing football in the park when he saw Jane.

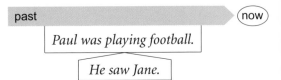

Here are some more examples:
> The phone rang while I **was making** a cake.
> It **was raining** when we left home.

3 We often use the Past Simple to talk about one event that followed another event:
> When Ann James **left** university, she **went** to work for a bank. She **left** the bank after five years, and **wrote** a book which ...

In a story we often use the Past Continuous to say what was in progress, when something happened:
> The sun **was shining**. People **were sitting** under the trees or **walking** around the park. Suddenly a car **drove** into the park ...

Practice

A **Use the Past Simple and the Past Continuous to make sentences from the words in brackets ( ).**

▶ (The police/arrive/while/I/have/breakfast)
  The police arrived while I was having breakfast.

1 (The storm/start/while/they/drive/home)
  ....

2 (I/see/an accident/while/I/wait/for the bus)
  ....

3 (Mary/go/to several concerts/while/she/stay/in London)
  ....

▶ (I/have/breakfast/when/the police/arrive)
  I was having breakfast when the police arrived.

4 (My father/cook/the dinner/when/he/burn/his fingers)
  ....

5 (The soldiers/prepare/to leave/when/the bomb/explode)
  ....

B Complete these texts using the Past Simple or the Past Continuous of the verbs in brackets ( ).

▶ Beethoven _wrote_......... (write) nine symphonies; he _was writing_.. (write) another symphony when he died.

1 Last Saturday Tom wanted to make two salads. He .... (make) the first one in five minutes. He .... (make) the second one when his guests .... (arrive), and they .... (help) him to finish it.

2 The artist Gaudi .... (design) several houses in Barcelona, Spain. Later he .... (start) work on a church. He .... (work) on the church when he .... (die).

3 Last month a bank robber .... (escape) while the police .... (take) him to prison. Later they .... (catch) him again, and this time they .... (lock) him up without any problem.

4 Philip's football team were lucky last Saturday. After twenty minutes they .... (lose), but in the end they .... (win) the game by four goals to two.

5 John Lennon .... (sing) and .... (play) on many records with the Beatles. After that he .... (record) several songs without the Beatles. He .... (prepare) a new record when Mark Chapman .... (shoot) him.

6 The evening was getting darker; the street lights .... (come) on. People .... (hurry) home after work. I .... (stand) in a queue at the bus stop. Suddenly somebody .... (grab) my bag.

C A policewoman is interviewing Mary Croft about last Friday evening. Look at the pictures and complete the conversation. Use the Past Simple or the Past Continuous of the words in brackets ( ).

Policewoman: What time (▶) _did you get_......... (you/get) home from work?
Mary: At about six o'clock.
Policewoman: And what (1)....................... (you/do) after you got home?
Mary: I read the newspaper.
Policewoman: Did anything happen while (2)....................... (read) the paper?
Mary: Yes, the phone (3)....................... (ring).
Policewoman: What (4)....................... (you/do) when your husband came home?
Mary: I was watching TV, and I (5)....................... (drink) a cup of coffee.
Policewoman: Did you and your husband stay at home?
Mary: No, I (6)....................... (drink) my coffee. Then I put on my raincoat, and we (7)....................... (go) out at seven o'clock.
Policewoman: Why (8)....................... (you/put) your raincoat on?
Mary: Because it (9)....................... (rain), of course.

13 Present Perfect (1)

1 We form the Present Perfect using the present tense of **have** + a past participle:

POSITIVE

FULL FORM	SHORT FORM
I/you **have arrived**	I've **arrived**
he/she/it **has arrived**	he's **arrived**
we/you/they **have arrived**	we've **arrived**

NEGATIVE

FULL FORM	SHORT FORM
I/you **have not arrived**	**haven't**
he/she/it **has not arrived**	**hasn't**
we/you/they **have not arrived**	**haven't**

QUESTIONS

Have I/you **arrived?**
Has he/she/it **arrived?**
Have we/you/they **arrived?**

2 Regular past participles end in **-ed** or **-d**:

played   travelled   arrived   washed

(For more regular past participles see Appendix 2, page 243.)

Many past participles are irregular:

buy → bought   go → gone
make → made

(For irregular past participles see Appendix 3, page 244.)

3 We use the Present Perfect:

▶ to talk about recent actions:

At 18.00, Anne arrived home.
At 18.01, we can say:
  Anne **has arrived** home.

From 18.30 to 19.00, Anne ate her dinner.
At 19.01, we can say:
  She's **eaten** her dinner.

▶ to talk about our lives:

*I've **sailed** across the Atlantic.*
*I've **seen** gorillas in Africa.*
*I **haven't danced** the Flamenco.*

4 When we ask people about their lives, we often use **ever** (= at any time):
  *Have you **ever** been to Australia?*

When people talk about their lives, they sometimes use **never** (= not at any time):
  *I've **never** learnt French.*

Note that **ever** and **never** come before the past participle.

Practice

A Use short forms (*I've seen, she's gone*) of the Present Perfect to make positive or negative sentences.

▶ (He/lose/his passport)   He's lost his passport.
▶ (She/not/see/her sister)   She hasn't seen her sister.
1 (We/finish/our work)   ....
2 (They/buy/a new house)   ....
3 (They/not/phone/the doctor)   ....
4 (They/go/to the cinema)   ....
5 (You/eat/four bananas!)   ....
6 (You/not/take/any photographs) ....

Now use the Present Perfect to make questions.

▶ (you/see/John?)   <u>Have you seen John?</u> ....

7 (you/be/to Canada?)   ....

8 (they/cook/our breakfast?)   ....

9 (Jane/make/any mistakes?)   ....

10 (we/visit/all the museums?)   ....

B James is talking about his life. Put the correct past participles in the gaps.

I've (▶) <u>seen</u>.......... (see) a lot of beautiful places in my life,
and I've (1)................ (do) a lot of interesting things. I've
(2)................ (travel) in North and South America, for
example. I've (3)................ (visit) all the big American cities.
I've (4)................ (drive) across Mexico. I haven't
(5)................ (be) to Argentina, but I've (6)................
(work) in Peru and Bolivia. I've (7)................ (swim) in the
Pacific Ocean, the Atlantic Ocean, and the Mediterranean
Sea. I've (8)................ (eat) in the best restaurants in Paris,
and I've (9)................ (sing) Italian songs in Rome. I haven't
(10)................ (make) much money in my life, but I've
(11)................ (meet) a lot of interesting people and I've
(12)................ (take) a lot of wonderful photographs!

C Read the questions. If they refer to a recent event, put a tick (✓). If they refer to someone's life rewrite the sentence using *ever*.

▶ Have you had coffee?   ✓...

▶ Have you eaten elephant meat?   <u>Have you ever eaten elephant meat?</u>....

1 Have you bought a newspaper?   ....

2 Have you flown in a military aeroplane?   ....

3 Have you washed your hands?   ....

4 Have you spoken to a prince or princess?   ....

5 Have you had anything to drink?   ....

D Now write true answers to these questions, using either *this morning* or *never*.

▶ <u>No, I haven't had coffee this morning.</u>..

▶ <u>No, I've never eaten elephant meat.</u>..

1 ....

2 ....

3 ....

4 ....

5 ....

14 Present Perfect (2)

1 We use the Present Perfect to talk about something that happened in the past, but we do not say exactly when it happened:
I've seen this film before. (= before now)

We often use the Present Perfect in this way for things that happened in the past, and that have a result now:
I've seen this film before. I don't want to see it again now.
She's left the company. She doesn't work there now.

We often use the Present Perfect with **ever** (= at any time) and **never** (= at no time):
Have you ever met a famous person?
He has never worked in a factory.

2 We can use the Present Perfect with **for** and **since**, to talk about situations or actions in a period of time from the past until now. We use **for** with a period of time (e.g. **three months**), and **since** with a point in time (e.g. **Tuesday**):

past	1	2	3	4	5	6	now

for six months

*We've lived here **for six months.***

past	Monday	Tuesday	Wednesday	now

since Tuesday

*I haven't seen Tom **since Tuesday.***

3 **Gone** and **been**
Look at the difference between these two sentences:
*He's **been** to Paris.* (= He is now at home again.)
*He's **gone** to Paris.* (= He is in Paris now.)

He's been means 'he has finished his trip'.
He's gone means 'he has begun his trip'.

Practice

A Look at the pictures that show what Jenny has done in her life. Complete the sentences about her, using the Present Perfect form of the verbs in brackets ( ).

▶ She has worked .... (work) as a secretary and as a schoolteacher.
1 She .... (live) in Paris since 1991.
2 She .... (visit) Canada and the USA.
3 She .... (be) married for four years.
4 She .... (write) four books.
5 She .... (climb) Mont Blanc twice.

B Complete the sentences using the Present Perfect form of the verbs in brackets ( ).

▶ Don't take my plate away. I _haven't finished_ .... (not/finish) my meal.

1 A: What's that book about?
B: I don't know. I .... (not/read) it.

2 I .... (lose) my pen. Can I borrow yours, please?

3 My father .... (buy) an expensive new car.

4 A: I .... (book) a room here for tonight.
B: Yes madam, what's your name, please?

5 I .... (make) some sandwiches. Would you like one?

6 I'm not sure what the problem with the car is. It .... (not/happen) before.

7 A: .... (you/reply) to that letter from the bank?
B: No I haven't, but I'll do it soon.

C Write this conversation using the Present Perfect and the words in brackets ( ).

Rob: (you/ever/want/to work in another country?)

▶ _Have you ever wanted to work in another country?_ ....

Brian: (Yes, in fact I/work/abroad.)

1 ....
(I/work/in Ireland and in Brazil.)

2 ....
(What about you?/you/ever/have/a job abroad?)

3 ....
Rob: (No, I/never/want/to leave my home town.)

4 ....
(I/live/here for twenty years, and I/never/think/of working abroad.)

5 ....
Brian: (Really? Well, I/apply/for another job abroad.)

6 ....

D Make sentences with the Present Perfect and *for* or *since*.

▶ (I/not/play/tennis/last Summer.)
I haven't played tennis since last Summer. ....

1 (I/know/her/more than ten years.)
....

2 (I/not/eat/anything/lunchtime.)
....

3 (you/live/in this town/a long time?)
....

4 (Jill/be/a good friend/we were at school together.)
....

5 (you/see/Jack/the party last week?)
....

15 Present Perfect (3)

1 We use **just** with the Present Perfect to talk about things that happened a short time before now:

> **have** + **just** + PAST PARTICIPLE
> *It has **just** finished.*

> *Could I speak to Jane, please? ~ I'm afraid she **has just left**.*
> (= She left a short time ago.)
> *Is that a good book? ~ I don't know. I've **just started** it.*
> (= I started it a short time before now.)

2 Look at this example with **already**:
> *Do you want something to eat? ~ No thanks, I've **already eaten**.*
> (= I ate before now.)

We use **already** with the Present Perfect to emphasize that something happened before now, or before it was expected to happen. We use **already** like this:

> **have** + **already** + PAST PARTICIPLE
> *I've **already** heard that story.*

Here is another example:
> Nicola: *Is Sarah going to phone you later?*
> Robert: *No. She's (= She has) **already** phoned me.*
> (= Sarah phoned before Nicola expected her to phone.)

3 We use **yet** with a negative verb to say that something has not happened, but we think that it will happen:

> *The post **hasn't arrived yet**.*
> (= The post has not arrived, but it probably will arrive.)
> *I **haven't finished** this work **yet**.*
> (= I haven't finished this work, but I will finish it.)
> *They **haven't replied** to my letter **yet**.*

We use **yet** in questions to ask whether something that we expect to happen has happened:
> *Have you paid the bill **yet**?*
> (= Perhaps you have not paid the bill, but you are going to pay it soon.)
> *Has it stopped raining **yet**?*
> (= Perhaps it has not stopped raining, but it will stop raining soon.)
> *Have you found a job **yet**?*

Notice that we usually put **yet** at the end of a negative statement or question:
> *They haven't replied to my letter **yet**. Have you found a job **yet**?*

Practice

A Complete the dialogues, using *just* and the words in brackets ( ).
Use the Present Perfect.

▶ A: What's happening in this programme?
   B: I don't know. <u>It's just started.</u> .... (It/start).

1 A: .... (I/come) back from my holiday.
   B: Did you have a good time?

2 A: Could I have a copy of *Sports World*, please?
   B: Sorry. .... (I/sell) the last copy.

3 A: How's Lucy?
   B: She's very happy. .... (She/finish) her exams.

4 A: .... (I/have) a letter from Mike.
   B: Oh yes? What did he say?

5 A: Have you heard from Alison and Frank recently?
B: Yes, ... (they/move) to another town.
6 A: Have you still got the same car?
B: No, ... (I/buy) a new one.
7 A: Would you like something to eat?
B: No, thanks. .... (I/have) breakfast.

B **Make sentences using the Present Perfect with *already* or *yet*.**

▶ (I/not/read/today's newspaper) yet.
<u>I haven't read today's newspaper yet.</u> ....

1 (you/decide/which one to buy) yet?
....

2 (I/explain/this to you three times) already.
....

3 (Their baby son/start/talking) already.
....

4 (you/phone/Jane) yet?
....

5 (The game/not/finish) yet.
....

6 (I/have/lunch) already.
....

7 (He/spend/all his money) already.
....

C **Complete the conversation using *just*, *already* or *yet* and the words in brackets ( ).**
Put the verbs into the Present Perfect.

Julia: Are you having a good time here?
Anna: Yes, I haven't been here long, and (▶) <u>I've already visited</u> .... (I/visit) a lot of
         interesting places.
Julia: (1)............................. (you/visit/the Art Gallery/?)
Anna: No, (2)............................. (I/not/do/that), but I'm going to do it.
Julia: What about the theatre? (3)............................. (you/see/a play/?)
Anna: No, but (4)............................. (I/book/a ticket) for one. It's called *The Friends*.
         I rang the theatre five minutes ago. Would you like to come with me?
Julia: Thanks, but (5)............................. (I/see/that play). I saw it last month.
Anna: (6)............................. (I/read) in the newspaper that The Adventurers are
         going to give a concert next week. Do you like them?
Julia: Yes, I do. (7)............................. (they/make) a really good, new record. It
         came out a couple of days ago.
Anna: I really want to get a ticket.
Julia: (8)............................. (they/not/sell/all the tickets). But be quick! They're a
         very popular group.

16 Past Simple or Present Perfect

Compare the Past Simple and the Present Perfect:

1   We use the Past Simple to talk about something that happened at a particular time in the past:

I met John at four o'clock.
When did Jane go to India? ~ In June.
Martin bought a new car last week.

We use the Present Perfect to talk about the past, but not about when things happened:

I've met John's girlfriend. She's nice.
Have you ever been to India? ~ Yes, I have.
I have never bought a new car.

2   We use the Past Simple for situations or actions during a period of time that ENDED in the past:

I worked there for two years. I left last year.

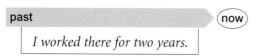

We use the Present Perfect for situations or actions during a period of time from the past to NOW:

He has worked here for two years.
(He still works here.)

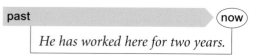

We lived in that house for a long time; then we moved to this one.
Our company opened two new shops last summer.

We've lived in this flat since we got married.
(We still live in it.)
We opened two shops last summer. Since then (= since that time), we have opened two more.

3   Notice how we often move from the Present Perfect to the Past Simple:

Peter: *Have you ever played this game before?*
Maria: *Yes, I played it once when I was in England.*
Peter: *Did you win?*
Maria: *No, I lost.*

Practice

A   Complete the conversation by choosing the correct form in brackets ( ).

Sarah: (▶) Have you ever been .... (Have you ever been/Did you ever go) to the United States?

Jim: Yes, (1)............................. (I've been/I went) to California last year.

Sarah: (2)............................. (Have you liked/Did you like) it?

Jim: Yes, (3)............................. (I've enjoyed/I enjoyed) the trip a lot.

Sarah: What (4)............................. (have you done/did you do) there?

Jim: (5)............................. (I've visited/I visited) Hollywood, Disneyland and San Francisco.
(6)............................. (Have you been/Did you go) to California, Sarah?

Sarah: No, but (7)............................. (I've booked/I booked) a holiday there. I've got my ticket and I'm going next week!

B Complete the dialogues using the Present Perfect (*I have seen*) or Past Simple (*I saw*).

A: I (▶) saw........................... (see) Jack last night.
B: Oh really. I (1)................................. (not/see) him for months. How is he?

A: We (2)............................... (go) to the theatre last Saturday.
B: (3)............................... (you/enjoy) the play?
A: Yes, it (4)................................ (be) very good.

A: I (5)................................. (never/hear) of this group before. Are they famous in your country?
B: Yes, they are very popular. They (6)............................... (be) famous in my country for years.

A: What (7)................................ (you/do) last weekend?
B: I (8)........................... (stay) at home. I (9)................................ (need) a rest.

A: (10)................................ (you/ever/win) a competition?
B: Yes, I (11)............................ (win) a photographic competition in 2001.

A: So, John is your best friend. (12)............................... (you/meet) him when you were at university?
B: Yes. We (13)................................ (be) friends for more than ten years.

C Complete this paragraph about the London Underground by putting in the Present Perfect or Past Simple forms of the verbs in brackets ( ).

THE LONDON UNDERGROUND

London (▶) has had.............. (have) an underground train system since the ninteenth century. The London Underground (1)........................ (start) in 1863, when Victorian engineers and workers (2)........................ (build) the Metropolitan railway. This railway line (3)........................ (go) from Paddington Station to Farringdon Street Station, and steam engines (4)........................ (pull) the coaches. Eleven more lines (5)........................ (open) since then. The world's first underground electric railway (6)........................ (open) in 1890. This line (7)........................ (go) from the City of London to Stockwell in South London. The most modern line is the Jubilee line, which (8)........................ (open) in 1979. Since the London Underground (9)........................ (begin), many other cities, such as New York and Moscow, (10)........................ (build) their own systems.

17 Present Perfect Continuous

1 We form the Present Perfect Continuous like this:

POSITIVE		
	FULL FORM	*SHORT FORM*
I/You/We/They	have	've
	been cooking.	been cooking.
He/She/It	has	's
	been cooking.	been cooking.
NEGATIVE		
I/You/We/They	have not	haven't
He/She/It	has not	hasn't
	been cooking.	been cooking.
QUESTIONS		
Have	I/you/we/they	been cooking?
Has	he/she/it	been cooking?

(For details about **-ing** forms see Appendix 2, on page 243.)

2 We use the Present Perfect Continuous for an action or situation that began in the past and continues until now:

You're late! I've been waiting for you.

We often use **for** and **since** with the Present Perfect Continuous. We use **for** with a period of time, and **since** with a point in time:

I've been waiting for you for two hours.
I've been waiting for you since six o'clock.

3 Here are some more examples:

PAST   NOW

*Julia **has been talking** on the phone for an hour.* (= She started talking on the phone an hour ago and she is still talking.)
*You've **been sitting** there since one o'clock.* (= You started sitting there at one o'clock and you are still sitting there.)

4 We use the Present Perfect Continuous for actions that are done many times in a period of time from the past until now:

*She's **been having** driving lessons for a couple of months.* (= She started a couple of months ago; she is still having lessons.)
*I've **been playing** tennis since I was a small child.*

5 We can use **How long ...?** with the Present Perfect Continuous:

*How long **have** you **been living** here? I **have been living** here for three years.*

Practice

A Complete the sentences by putting the verbs in brackets ( ) into the Present Perfect Continuous.

▶ She *has been leaning* .... (she/learn) Spanish for six months.

1 The roads are very wet; .... (it/rain) for hours.

2 .... (we/play) this game for hours. Let's stop now!

3 .... (Wendy/learn) French at school for three years.

4 .... (I/read) this book for months, but I haven't finished it yet.

5 .... (we/watch) this programme for hours.

6 .... (the neighbours/make) a lot of noise again today?

7 .... (I/save) my money for a holiday.

8 .... (you/listen) to me carefully?

B Put *for* or *since* into the gaps.

▶ I've been working in this office *since*......... last summer.

1 Have you been doing this course .... a long time?

2 I've been driving this car .... more than ten years.

3 She has been planning the party .... the beginning of the month.

4 George has been telling the same stories .... several years.

5 We've been waiting for a reply .... we wrote to them last week.

6 What have you been doing .... the last time that I saw you?

7 You've been writing that letter .... more than two hours.

8 He's been feeling ill .... a few days.

C Write sentences to describe what each member of the Wyatt family has been doing to prepare for Christmas. Use words from the box and the Present Perfect Continuous to describe the pictures.

wrap	make
decorate	shop
write	put up
a cake	cards
~~decorations~~	presents
the tree	for food

▶ *John has been putting up decorations.*...

1 Mary and Stephen ....

2 Martha ....

3 Delia ....

4 Tom ....

5 Joanna ....

D Write a sentence for each of the following situations, using the Present Perfect Continuous and *for* or *since*.

▶ She started her course a month ago and she is still doing it.
   She has been doing her course for a month..............................

▶ I started reading this novel last weekend and I'm still reading it.
   I have been reading this novel since last weekend......................

1 It started raining at three o'clock and it is still raining.
   ....

2 He started playing chess when he was ten and he still plays it.
   ....

3 I started work at eight o'clock and I'm still working.
   ....

4 Helen started looking for another job two months ago and she's still looking.
   ....

5 We arrived here two hours ago and we're still waiting.
   ....

18 Present Perfect Simple or Continuous

Compare the Present Perfect Simple and Present Perfect Continuous:

1 We use the Present Perfect Simple (**have painted**) to talk about a past activity that is now completed:

> *We've painted the rooms.* (= The rooms are now painted.)
> *Anna's mended her bike.* (= She can ride it now.)

We use the Present Perfect Continuous (**have been painting**) to emphasize the activity itself, which may or may not be completed:

> *We've been painting the flat. That's why it smells.*
> *We still have three rooms to paint.*
> *Anna's hands are dirty because she's been mending her bike.*

2 We use the Present Perfect Simple to ask and answer **How many?** and **How much?**:

> A: *How many rooms have you painted?*
> B: *We've painted three of them.*

We usually use the Present Perfect Continuous to ask **How long?**, and with **since** and **for**:

> *I have been travelling for six months.*

A: *How long have you been waiting? Have you been queuing for a long time?*
B: *Yes, I've been waiting since two o'clock.*

For more details about **How long?**, **How many?** and **How much?** see Unit 32.

3 Note that we usually use the Present Perfect Simple (not the Continuous):

> ▶ to talk about short actions with **have, stop, break,** etc.
> *Tony has had an accident on his bike.*

> ▶ with verbs of thinking (e.g. **know, decide, forget, notice**):
> *I'm sorry. I've forgotten your name.*

> ▶ to talk about the last time that something happened:
> *I haven't eaten meat for two years.*
> (= *I last ate meat two years ago.*)

Note that we can use the Present Perfect Simple or the Continuous with **work, teach,** and **live,** with no difference in meaning:

> *I have taught here for two years.*
> OR *I have been teaching here for two years.*

Practice

A Write out the sentences in brackets ( ). Use the Present Perfect Simple (e.g. *I have done*).

▶ He's late again. (How many times/he/arrive/late this month?)
  How many times has he arrived late this month?

1 What a good week! (We/sell/much more than we expected.)
  ....

2 (How much money/you/spend/this week?)
  ....

3 (How many people/Jane/invite/to her party?)
  ....

Now use the Present Perfect Continuous (*I have been doing*).

4 It's still raining. (It/rain/for hours.)
  ....

5 That noise is awful. (They/drill/holes in the wall all morning.)
  ....

6 Are you still here? (How long/you/sit/here?)
  ....

B Five friends have just finished some jobs. Look at the table.

	ACTIVITY	NOW
Neil	sweep the floors	he is sweating
Rachel	cut the grass	she is tired
Paul	do the washing-up	he has soft hands
Carol	peel the onions	she has red eyes
Tim	defrost the fridge	he has cold hands

Complete the dialogues from this information. Use the Present Perfect Simple or the Present Perfect Continuous.

▶ Neil, why are you sweating? ~ Because I <u>have been sweeping the floors.</u>

▶ Is the lawn finished? ~ Yes, Rachel <u>has cut the grass.</u>

1 Paul, why are your hands so soft? ~ Because I ....

2 Are the onions ready for the pan? ~ Yes, Carol .... them.

3 Rachel, you look tired. ~ Yes, I ....

4 Tim, your hands are very cold. ~ Yes, I ....

5 Are the floors clean? ~ Yes, Neil .... them.

6 Why are your eyes red, Carol? ~ Because I ....

7 Are the plates clean? ~ Yes, Paul ....

8 Is the fridge all right now? ~ Yes, Tim ....

C Put the verbs in brackets ( ) into the gaps in the right form. Use the Present Perfect Simple or the Present Perfect Continuous.

▶ Ellen: Where are you and your family going to live?

  Ian: Well, we've <u>been talking</u> .... (talk) about that for weeks, but we haven't <u>decided</u> .... (decide) anything yet.

1 Tina: Excuse me. Have you .... (stand) in this queue for a long time?

  Larry: Yes, I've .... (queue) for almost an hour.

2 Sara: Why are you crying?

  Joe: Because my brother has .... (have) an accident. He's .... (break) both his legs.

3 Susan: Excuse me. Has someone .... (leave) this bag here?

  Wally: I don't know. I've .... (sit) here all afternoon, but I haven't .... (notice) it until now.

19 Past Perfect

1 We form the Past Perfect with **had** and the past participle of a verb (e.g. started, taken):

	FULL FORM	SHORT FORM
I/You/He/She/It/ We/They	**had started.**	**'d started.**

> *I **had taken** it.* OR *I'd **taken** it.*
> *They **had not started.*** OR *They **hadn't** started.*

2 Look at this:

> A year ago:
> *Jenny is flying to Rome. She thinks, 'I have never been on a plane before now.'*
> Now:
> *Jenny flew to Rome last year. She **had** never **been** on a plane before that.*

When we talk about an event or situation in past time we use the Past Simple (e.g. flew); if we talk about an event before that time, we use the Past Perfect (e.g. **had been**). Here is another example:

> Last Saturday at the cinema:
> Mary: *We don't need to queue because I've already bought the tickets.*
> Now, talking about last Saturday:
> Mary: *We didn't need to queue because I **had** already **bought** the tickets.*

Note that we can use **never** and **already** before the past participle (e.g. **been**, **bought**).

3 If we talk about a series of past events in order, we use the Past Simple:
> A: *I saw a beautiful bird in my garden.*
> B: *I went to get my camera.*
> C: *The bird **flew** away.*
> D: *I returned with my camera.*

| past | A | B | C | D | | now |

We need the Past Perfect to make it clear that one of the events is not in order:
> D: *I returned with my camera.*
> C: *The bird **had** already **flown** away.*
> *(The bird had gone before I returned.)*

Also, compare these sentences using **when**:

Past Simple: ***When I returned with my camera, the bird flew away.*** (It went after I returned.)

Past Perfect: ***When I returned with my camera, the bird had flown** away.* (It went before I returned.)

4 The Past Perfect is used in reported speech:
> '*I have suffered from asthma for many years.*' *She told the doctor that she **had suffered** from asthma for many years.*

(For more on reported speech, see Units 100–102.)

Practice

A Write sentences about what these people had already done or had never done before. Use the Past Perfect, and *already* or *never*.

▶ Last summer Mary won a gold medal for the third time.
  She had already won two gold medals before that.

▶ Last year Ken visited Scotland for the first time.
  He had never visited Scotland before that.

1 Last weekend Tom rode a horse for the first time.
  He .... before that.

2 Last summer Jeff ran in a marathon for the sixth time.
  He .... before that.

3 Last week Susan wrote a poem for the first time.
  She .... before that.

4   Last week Ann appeared on TV for the first time.
    She .... before that.
5   Last summer Tony played tennis at Wimbledon for the fifth time.
    He .... before that.
6   Last year Jean wrote her third novel.
    She .... before that.

B   **In each case you have two events in the order in which they took place. Write the information in one sentence using the words in brackets ( ).**

► A: The driver started the car. B: Lady James appeared.
    (When Lady James/appear/, the driver/already/start/the car)
    <u>When Lady James appeared, the driver had already started the car.</u>

1   A: We put the fire out. B: The firemen arrived.
    (When the firemen/arrive/, we/already/put/the fire out)
    ....

2   A: Jim finished the work. B: The manager came back.
    (When the manager/come/back, Jim/already/finish/the work)
    ....

3   A: I went to bed. B: Philip telephoned.
    (When Philip/telephone/, I/already/go/to bed)
    ....

4   A: Alice and Jack had lunch. B: Their children came home.
    (When their children/come/home, Alice and Jack/already/have/lunch)
    ....

5   A: Ian prepared the supper. B: His wife got home from work.
    (When his wife/get/home from work, Ian/already/prepare/the supper)
    ....

6   A: The thieves spent the money. B: The police caught them.
    (The thieves/already/spend/the money, when the police/catch/them)
    ....

C   **Use the Past Perfect to complete the sentences.**

► Last summer Pam said, 'I've always wanted to fly in a helicopter.'
    Pam said that she <u>had always wanted to fly in a helicopter.</u>
1   Fred said, 'Jack has just gone out.'
    Fred told us that Jack ....
2   Robert said to Jill, 'Have you been to Cambridge?'
    Robert asked Jill if she ....
3   When the boys came home, Mrs Brock said, 'I've made some sandwiches.'
    Mrs Brock told the boys that she ....
4   'I know your cousin,' said Tom. 'I met her in Amsterdam.'
    Tom said he knew my cousin because he ....
5   Bob was talking to Jean, and he said, 'Have you ever been to Japan?'
    Bob asked Jean if she ....

20 Used to

1 We can use the Present Simple to talk about present situations or habits:

> ▶ situations:
> *My sister **works** as a translator.*
> *Andrew **lives** in London.*

> ▶ habits:
> *Peter usually **wears** jeans.*
> *I often **eat** a sandwich for lunch.*
> *Mike **doesn't smoke** anymore.*
> ***Does** John **drive** to work every day?*

2 Look at these sentences with the Past Simple:

> ▶ situation:
> *Henry **lived** in France for many years.*

> ▶ habit:
> *When I was young, I **ran** three miles every day.*

The verbs are in the Past Simple and the sentences are about past situations or habits.

3 Look at these sentences with **used to**:
> *Jill **used to live** in Ireland.*
> *Many people **used to make** their own bread.*
> *My husband **used to work** at home.*

We use **used to** to talk about a past situation or habit that continued for months or years, and to emphasize that the situation today is different:
> *Jill doesn't live in Ireland **now**.*
> ***Nowadays** people usually buy bread from a shop.*
> *My husband doesn't work at home **now**.*

Compare the Past Simple and **used to**:

> ▶ Past Simple:
> *When he was young, he **ran** three miles every day.* (He may or may not run three miles every day now.)
> ▶ used to:
> *When I was young, I **used to run** three miles every day. I don't do that now.* (I don't run three miles every day now.)

We make negative sentences and questions with **did + use to**:
> *Sue **didn't use to like** black coffee.*
> *Paul **didn't use to smoke** a pipe.*
> ***Did** Alan **use to cycle** to school?*
> ***Did** your parents **use to read** to you?*

4 We do not use **use to** for present situations or habits; we use the Present Simple:
> *Ann **sings** in a band.* (NOT ~~Ann uses to sing in a band.~~)
> *Joe **doesn't cycle** to school.* (NOT … ~~doesn't use to cycle…~~)

Practice

A Look at this table of people who have changed what they eat or drink.

name		in the past		now	
Ann	Pam	meat	tap water	fish	bottled water
Tom	Mary	coffee	tinned fruit	tea	fresh fruit
Robert	Susan	white bread	margarine	brown bread	butter

Now make sentences, as in the examples.

▶ Ann _used to eat_ meat, but now she _eats fish_ .

▶ Tom _drinks tea_ now, but _he used to drink_ coffee.

1 Robert .... white bread, but now .... brown bread.

2 Pam .... tap water, but now .... bottled water.

3 Mary .... fresh fruit now, but .... tinned fruit.

4 Susan .... butter now, but .... margarine.

Now complete these questions.

▶ *Did Ann use to eat meat?*   ~ Yes she did, but now she eats fish.

5   white bread? ....   ~ Yes he did, but now he eats brown bread.

6   tinned fruit? ....   ~ Yes she did, but now she eats fresh fruit.

7   tap water? ....   ~ Yes she did, but now she drinks bottled water.

Now complete these sentences.

▶ Ann *didn't use to eat* .... fish, but she does now.

▶ Tom drinks tea now, but he *didn't use to drink* .... it.

8   Susan .... butter, but she does now.

9   Mary eats fresh fruit now, but she .... it.

10   Pam drinks bottled water now, but she .... it.

B   **Cross out all the sentences which are incorrect, as in the example.**

▶ When he was at primary school, Tony used to work very hard.

▶ ~~Last year Peter used to get a new bicycle for Christmas.~~

1   I didn't use to watch TV much, but I do now.

2   When he was a teenager, my father used to buy all the Beatles' records.

3   Paul used to go the cinema almost every weekend.

4   Did Pamela used to go to the concert last night?

5   Paul used to be really fit when he played a lot of volleyball.

6   John use to spend a lot of money on that new jacket he bought last week.

7   Kate didn't use to come to school yesterday because she was sick.

8   Jane used to play tennis a lot, but she doesn't have time now.

9   Did you use to go to the seaside for holidays when you were a child?

10   We used to live in Canada before we came here.

C   **Complete the sentences to say what these people used to do and what they do now, as in the example.**

▶ Andrew/get up/seven o'clock/now/half past seven

   Andrew used to get up at seven o'clock, but now he gets up at half past seven. ....

▶ I/swim/before work/now/after work

   I used to swim before work, but now I swim after work. ....

1   Dan/play/violin/now/guitar

   ....

2   Anna/be/best friends/Angela/now/Cathy

   ....

3   Susan/have/dancing lessons/now/riding lessons

   ....

4   I/buy cassettes/now/CDs

   ....

5   John and Jean/live/London/now/Cardiff

   ....

6   David/drive/Fiesta/now/Jaguar

   ....

Test B: Tenses – past

A Anne is emailing her new Spanish friend Pilar. If the <u>underlined</u> verb tenses are wrong, correct them. If they are right, put a tick (✓).

I'll try to answer some of your questions. (►) <u>I have moved</u> *I moved* .... to London from Bristol in 1995. That means I've been here (►) ✓. for almost ten years now. (Wow! Time flies, doesn't it?) (1) <u>I was living</u> .... in the south of the city when (2) <u>I was starting</u> .... going out with my husband, Mel. (We were both studying French at the time (3) <u>we have met</u> .... at University College.) In fact, (4) <u>I've stayed</u> .... in flats all over London! My favourite flat (5) <u>had</u> .... a balcony and you could see a small park in the square. (6) <u>I had never forgotten</u> .... that flat, or my flatmates. Anyway, that's enough about me. How long (7) <u>have you lived</u> .... Madrid? (8) <u>Have you been</u> .... born there? London and Madrid are so big, aren't they? (9) <u>I didn't see</u> .... all the different parts of London yet! I saw an old friend by chance about a week ago when (10) <u>I walked</u> .... to work, and she lives on a boat in north London. (11) <u>I have visited</u> .... her last week. (12) <u>I've never seen</u> .... such a small kitchen! My friend cooked a meal for us.

B Sara is talking to her husband. They've been married for forty years. Six Past Simple verb forms should be Past Perfect. One has been corrected for you as an example. Find the other five, cross them out and rewrite them.

Sara:	We first met in 1960, didn't we, at the cinema?	....
Brian:	Yes. When we arrived, (►) ~~the film already began~~.	*the film had already begun* ....
Sara:	I saw it before anyway.	....
Brian:	Really? You didn't tell me that.	....
Sara:	No. I wanted you to take me to the cinema the following week!	....
Brian:	So you already decided you liked me!	....
Sara:	And then you took me to your favourite restaurant, but it closed a week before!	....
Brian:	Oh dear. What did we do next?	....
Sara:	We went to a pub to meet your friends, but it was empty. Everyone went home, because England was playing Germany at Wembley.	....
Brian:	What an evening!	....
Sara:	That's not all! When I got home I couldn't open the front door because I left my keys at the pub.	....

C Anne is talking to her mother on the phone. <u>Underline</u> the verbs that should be in Present Perfect Continuous or Past Continuous form, and then change them. One has been done as an example. Find five more.

       I've been studying

'I'm so tired, Mum. <u>I've studied</u> all day from five o'clock this morning. In fact, I did some

maths when you rang just now. I still haven't finished and now I've got a headache because

I've worked harder than I've ever done before! Sorry, what did you say? You've never had a

problem with maths? But you're a teacher! You've read books and things all your life! Dad

says you learnt French verbs on Saturday morning in the park when he first met you!

Anyway, I haven't finished yet. My friend Stevie will be OK, though. Every time I've visited

her in the last month, she has worked hard.'

D Paul, Caroline, Jo and Bob are talking about some of the holidays they've had. Put the verbs in the Past Simple, Past Continuous or Present Perfect tenses.

Paul: Do you remember when (▶) *we went*.............. (we go) to Morocco, Caroline?

Caroline: Unfortunately, yes. (1)........................ (You/lose) your passport, just after we arrived.

Paul: That's right. (2)........................ (We/sail) near the coast, and I was looking at the fish, and (3)........................ (it/just drop) into the sea!
           (4)........................ (you/two/visit) North Africa?

Jo: No. (5)....................(We/be) to Ghana, though. (6)........................ (We/fly) there in 2001, didn't we, Bob?

Bob: Sorry, Jo. (7)........................ (I/not/listen). (8)........................ (I/have) such a busy day today! Actually, (9)........................ (I/fall) asleep on the sofa when (10)........................ (Paul/ring) and invited us around.

Jo: So you need a holiday, don't you?

Caroline: (11)........................ (Paul and I/go) to this really great country hotel, The Woodland Spa, about a month ago. (12)........................ (We/read) the Sunday newspapers, and (13)........................ (we/see) this advertisement. (14)........................ (Paul/not/stop) talking about it since we got back!

Paul: It was fantastic!

Bob: (15)........................ (it/have) a jacuzzi in the bathroom?

Jo: (16)........................ (be/there) a bowl of fruit in your bedroom?

Caroline: All of that. And (17)........................ (you/never/see) such a beautiful swimming pool in your life!

Jo: It sounds lovely. Better than that hotel (18)........................ (Bob and I/stay) in last year in Devon.

Bob: Oh dear. (19)........................ (It/be) terrible. One night (20)........................ (we/talk) in our room, and the owner knocked on the door at ten o'clock in the evening and told us to go to sleep!

Jo: (21)........................ (I/not/enjoy) a holiday in the UK for years, I'm afraid.

21 Be going to

1 We form sentences with **be going to** like this:

	be going +	to	+ INFINITIVE
It	is going	to	snow.

POSITIVE
I am
He/She/It is   } going to leave.
We/You/They are

NEGATIVE
I am
He/She/It is   } not going to leave.
We/You/They are

QUESTIONS
Am I
Is he/she/it   } going to start?
Are we/you/they

2 Note that we usually use the short form of **be** (I'm, he/she/it's, we/you/they're):
They're going to leave.
He's going to spend a week by the sea.

3 The negative short form is **I'm not going to:**
I'm not going to play tennis today.

With **he, she, it**, there are two negative short forms:
*He/she/it **isn't** going to come.*
*He/she/it's **not** going to come.*

With **you, we** and **they**, there are also two negative short forms:
*You/we/they **aren't** going to come.*
*You/we/they're **not** going to come.*

4 We use **be going to** for the future. We use it:

▶ to talk about things we have decided to do in the future:
A: *What **are** you **going to do** tomorrow?*
B: *I'm **going to visit** Paul in Brighton.*
A: *Are you **going to drive**?*
B: *No, I'm **going to take** the train.*

▶ to predict the future, using information we know now:
*Look at that blue sky! It's **going to be** hot.*
*I've eaten too much. I'm **going to be** ill.*
*Look at the time. It's two o'clock. They **aren't going to come** now.*

Practice

A Paul has decided what he's going to do in his life. Complete the sentences, using short forms of *be going to* and the verbs in brackets ( ).

▶ I'm going to study .... (study) music at university.
1 I .... (travel) all over the world.
2 I .... (not/work) in an office.
3 I .... (marry) a very rich woman.
4 We .... (have) eleven boys.
5 They .... (become) a football team.
6 They .... (win) the World Cup.
7 I .... (play) the piano every night in a cafe.
8 My wife .... (not/cook) or clean.
9 We .... (eat) in restaurants every day.

B Write positive sentences with short forms of *be going to* and the words in brackets ( ).

▶ (I/see/a film tonight)   I'm going to see a film tonight. ....
1 (She/buy/a new car tomorrow)   ....
2 (They/work/hard this year   ....
3 (It/rain/this afternoon)   ....

Write negative sentences with short forms of *be going to*.

▶ (They/not/catch/that train!)   _They're not going to catch that train!_ ....

4 (Paul/not/drive/to Scotland.) ....

5 (We/not/finish/it today.) ....

6 (She/not/buy/a new house.) ....

Write questions with *be going to*.

▶ (you/have/a holiday this year?) _Are you going to have a holiday this year?_ ....

7 (they/win/the match?) ....

8 (Mary/leave/her job?) ....

9 (you/take/the exam in June?) ....

C Keiko is Japanese. She's going to spend a week by the sea in England. Ask her some questions. Use *be going to*, the verbs in brackets ( ), and the words in the box.

an umbrella	in a luxury hotel	to a disco	fish and chips
in the sea	~~a lot of English~~	golf every day	

▶ (speak) _Are you going to speak a lot of English?_ ....

1 (play) ....

2 (take) ....

3 (swim) ....

4 (eat) ....

5 (stay) ....

6 (go) ....

D Match the words in the box with the pictures, and write a sentence using short forms of *be going to*.

It/rain
They/eat/a pizza
They/not/play/tennis
He/not/win/the race
She/have/a swim
They/watch/a film
~~He/make/a phone call~~
He/play/the piano

▶ _He's going to make a phone call._

1 ....

2 ....

3 ....

4 ....

5 ....

6 ....

7 ....

22 **Will** and **shall**

1 We use **will** to talk about the future. Look at this example:

*It's now five o'clock. **I'll stop** work at six.*

2 We make sentences with **will** like this:

> **Will** + INFINITIVE
> *I **will stop**.*

We use **I will** or **I'll**, and **I will not** or **I won't**. We usually use the short forms (**I'll, he'll, I won't, he won't**) when we speak.

POSITIVE	*Full form*	*Short form*
I/He/She/It/We/You/ They	**will go.**	**'ll go.**
NEGATIVE		
I/He/She/It/We/You/ They	**will not go.**	**won't go.**
QUESTIONS		
Will I/he/she/it/we/you/they	**go?**	

3 We use **will** to talk about future facts, and things that we think will happen in the future:

> *My father **will be** fifty years old tomorrow.*
> *Jane **will love** your new dress.*
> *He's a good manager. He **won't make** any mistakes.*

We also use will to ask about the future:

> *Will they **win** this game?*

4 We use **I'll** when we make a decision to do something. For example, when the telephone rings, we say:

> *I'll answer it.*

Here is another example:

> A: *Does anyone want to come with me tonight?*
> B: *Yes, I'll come.*

5 We use **Shall I …?** or **I'll …** when we want to do things for other people:

> OFFER: ***Shall I make** you a cup of coffee?*
> OFFER: ***I'll make** you a cup of coffee.*

We use **Shall we …?** to suggest things that we can do:

> SUGGESTION: ***Shall we see** a film tonight?*

Practice

A Use the verbs in the box with *will* or *won't* to complete these dialogues. Use short forms of *will* where you can.

> have   take   ~~phone~~   finish   be (x2)   win   make

▶ A: Are you coming to the cinema on Sunday?
   B: I'm not sure. I'll *phone* .... you on Saturday.

1 A: Don't change your clothes now. We .... late.
   B: No, we won't. We .... a taxi.

2 A: George is going to have a party at the weekend.
   B: Why?
   A: It's his birthday. He .... thirty on Saturday.

3 A: She .... the tennis match tomorrow.
   B: Why not?
   A: She .... mistakes. She always makes mistakes in important matches.

4 A: .... Steve .... the work tonight?
   B: No, he won't finish. He .... time.

B Put the best phrase from the box in each gap. Start your sentences with *I'll*.

phone for a taxi	help you to look for it	~~carry some of them~~
go with you	give you some money	make you a sandwich
open a window	ask her to phone you tonight	give you the name of a language school

▶ A: I want to take these books home, but they're very heavy.
   B: *I'll carry some of them.* ....

1 A: I feel sick. It's so hot in this room.
   B: ....

2 A: I want a cup of coffee, but I don't have any money.
   B: ....

3 A: I'm hungry. I didn't have any lunch.
   B: ....

4 A: I want to learn Japanese.
   B: ....

5 A: I've lost my passport.
   B: ....

6 A: It's ten o'clock. I'll be late if I walk.
   B: ....

7 A: I want to speak to Jane. It's very important.
   B: ....

8 A: I want to go to the museum, but I don't know the way.
   B: ....

C Put *Shall I* or *Shall we* in the gaps in the dialogues.

▶ A: I'm hungry. Are you going to the shops?
   B: Yes. *Shall I* .... get you something to eat?

▶ A: We need a holiday.
   B: What a good idea! *Shall we* .... go to Florida?

1 A: I'm going to get some tickets for the concert next week. .... buy you
   one?
   B: Yes please. I'd love to come.

2 A: .... go to a restaurant tonight?
   B: OK, but I don't have any money. Will you pay for me?

3 A: I want to go to Italian classes, but I've never learnt a foreign language before.
   B: .... come with you?
   A: That's very kind of you.

4 A: Where is our meeting?
   B: At John's office on Baker Street.
   A: .... walk or take a taxi?

5 A: You look thirsty. .... get you a drink?
   B: Yes, please. Can I have an orange juice or some water?

6 A: It's a beautiful day! .... have a picnic?
   B: Wonderful idea! Who shall we invite?

23 **Will** or **be going to**

Compare **will** and **be going to**:

1 We use **will** with an infinitive (**do, go, be, arrive,** etc.):

> INFINITIVE
> *John will arrive tomorrow.*

2 We use **will** for actions that we decide to do NOW, at the moment of speaking:

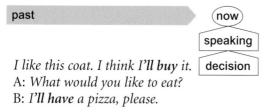

> *I like this coat. I think I'll buy it.*
> A: *What would you like to eat?*
> B: *I'll have a pizza, please.*

We can use will for offers and promises:
> *I'll carry your case for you.* (OFFER)
> *I won't forget your birthday again.* (PROMISE)

3 We use **will** to talk about things that we think or believe will happen in the future:
> *I'm sure you'll enjoy the film.*
> *I'm sure it won't rain tomorrow. It'll be another beautiful, sunny day.*

We use **be going** with **to** + infinitive (**to do, to be, to rain,** etc.):

> to + INFINITIVE
> *It's going to rain soon.*
> *My friends are going to come tonight.*
> *It isn't going to rain today.*
> *What are you going to do on Sunday?*

We use **be going to** for actions that we have decided to do BEFORE we speak:

> *I'm going to clean my room this afternoon.*
> (I decided to clean it this morning.)

We can ask questions about people's plans:
> *Are you going to take the three o'clock train?*
> (= Have you decided to take the three o'clock train?)

We use **be going to** for something that we expect to happen, because the situation now indicates that it is going to happen:
> *He's running towards the goal, and he's going to score.*

Practice

A Complete the sentences, using the words in brackets ( ) and *'ll* or a form of *be going to*.

▶ A: Are you going to watch TV tonight?
  B: Yes, I'm going to watch......... (I/watch) my favourite programme at nine o'clock.

1 A: What .... (you/eat) tonight? What food have you bought?
   B: I haven't bought any food. A: Well, why don't you come to my house?
   .... (I/cook) us something nice to eat.

2 A: I'm going into the centre of town tomorrow. .... (I/buy) some new
   clothes. B: Oh, what .... (you/get)? A: ....
   (I/look) for a T-shirt and some jeans. B: I'd like to go into the centre too.
   .... (I/come) with you.

3 A: .... (I/leave) work late tomorrow. There is a meeting at six p.m.
   B: Oh, I didn't know that. Well, ... (I/see) you after the meeting.

4 .... (I/phone) Tom at six o'clock. I promised to phone him this
   evening.

5 A: Are you going to have a holiday in the summer?
   B: Yes, ... (I/travel) around Europe with a friend.

3 Look at these office scenes. Choose the correct situation for each scene, then choose the correct sentence and cross out that which is incorrect.

▶ Relax, I'll answer it./ ~~Relax, I'm going to answer it.~~
a You look hot, I'll open a window./You look hot, I'm going to open a window.
b Next year, we're going to enter the Japanese market./Next year, we'll enter the Japanese market.
c Thanks, I'm going to have an orange juice./Thanks, I'll have an orange juice.
d Have a rest, I'm going to do the photocopying./Have a rest, I'll do the photocopying.
e Thursday is no good for me, I'm afraid. I'll meet the new manager of our Tokyo office./Thursday is no good for me, I'm afraid. I'm going to meet the new manager of our Tokyo office.

C You are at a party. Here are some of the questions you are asked. Reply using *will* or *be going to*.

▶ A: Hi, nice to see you. Would you like a drink?
  B: (I/have/a coke, please) I'll have a coke, please.
1 A: What are you doing these days?
  B: (Nothing much, but I/start/a new job soon) ....
2 A: Would you like something to eat?
  B: (Thanks, I/have/a sandwich) ....
3 A: What are your plans for the weekend?
  B: (I/do/some shopping tomorrow and I/go/for a swim on Sunday)
  ....
4 A: Why is Maria standing by the piano?
  B: (She/sing/, I'm afraid) ....
5 A: This cake looks delicious. Are you going to have some?
  B: (No, but I'm sure you/enjoy/it) ....
6 A: How are you getting home?
  B: (David/give/me a lift) ....

24 Present Continuous for the future

1 Look at these examples:
   I'm flying home tomorrow.
   He's starting a new job on Monday.
   Tony and Ann are coming at the weekend.

In each example, we are using the Present Continuous (see Units 5 and 6), but we are talking about the future, not the present.

2 Look at this example:

> You bought a plane ticket *last week.*
> You can now say:
> *I'm flying home next week.*
>
>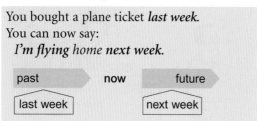

We use the Present Continuous to talk about things we have arranged in the past to do in the future.

Here are some more examples:

> A bank wrote to Steven and asked him to start work **next week.**
> We can now say:
> *He's starting a new job next week.*

> John said to Tony and Ann:
>   *Would you like to come for dinner on Sunday?*
> Tony and Ann said: *Yes.*
> John now says:
>   *Tony and Ann are coming on Sunday.*

3 The important part of a Present Continuous for the future sentence is often a time or day (e.g. **next week, in July, tomorrow, on Sunday**):
   PRESENT: *I'm leaving now.*
   FUTURE: *I'm leaving tomorrow.*
   PRESENT: *We're having a party at the moment. Can I phone you tomorrow?*
   FUTURE: *We're having a party in July.*

4 We do not use the Present Continuous for future events that we cannot arrange or have not arranged:
   NOT ~~The sun is shining tomorrow.~~
   (*The sun will shine …*)
   NOT ~~The Irish team are winning next week.~~
   (*The Irish team will win next week.*)

Practice

A Look at the past events in brackets ( ), and then write sentences using the words in the box. Use short forms of the Present Continuous for the future.

I/eat/in a new restaurant tonight	I/go/to the doctor tomorrow
I/fly/to Florida in August	~~I/study/English in London in May~~
I/go/to a concert next Tuesday	I/see/Mary this weekend

▶ (You paid for an English course in London yesterday.)
   I'm studying English in London in May.

1 (You booked a table at a new restaurant last week.)

   ....

2 (You bought a ticket for a concert last month.)

   ....

3 (You telephoned your doctor this morning.)

   ....

4 (You paid for a holiday at a travel agent's last week.)

....

5 (You talked to Mary on the phone this morning.)

....

B Mark is an explorer. Look at the things he has arranged to do. Match the pictures with the words in the box. Write sentences about what he is doing next year, using the Present Continuous. Say when he is doing each thing.

| he/drive/across the Sahara |
| he/walk/across the Antarctic |
| he/run/across/Africa |
| he/fly/over the Amazon |
| he/climb/Mount Everest |
| he/sail/across the Pacific |

JANUARY   MARCH   MAY

JULY   SEPTEMBER   NOVEMBER

▶ He is running across Africa in January. ....

1 ....

2 ....

3 ....

4 ....

5 ....

C Finish these dialogues using the Present Continuous for the future, and the words in brackets ( ). Use short forms where possible.

▶ Steve: Are you doing .... (you/do) anything this weekend?

Lynn: I'm seeing .... (I/see) a film on Sunday. Do you want to come?

1 Pete: Jane, Joe and Sally .... (come) to my house on Friday night.

Mark: .... (you/have) a party?

Pete: No, we aren't. .... (We/play) cards. Would you like to come?

2 David: .... (I/fly) to New York on Sunday.

Chris: .... (you/see) John there?

David: Yes, ... (we/meet) at the airport.

3 Philip: Mary and I .... (drive) to Scotland next Wednesday.

Mike: .... (you/stay) in Edinburgh?

Philip: No. .... (we/visit) my mother in Aberdeen.

4 Paul: .... (I/start) a new job on Monday.

Clive: Really? What is it?

Paul: .... (I/sell) cars. Do you need a new car?

25 Present tense: **when, before, after, until,** etc.

1 Look at this sentence:
> **When** the programme **ends,** I'll do the washing-up.

To talk about an event in the future, we usually use the Present Simple (e.g. **ends**) after **when, before, after, until** and **as soon as.** We do not use **will:**
> I'm going to finish this work **before I go.** (NOT … ~~before I will go.~~)
> Wait here **until I get** back.
> I'll phone you **as soon as I arrive.**

2 We can use **when** + Present Simple to refer to a time when something will happen:
> I'll buy an ice-cream **when I'm in the newsagent's.**

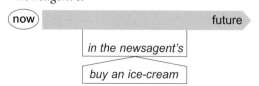

> **When** you **see** her, give her my message.

We use **until** + Present Simple to mean from now to a time in the future:
> We'll sit outside **until it gets** dark. (= We'll sit outside from now to when it gets dark.)

We use **as soon as** + Present Simple with the meaning 'immediately after':
> They'll start playing **as soon as it stops** raining. (= They will start playing immediately after the rain stops.)

3 We use **when** + Present Perfect (e.g. **I have done**) to talk about an action that must, or will, happen before the next action can happen:
> **When I've found** a job, I'll look for a place to live. (= First I will find a job; then I will look for a place to live.)

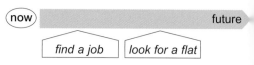

> **When** Simon **has saved** enough money, he'll buy a car. (= First Simon must save the money; then he can buy a car.)

4 With **after** we can use either the Present Simple or the Present Perfect with no difference in meaning:
> After she **takes/has taken** the course, she'll be a qualified teacher. (= When she has done her course, she'll be a qualified teacher.)

Practice

A Complete the sentences by putting *when, before, after, as soon as* or *until* into the gaps. Sometimes more than one answer is possible.

> ▶ I'll stay in this job <u>until</u>.......... I find a better one.
> 1 I'm going to keep working .... I finish this.
> 2 Remember to buy some stamps .... you're in the post office.
> 3 .... I speak to him on the phone tonight, I'll ask him.
> 4 We can go for a meal .... we've seen the film.
> 5 I'll keep looking for it .... I find it.
> 6 I'll wait for them .... it gets dark, and then I'll leave.
> 7 Don't forget to lock the door .... you go out.
> 8 .... I've found the information, I'll phone you.
> 9 We'll wait .... it stops raining, and then we'll go out.
> 10 .... you see John, give him my regards.
> 11 Put in your application .... the closing date arrives.
> 12 You shouldn't wait. You should reply .... you receive the invitation.
> 13 Book a table .... you go to the restaurant. It's often full.

B Complete the dialogues, using the Present Simple or *will* forms of the verbs in brackets ( ). Sometimes you do not need to change the word in brackets.

▶ A: Could you post this letter for me today, please?
B: Yes, I'll do......... (do) it when I go............ (go) to the shops.

1 A: I might be late tonight.
B: OK. I .... (wait) until you .... (arrive).

2 A: I'm leaving next week.
B: I .... (see) you before you .... (go), won't I?

3 A: Have you decided what you're going to do at the weekend yet?
B: No, but I .... (phone) you as soon as I .... (know) what I'm going to do.

4 A: Have you done that homework yet?
B: No, not yet. I .... (do) it when I .... (have) enough time.

5 A: I don't want to go to that party tonight.
B: Well, I'm sure you .... (enjoy) it when you .... (get) there.

6 A: Could you tell Tom to ring me, please?
B: Yes, I .... (tell) him when I .... (see) him tomorrow.

7 A: Mr Jackson isn't in at the moment.
B: I see. Well, I .... (wait) until he .... (come) back.

8 A: Have you booked a hotel in London yet?
B: No, but we .... (book) one before we .... (go) there.

9 A: Don't forget to write to Peter.
B: OK. I .... (do) it as soon as I .... (get) home.

10 A: .... (you/see) Jack when you .... (be) in Madrid?
B: Yes, I hope I will. I .... (phone) him when I .... (arrive) in Spain.

C Complete the sentences using the Present Perfect or *will* forms of the verbs in brackets ( ).

▶ When you have written....... (write) that letter, I'll post....... (post) it for you.

1 I .... (pay) the bill when I have borrowed some money from somebody.

2 When I've found a car that I want to buy, I .... (ask) my bank to lend me the money to buy it.

3 After the plane .... (land), you may unfasten your safety belts.

4 When you .... (check) all your answers, hand in your question paper.

5 I .... (read) this book when I'm on holiday.

6 When I .... (read) this magazine, I'll start work.

7 You .... (feel) better when you have had something to eat.

8 When you .... (finish) your work, you can go home.

9 She .... (be) pleased when she hears the news.

10 Let's go for a walk after we .... (have) dinner.

26 Future

1 We can talk about future time with different verb forms, for example:

- ► will: *I'll come with you.*

- ► be going to: *He's going to come with us.*

- ► Present Continuous:
  We're coming tomorrow.

- ► Present Simple:
  When he arrives, we'll have dinner.

2 When we talk about events in the future that we expect to happen but that are not in our control, we can use **will** or **be going to**:
  *Ann **will be** (OR **is going to be**) 12 next week.*
  *We **won't see** (OR **aren't going to see**) those birds again until next spring.*
  ***Will** they **finish** (OR **Are** they **going to finish**) the building soon?*

3 When we talk about events in the future that are in our control (i.e. we can decide what will happen), we use **will** differently from **be going to**. We use **will** at the time we decide what to do; we use **be going to** after we have decided what to do. Look at these examples:
  John: *Can somebody help me, please?*
  Helen: *Yes, I'll help you.*
  (Here Helen decided <u>after</u> John asked.)

Now compare:
  Carol: *John needs some help.*
  Helen: *I know. I'm going to help him.*
  (Here Helen had decided <u>before</u> Carol spoke.)

4 Look at these examples:
  If it rains, they'll stay (OR they're going to stay) at home.
  We'll have (OR we're going to have) lunch after the programme finishes.

When a sentence has two parts that refer to the future, we use the Present Simple after **if**, **when**, **before**, **after**, **as soon as** and **until**, and in the other part of the sentence we use **will** or **be going to**:

When/ after etc.		SIMPLE PRESENT		will/ be going to
After	+	*it finishes*	+	*we'll have* lunch.

5 We use the Present Continuous to talk about a future arrangement that we have made with someone else:
  A: *Can you come and see us this evening?*
  B: *I can't. I'm playing squash with Sam.*

  Peter can't come to the cinema with us tonight because he's meeting Jane for dinner.

Practice

A Liz has come back to London from Holland. Her brother Tom has just met her at Liverpool Street Station. In the sentences below, think about when the person decides to do something. Put a tick if you think the phrase <u>underlined</u> is correct. Otherwise write in the correct form of *will* or *be going to*.

Tom: Hi Liz. Do you want some tea or coffee after your journey?
Liz: Thanks. <u>I'll</u> (►) ✓.............. have a tea.
Tom: <u>I'm going to</u> (►) !'ll.............. carry your bag – you look tired. <u>We'll</u> (1)................ go to that café, over there. Here we are. So, welcome back to England. How was Holland?
Liz: Well, it was great to have some time to think, and I've made some decisions. <u>I'll</u> (2)............... talk to the boss tomorrow, and I'll (3)................ ask him if I can move to another department.
Tom: Good. I'm sure <u>he'll</u> (4)................ give you what you want. Now, would you like something to eat?

Liz: Um, yes. <u>I'm going to</u> (5)............... have a sandwich. Thanks. What about you?

Tom: No, thanks, I don't want to spoil my appetite. I've reserved a table for this evening at the Mexican restaurant in Leicester Square. <u>I'll</u> (6)............... take Jill. What are you going to do this evening?

Liz: I haven't thought about it. <u>I'll</u> (7)............... probably cook something. Oh, and I must ring Dad. Did you remember that it's his birthday tomorrow?

Tom: Yes, I remembered. <u>He'll</u> (8)............... be fifty. Promise me you'll relax a bit?

Liz: Sure.

Tom: OK. <u>I'll</u> (9)............... get you a taxi. Call me tomorrow. <u>You won't</u> (10)............... forget, will you?

B Use the words in brackets ( ) to write sentences using *will* and the Present Simple.

▶ (Tom/help/us/when/he/come/home) Tom will help us when he comes home...............

1 (I/buy/the tickets/before/I/go/to work) ....

2 (As soon as/Henry/arrive/, we/have/something to eat) ....

3 (The play/start/after/the music/stop) ....

4 (He/not/stop/until/he/finish/the job) ....

5 (When John/get/here, we/go/to the beach) ....

C Look at Ann's diary for next week.

	MORNING	AFTERNOON/EVENING
Monday	10.00 take Tim to the airport	wash the car
Tuesday	buy some stamps	write some letters
Wednesday	11.00 take the dog to the vet	tidy my flat
Thursday	12.30 cook lunch for mother	buy a new squash racket
Friday	9.00 play squash with Mary	do the shopping
Saturday	wash my hair	6.00 meet Tim at the airport

If Ann has an arrangement with someone else, use the Present Continuous, but if she does not, use *be going to*.

▶ Ann _is taking_.................. Tim to the airport on Monday morning

▶ On Monday evening Ann _is going to wash_............ the car.

1 On Tuesday she .... some stamps because in the evening she .... some letters.

2 She can't see anyone on Wednesday morning because she .... the dog to the vet.

3 On Wednesday evening she .... her flat.

4 On Thursday afternoon she .... a new squash racket because .... squash with Mary on Friday morning.

5 On Friday afternoon she .... the shopping

6 She .... her hair on Saturday morning because she .... Tim at the airport at six o'clock.

Test C: Tenses – future

A Alex is talking on the phone to his girlfriend, Rosemary. Use *shall* or short forms of *will* or *be going to* to complete the conversation.

Alex: Hi! It's Alex here.

Rosemary: Hi! I'm drying my hair at the moment.

Alex: (▶) <u>Shall I ring</u>.......... (I/ring) you back?

Rosemary: No, it's OK. (1)...................... (I/finish) drying it later. How are things going?

Alex: Not bad, thanks. What (2)....................... (you/do) on Saturday after you've seen your mum?

Rosemary: I'm not really sure. (3)....................... (we/meet up) around six in the evening?

Alex: OK. But I may be a little late. (4)....................... (I/watch) the final at tennis club in the afternoon. (5)....................... (I/get) you a ticket, if you like.

Rosemary: No thanks. It sounds a bit boring. I'm sure (6)....................... (you/enjoy) it more on your own. Anyway, (7)....................... (I/buy) some new shoes in town, I think, if I've got enough money.

Alex: (8)....................... (I lend) you some. I've just been paid.

Rosemary: Don't worry. I'll have my credit card.

B Steve is writing an email to Joanna, a work colleague. Use the Present Continuous or *shall* or a short form of *will* to complete the message.

I've just arrived in Mexico City. I didn't get much sleep on the plane so I think ▶ <u>I'll go</u>................ (I/go) to bed for an hour or two this morning. As you know from my schedule, (1)....................... (I/meet) Carl this afternoon, and then (2)............... (I/fly) to Monterrey tomorrow morning. (3)....................... (I/fax) you the documents after Carl has signed them? By the way, Carl says (4)....................... (you/come) to Mexico at the weekend. If (5)....................... (you/stay) near the Hotel Victoria, (6)....................... (you/bring) me the green folder on my desk? I forgot it, I'm afraid. Also, I'm sorry but (7)....................... (not/be able) to meet you at the airport. I'm sure you've heard already that (8)....................... (I/visit) the new headquarters building of Carl's company in Acapulco.

C Mike is talking to his teenage daughter about the visit of her uncle and his children. Fill in the gaps with one of the following words:

I'm/taking/you're/is/I'll/am/won't/will/Shall/arrive

Sally: I just want to go out, Dad.

Mike: I know, but your Uncle Paul (▶) <u>is</u>..................... coming tomorrow with Steve and Sara.

Sally: So? What's it got to do with me?

Mike: You know (1)....................... moving out of your room tomorrow morning, don't you?

Sally: I (2)....................... move! I don't want to! Why should I?

Mike: We've talked about this already. (3)....................... I tell Uncle Paul that he can't come?

Sally: Where (4)....................... I going to sleep then?

Mike: Before they (5).......................... , we'll make a bed for you in my room.

Sally: OK. But that's all (6)........................ going to do.

Mike: Almost. Remember you're (7)........................ the children to the circus on Sunday.

Sally: I won't go. Circuses are cruel to animals!

Mike: It's a circus without animals. We've talked about this before. I'll give you some money. When you get there, the kids (8)........................ want some ice cream.

Sally: OK. I'll sleep in your room and (9)........................ take little Steve and Sara to the circus, but next weekend I'm going to Sharlene's party, and I'll need a new pair of jeans, but I don't have any money. Can you help?

D Jane is telling her classmates what will happen when they arrive at the school's mountain centre in Scotland. Cross out the word *will* or the form *'ll*, if they are wrong.

'You'll meet Tim, one of the team of guides, as soon as you ~~will~~ arrive at the centre. He'll show you where to eat and sleep. Tim will check your bags when you will get up, to make sure you're ready for the day. It's important to have food and drink and an extra pullover. Before you'll start walking, Tim will make sure you have your own map, in case you get lost. It's a fantastic place to go walking. You'll be able to see the sea after you will get to the top of the mountain! But it can become cold very quickly. You'll have to listen to Tim until you'll know the right thing to do if the weather changes suddenly. Don't worry, though. You'll have a good time. You'll enjoy the views as soon as you will get there!'

E Four friends are in a restaurant on holiday. Cross out one of the **bold** future forms each time.

Laura: (▶) **Are you going to/~~Shall you~~ order** some food, Tom?

Tom: Yes, but I'll have a chat with the waiter first when he (1) **comes/will come** to the table. There are some dishes I just don't understand.

Ben: We haven't made any plans for this afternoon, have we? What are we (2) **doing/going to do**?

Karen: It's too hot to go for a walk again.

Tom: Don't worry. (3) **I'm carrying/I'll carry** you!

Ben: After you (4) **finish/will finish** lunch, you won't be able to carry anyone!

Karen: Don't order too much food, Tom. (5) **I'm playing/I'll play** in a volleyball match on the beach this evening. It's not a serious game, but there is an interesting prize.

Ben: What is it?

Karen: (6) **I'll/I'm going to tell** you if you agree to play a practice match with me this afternoon.

Tom: (7) **Am I calling/Shall I call** the waiter? (8) **I'm dying/I'm going to die** of hunger in a moment.

Laura: Look. He's coming over. Ben, for the first time in your life, why don't you have something different from a pizza?

27 Nouns, verbs, adjectives, etc.

1 Look at this:

NOUNS

VERBS   ADJECTIVES

Steven bought an expensive new car on Friday.

He drove it carefully to Manchester.

PRONOUNS   ADVERBS   PREPOSITIONS

2 Nouns describe things or people or animals:

butter	car	woman	dog	problem

Some nouns (proper nouns) are the names of people, places and things. We begin proper nouns with capital letters (A, B ...):

Jane	Paris	Oxford Street	June
a Rolls-Royce		the Tower of London	

3 Verbs describe actions or situations:

work	play	live	meet	stay	see

*They **work** hard.* (**work** = verb)
*I **saw** Peter.* (**saw** = verb)

4 We use auxiliary verbs (**be, have, do, will, can, may, must,** etc.) before another verb:
*They **are** working hard.* (**are** = auxiliary)
*I **have** seen Peter.* (**have** = auxiliary)
*I **must** go now.* (**must** = auxiliary)

5 We put adjectives (e.g. **wonderful**) before nouns:
*We had a **wonderful** day.*

We can also use adjectives after the verbs **be, look, seem, feel:**
*He's **hungry**.*   *She **looks** tired.*

Sometimes we put **very** before adjectives:
*It's **very hot** today.*
*He bought a **very expensive** car.*

6 We normally use adverbs to describe verbs:
*She walked **quickly**.*   *He sings **well**.*

Most adverbs end in -**ly**:

clearly	slowly	badly

7 We use pronouns (**I, you, he, she,** etc.) to replace nouns:
*David has a new job. **He** is enjoying **it**.*

8 We use prepositions (**in, on, at,** etc.) when we are talking about places and times:

PLACE:	*She's **at home**.*
	*It's **in the box**.*
TIME:	*I'll see you **on Monday**.*
	*They went on holiday **in June**.*

Practice

A Put the <u>underlined</u> words in the correct columns in the box.

noun:	verb:	auxiliary:	adjective: wonderful	adverb:	pronoun:	preposition:

I had a <u>wonderful</u> holiday in <u>Spain</u> last year.
She <u>lives</u> in a <u>large</u> flat in New York.
Peter walked <u>quickly</u> <u>to</u> work.
We <u>met</u> them in Green Street <u>on</u> Friday.
<u>You</u> <u>must</u> come and visit me in Scotland.
My teacher spoke <u>slowly</u> but I didn't understand her.
<u>Mary</u> and Jackie <u>are</u> studying Japanese at college.
I <u>have</u> lost my <u>bag</u>.
They bought a <u>big</u> old <u>house</u> in the country.
She <u>swims</u> fast, and <u>she</u> can ski <u>well</u> too.

B Put words from the box in the sentences. Use each word once.

noun:	verb:	auxiliary:	adjective:	adverb:	pronoun:	preposition:
job	find	~~has~~	beautiful	badly	I	on
match	pass	must	sick	easily	you	at
Saturday		do		carefully		in

▶ Paul *has* .... just started a new job .
1 You'll .... the books .... the table.
2 .... bought some .... flowers and gave them to my wife.
3 She played .... and lost the tennis ....
4 .... haven't seen your grandfather for a long time – you .... visit him at the weekend.
5 Don't worry! You'll .... the exam ....
6 Listen ....! The money is .... the box.
7 I'm playing golf on .... you want to play with me?
8 I feel .... What did we eat .... the restaurant?

C In this text, circle the letters that should be capital letters.

Josephine got a job in ⟨n⟩ew ⟨y⟩ork in june. She went there with her husband, mike. They are living in an apartment on madison avenue. Yesterday, they wanted to look at the sights. They saw the statue of liberty and walked through manhattan. Last monday, josephine started her new job. Josephine and mike want to live the rest of their lives in america.

D Say what is the correct place (*a* to *i*) to put the word in brackets ( ).

▶ (on) I'm ᵃflying ᵇto ᶜMexico ᵈSunday.   *d*..
1 (interesting) I ᵃsaw ᵇa ᶜvery ᵈfilm ᵉlast ᶠnight.   ....
2 (quickly) Go ᵃor ᵇyou'll ᶜmiss ᵈthe ᵉtrain!   ....
3 (can) I ᵃsee ᵇthe ᶜmountains ᵈfrom ᵉmy ᶠwindow.   ....
4 (it) She ᵃsent ᵇme ᶜa ᵈticket ᵉbut ᶠI ᵍleft ʰat ⁱhome.   ....
5 (go) You ᵃlook ᵇsick. You ᶜmust ᵈand ᵉsee ᶠa ᵍdoctor.   ....
6 (in) I ᵃstayed ᵇthere ᶜfor ᵈa ᵉweek ᶠJune.   ....
7 (very) Mary ᵃgave ᵇChristopher ᶜa ᵈexpensive ᵉpresent.   ....
8 (road) There's ᵃsnow ᵇon ᶜthe ᵈso ᵉdrive ᶠcarefully.   ....

28 Word order: subject, verb, object

1 In English, the order of words in a statement is subject + verb + object:

SUBJECT	+ VERB	+ OBJECT
I	*enjoy*	*good food.*
Peter	*is watching*	*TV.*
She	*drank*	*a cup of coffee.*

2 Some verbs (e.g. **go**) do not have an object:
> Steven **has gone**.
> The train **didn't arrive**.
> Ann and Tom **are swimming**.

Some verbs (e.g. **like**) always need an object:

SUBJECT	+ VERB	+ OBJECT
I	*like*	*music.*
She	*wants*	*a drink.*

3 After the verb **be**, we can use an object or an adjective:

She is | OBJECT
         a doctor.

Mary is | ADJECTIVE
          tired.

We can also put adjectives after the verbs **look**, **seem** and **feel** (see Unit 65):
> Mary **looks tired**.

4 Now look at this example:

> John gave **Mary** an apple.
> John gave **her** an apple.

After some verbs (e.g. **give**, **send**, **bring**), we can talk about a person (**Mary**, **her**) and an object:

	VERB	+ PERSON	+ OBJECT
He	*sent*	*Jane*	*a book.*
Ann	*made*	*Tom*	*a cup of tea.*
Ann	*brought*	*him*	*a cup of tea.*
He	*left*	*them*	*some money.*
She	*wrote*	*him*	*a letter.*

5 We usually put information about times or places at the end of the sentence:

I had a holiday | PLACE
                  in Spain.

They gave their son a watch | TIME
                              yesterday.

Practice

A **There are ten sentences in the box. Circle each sentence.**

(She didn't come) he is rich they like sport we are studying she is a teacher the bus hasn't arrived they've gone I didn't like the programme they sent me a postcard Paul and Joe have left

B **Put the words in brackets ( ) in the correct order.**

▶ (bought – she – a TV)   *She bought a TV.*...................
1 (the match – won – they)   ....
2 (is eating – he – a pizza)   ....
3 (Anna – films – loves)   ....
4 (saw – three cats – I)   ....
5 (tennis – we – played)   ....
6 (wants – a new house – Steve)   ....
7 (forgot – my passport – I)   ....
8 (a photo – she – is taking)   ....
9 (drank – an orange juice – he)   ....

10 (golf – they – like)   ....
11 (Joe – Mexico – visited)   ....
12 (lost – we – our money)   ....

C If the words are in the correct order, put a tick (✓). If not, write the correct sentence.

▶ Mary has phoned.   ✓...
▶ Brilliant was the film.   The film was brilliant............................
1 The boys are playing football. ....
2 Michael not has come.   ....
3 The children are looking tired. ....
4 Ann eggs does not eat.   ....
5 Mary ate a large piece of cake. ....

D Write sentences, putting the word in brackets ( ) in the correct place.

▶ She wrote a letter. (me)   She wrote me a letter..........................
1 They sent an invitation. (us)   ....
2 Sheila gave a present. (Mike)   ....
3 I made a sandwich. (her)   ....
4 Tom brought a newspaper. (Sally) ....
5 My uncle gave a job. (me)   ....
6 She left a message. (you)   ....
7 Mary is sending some flowers. (them) ....
8 She brings a coffee every day. (him) ....

E Put the word in brackets ( ) in the correct place in the sentence.

▶ (bought) We bought........ a house .... in Italy ....
1 (him) They .... gave .... a new car ....
2 (was) I .... thirsty .... this morning.
3 (last night) My friends .... didn't arrive ....
4 (her bag) She .... lost ....
5 (an actor) David .... is ....
6 (a photograph) I .... sent .... her ....
7 (stayed) We .... in Turkey .... for a week.
8 (his wife) Paul .... met .... in Scotland ....
9 (yesterday) We .... didn't win .... the match ....
10 (her) I .... wrote .... a letter ....
11 (wonderful) The film .... was ....
12 (today) They .... left ....
13 (me) She .... brought .... a cake ....
14 (ate) They .... their dinner .... at seven o'clock ....

29 'Yes/no' questions

1 Here are some 'yes/no' questions:
Are you hungry?
Shall I answer the phone?
Did you enjoy the film?

We call them 'yes/no' questions because the answer is either 'yes' or 'no':
Are you hungry?   *Yes, I am.*
                   No, I'm not.

2 We form 'yes/no' questions like this:

▶ We put the verb **be** before the subject:

be	+	SUBJECT	
Are		*they*	*busy?*
Is		*he*	*ready?*
Was		*she*	*here?*

▶ Or, we put an auxiliary verb (**be, have, will, shall, can, may,** etc.) before the subject:

AUXILIARY	+	SUBJECT	+	VERB
Is		*Mark*		*leaving?*
Have		*they*		*gone?*
Will		*they*		*win?*
Can		*you*		*sing?*

(For auxiliary verbs, see Unit 27.)

▶ With Present Simple verbs, we put **do** or **does** before the subject:

do	+	SUBJECT	+ VERB	
Does		*she*	*work*	*in Paris?*
Do		*they*	*live*	*in New York?*
Do		*you*	*play*	*tennis?*
Does		*he*	*like*	*ice-cream?*

Note that we say:
Does she play tennis?
(NOT *Does she plays tennis?*)

▶ With Past Simple verbs, we put **did** before the subject:

did	+ SUBJECT	+ VERB	
Did	*she*	*visit*	*Paris?*
Did	*he*	*go*	*to Spain?*

3 Here are all the forms of **do** questions:

PRESENT SIMPLE		
Do	*I/you/we they*	}*work?*
Does	*he/she/it*	

PAST SIMPLE		
Did	*I/he/she/it/you/we/they*	*work?*

Practice

A Make 'yes/no' questions from these statements.

▶ You are learning a language.   *Are you learning a language?*
1 She is thirsty. ....
2 He can swim well. ....
3 They were tired after the match. ....
4 She will return to Mexico. ....
5 I may leave now. ....
6 They have all left. ....
7 We shall wait a little longer. ....

B Now make questions from these statements. Start your questions with *Do, Does* or *Did*.

▶ You listen to the radio.   *Do you listen to the radio?*
1 They work in London. ....
2 She visits her uncle. ....
3 We began the course in March. ....
4 Her car goes very fast. ....
5 You bought a new table. ....

C You have met Jane, an English girl, in Paris. Use the words in brackets ( ) to ask her some questions. Her answers are on the right. They will help you choose the right tense for your questions.

▶ (like/it here)　　　　　You: Do you like it here .... ?　～ Jane: Yes, I do.
▶ (studying/French)　　　You: Are you studying French .. ?　～ Jane: Yes, I am.
1 (like/French music)　　　You: .... ?　～ Jane: Yes, I do.
2 (staying/in the centre)　 You: .... ?　～ Jane: No, I'm not.
3 (come/by plane)　　　　You: .... ?　～ Jane: Yes, I did.
4 (have got/a flat)　　　　You: .... ?　～ Jane: Yes, I have.
5 (working/in Paris)　　　　You: .... ?　～ Jane: No, I'm not.
6 (visited/the museums)　 You: .... ?　～ Jane: Yes, I have.
7 (find/your flat easily)　　You: .... ?　～ Jane: No, I didn't.
8 (like/French food)　　　　You: .... ?　～ Jane: Yes, I do.

D You want to study English in London. You telephone a language school to ask some questions. Put the words in brackets ( ) in the right order to make questions.

▶ (of London? – Is – near the centre – the school) Is the school near the centre of London?
1 (homework? – give – Do – the teachers) ....
2 (the classes – small? – Are) ....
3 (organize – trips? – Does – the school) ....
4 (a certificate – I get – Will – at the end of the course?) ....
5 (a place now? – I – reserve – Shall) ....
6 (pay – I – Can – by credit card?) ....

E David has just spent a week on holiday in Greece with his wife Mary. Ask him some questions about his holiday using words and phrases from the box. Use his answers to help you.

~~Did~~	Was	the sea	~~Mary~~	~~enjoy~~	comfortable?	
Did	Was	the airport	Mary	busy?	the beaches?	
Did	Was	the restaurants	learn	expensive?	any Greek?	
Were	the hotel	you	like	warm?	~~the holiday?~~	

▶ You: Did Mary enjoy the holiday? ...... 　～ David: Yes, she had a good time.
1 You: .... 　～ David: Yes, there were thousands of people at the airport.
2 You: .... 　～ David: Yes, the water was very warm.
3 You: .... 　～ David: No, they were quite cheap.
4 You: .... 　～ David: No, it's a difficult language for me.
5 You: .... 　～ David: Yes, she swam and sunbathed every day.
6 You: .... 　～ David: Yes, it was a lovely hotel.

30 Where, when, why, how

1 **Where**, **when**, **why**, and **how** are question words. We use them like this:

▶ **Where**
We use **where** to ask about places:
*Where is Mike? – He's **at home.***

▶ **When**
We use **when** to ask about times and dates:
When** will you phone? – **At six o'clock.

▶ **Why**
We use **why** to ask about the reason for something:
Why** is Mary taking a taxi ? – **Because her car isn't working.

▶ **How**
We use **how** to ask 'in what way?':

***How** did he get to Brighton? ~ He went **by train**.*

We also use **how** to ask about people's health or happiness:
*Hello. **How** are you? ~ I'm **fine**, thanks.*

2 We form questions with **where, when, why** and **how** like this:

▶ In questions with **be**, we put the subject after **be**:

	be +	subject	
Why	*is*	*Paul*	*angry?*
Where	*are*	*they?*	
Why	*is*	*he*	*here?*

▶ In questions with an auxiliary verb (**will, is, are, can, must,** etc.), we put the subject after the auxiliary verb:

	verb +	subject +	verb	
Why	*are*	*they*	*leaving?*	
How	*will*	*she*	*get*	*there?*
When	*will*	*you*	*phone?*	

(For auxiliary verbs, see Unit 27.)

▶ In questions with a Present Simple or Past Simple verb, we put a form of **do** before the subject:

	do +	subject +	verb	
Where	*does*	*she*	*live?*	
Why	*did*	*you*	*phone*	*the police?*
Where	*did*	*he*	*live?*	

Practice

A Put the words in brackets ( ) in the right order to make questions.

▶ (you – where – live – do – ?)   *Where do you live?* ....
1 (do – get up – you – when – ?) ....
2 (she – does – where – come – from – ?) ....
3 (leaving – they – are – when – ?) ....
4 (he – is – why – waiting – ?) ....
5 (are – you – how – ?) ....
6 (did – to Scotland – how – get – you – ?) ....
7 (is – where – the town centre?) ....
8 (Paul – drive – so fast – does – why – ?) ....
9 (when – the film – does – start – ?) ....
10 (will – how – you – travel – ?) ....
11 (is – running – she – why – ?) ....
12 (did – where – buy – you – that picture – ?) ....

B Put *where*, *when*, *why* or *how* in the gaps.

▶ *Where* .... are you going? ~ To the shops.

1 .... are you leaving? ~ At six o'clock.

2 .... does she take a taxi to work? ~ Because she doesn't have a car.

3 .... did they get to France? ~ By boat.

4 .... is he studying Spanish? ~ Because he wants to work in Spain.

5 .... do you have breakfast? ~ At half past seven.

6 .... is the restaurant? ~ In Carlton Street.

7 .... are you feeling today? ~ I've got a headache.

8 .... did she buy that dictionary? ~ In the bookshop near the station.

9 .... did Pam go to the police? ~ Because she lost her passport.

C Use the 'full' answers to write questions with *where*, *when*, *why* or *how*.
(We usually use the short, <u>underlined</u> answers when we reply to a question.)

▶ Question: *When did you lose your bag?* ....
Answer: (I lost my bag) <u>On Saturday morning</u>.

1 Question: ....
Answer: (I met Joanna) <u>At a disco in the centre of town</u>.

2 Question: ....
Answer: (I went to the disco) <u>By bus</u>.

3 Question: ....
Answer: (I'm looking for a new job) <u>Because I want more money</u>.

4 Question: ....
Answer: (The nearest hospital is) <u>In Park Street</u>.

5 Question: ....
Answer: (You get to Park Street) <u>On the number 38 bus</u>.

6 Question: ....
Answer: (They're going to see the film) <u>On Friday evening</u>.

7 Question: ....
Answer: (She left the party at ten o'clock) <u>Because she was tired</u>.

8 Question: ....
Answer: (He's studying English) <u>At a language school in Edinburgh</u>.

D If the <u>underlined</u> words are wrong, change them. Put a tick (✓) if they are right.

▶ How <u>is</u> *does* .... she get to work in the mornings?

▶ Where <u>do</u> ✓ .... you normally go for your holidays?

1 How <u>is</u> .... your father?

2 Why <u>do</u> .... you working so hard at the moment?

3 When <u>does</u> .... she finish work yesterday afternoon?

4 Why <u>do</u> .... you go to the bank every day?

5 Where <u>does</u> .... Peter yesterday?

6 Where <u>do</u> .... Mike live?

7 How <u>do</u> .... you get from the art gallery to the swimming pool?

31 Who, what, which

1 We use **who** to ask about people:
   A: *who are you going to visit?*
   B: *I'm going to visit my sister.*
   who did Jane invite to her party?

2 We use **what** and **which** to ask about things:
   What film did you see at the cinema?
   Which newspaper do you want, The Times
   or the Daily Telegraph?

We normally use **what** when there are many
possible answers:

We normally use **which** when there is a small
number of possible answers:

3 When we form questions, we normally put a
   form of **be** or an auxiliary verb (e.g. **can,
   will, do**) after **who, what** and **which**:
   Who is the President of Peru?
   Who can speak Chinese?
   Who did you meet at the party?
   What's the capital of India? ~ *New Delhi.*
   What's she doing?
   What was the name of your teacher?
   What does your father do?
   *Which car will you buy, the Fiat or the
   Ford?*
   *Which shirt do you prefer, the red one or the
   blue one?*

Practice

A Put *who, what* or *which* in the gaps.

	QUESTIONS	ANSWERS
▶	*What* .... did you eat last night?	~ Fish, peas and potatoes.
1	.... are you writing to?	~ George and Mary.
2	.... restaurant do you prefer, the Pizza Palace or the Spaghetti King?	~ The Pizza Palace.
3	.... 's the answer to question 13?	~ I don't know.
4	.... bus do we take to the museum, the number 24 or the number 38?	~ The number 38.
5	.... did you invite to the party?	~ Tony, Steve and Kathryn.
6	.... are you doing at the weekend?	~ I'm driving to Bristol.
7	.... pen is yours, the green one or the blue one?	~ The green one.
8	.... has been to Africa?	~ I have.
9	.... 's the capital of Scotland?	~ Edinburgh.
10	.... 's the boy in the photo?	~ My cousin.

B Use the words in the box to complete the questions. Use each word once.

is	~~What~~	do	Who	is	are	What
did	Who	is	are	Which	were	

▶ A: *What* .... did you do this morning? ~ B: We bought a new car.
1 A: Where .... you buy that painting? ~ B: We bought it in Mexico.

2 A: Where .... the nearest bank? ~ B: In the High Street.

3 A: Why .... you tired yesterday evening? ~ B: I worked very hard all day.

4 A: When .... you get up in the morning? ~ B: I get up at seven o'clock.

5 A: .... car do you prefer, the family car ~ B: The sports car.
 or the sports car?

6 A: What .... they doing? ~ B: They're playing tennis.

7 A: .... did you meet at the station? ~ B: I met Jane.

8 A: Who .... they? ~ B: They're my sisters.

9 A: .... is the name of the hotel? ~ B: It's called the Bridge Hotel.

10 A: .... does she like best? ~ B: Tom.

11 A: Who .... the richest person in the world? ~ B: I don't know!

12 A: Which film .... better? ~ B: The French one.

C Complete the questions. (We usually use the short, <u>underlined</u> answers when we reply to a question.)

▶ A: Which *song do you prefer?* ....
 B: (I prefer) <u>The Spanish song</u>.

1 A: What ....?
 B: (She bought) <u>Bread and milk</u>.

2 A: Which ....?
 B: (They use) <u>The blue book</u>.

3 A: What ....?
 B: (I saw) <u>The Arc de Triomphe and the Eiffel Tower</u>. (in Paris)

4 A: Who ....?
 B: (I met) <u>My aunt and uncle</u>. (at the airport)

5 A: Which ....?
 B: (I am catching) <u>The 13.30</u>. (train)

6 A: Who ....?
 B: (I will visit) <u>My sister and her family</u>. (in Paris)

D Write questions to match the answers. Begin your questions with *who*, *what* or *which*.

▶ *Who is he?* ....
▶ He's my brother.

1 ....?
 Jack drinks coffee in the morning

2 ....?
 I'm going to see a film tomorrow.

3 ....?
 They are playing cricket.

4 ....?
 I prefer the blue book.

5 ....?
 She likes Peter.

6 ....?
 He bought the small car.

32 How long/far/often . . .?

1 We use **How long ...?** to ask about a period of time:

> *How long have you been waiting? ~ About twenty minutes.*
> *How long will the journey take? ~ Three hours.*

We use **from ... to** or **from ... until** to talk about a period of time:

> *She was a student from 1995 to 2000.*
> *Tomorrow I'm working from 8.30 until 6.*

2 We use **How far ...?** to ask about the distance from one place to another. We can use **from** and **to** with the places we are asking about:

> *How far is it from Amsterdam to Paris? 475 kilometres.*
> *How far are the shops from here? ~ Not far.*

3 We use **How often ...?** to ask about the number of times something happens. We can use phrases like **every day**, **once a week**, etc. in the answer:

> *How often do the buses run? ~ Every hour.*
> *How often do you play squash? ~ Twice a week.*

4 We can use **How much ...?** to ask about the price of something:

> *How much is a return ticket to Florence?*
> *How much did you pay for this car?*

5 We use **How much ...?** with an uncountable noun to ask about the amount of something. An uncountable noun cannot be plural because it describes something that cannot be counted (e.g. **bread, work, weather, money, music, meat, milk, cheese**).

> *How much bread is there in the cupboard?*
> *How much work have you done today?*

6 We use **How many ...?** with a plural noun to ask about numbers:

> *How many students are in your class? ~ Fifteen.*
> *How many people went to the party? ~ Ten.*

7 We use **How old ...?** to ask about someone's age:

> *How old are you? ~ I'm 19.*

Note that we say:

> *I am 19,* OR: *19.* (NOT ~~I have 19.~~)

We can also say: *I'm 19 years old.* But we cannot say: ~~I'm 19 years.~~

Practice

A Complete the questions using *How long*, *How old*, *How often*, etc. Put the verbs into the correct tense.

QUESTIONS

► (How/you/stay/in New Zealand?)
How long did you stay in New Zealand?..........

1 (How/he/read/a newspaper?)
....

2 (How/a single room/cost?)
....

3 (How/be/you when you went to live in Australia?)
....

4 (How/exams/you/going to take?)
....

5 (How/the course/last?)
....

6 (How/be/it from here to the nearest bus stop?)
....

ANSWERS

~ I stayed there for six months.

~ He reads one every day.

~ It costs £50 a night.

~ I was 15 when I went there.

~ I'm going to take three exams.

~ It will last for two years.

~ It's about 200 metres.

B Make each question using the words in brackets ( ), and *How old*, *How much*, *How many*, etc. Put the verbs into the correct tense.

▶ A: How old is your husband .... (your husband/be)?
    B: He is 34. He'll be 35 next month.
1 A: .... (languages/you/speak)?
    B: I speak three – English, French and Chinese.
2 A:.. (it/be) from here to the airport?
    B: It's about 25 kilometres.
3 A: .... (the meal/cost)?
    B: I can't remember, but it wasn't very expensive.
4 A: .... (you/stay) there?
    B: I stayed there from June until October.
5 A: .... (the postman/come)?
    B: He comes twice a day.
6 A: .... (cheese/you/buy)?
    B: I bought half a kilo.

C Complete each of these sentences by putting one word into each gap.

▶ It was my birthday last week. I am............ 21.
1 The programme lasts .... 8.30 .... 10 o'clock.
2 There is a train to the centre .... thirty minutes in the morning.
3 How .... money have you got?
4 How far is it .... here .... the city centre?
5 My grandfather is seventy ....
6 How .... countries have you visited?

D Complete the conversation by putting in Bob's questions. Start with *How ...* each time.

Anne: I'm doing a course in computing.
Bob: Oh really. (▶) How long have you been doing it? ....
Anne: I've been doing it for about a month. It's at the local college.
Bob: (1)...?
Anne: I go there twice a week.
Bob: (2)...?
Anne: The lessons last for three hours, from two o'clock until five.
Bob: (3)...?
Anne: I study at home every evening.
Bob: (4)...?
Anne: There are about twenty-five people in my class.
Bob: (5)...?
Anne: They're all about the same age as me.
Bob: (6)...?
Anne: It's not far from my home.
Bob: (7)...?
Anne: It doesn't cost anything. My company is paying.

33 What ... like?

1 Look at this question and answer:
A: **What's** Julie **like?**
B: *She's very pretty and she's very kind, but she's not very clever.*

We use **What ... like?** to ask about a person's physical appearance (tall, short, pretty, etc.) or character (interesting, boring, friendly, unfriendly, etc).

We can also use **What ... like?** to ask about places, books, films and events (e.g. a party, a football match):
A: **What's** Rio de Janeiro **like?**
B: *Well, the beaches are wonderful but the traffic is awful.*
A: **What's** Spielberg's latest film **like?**
B: *It's excellent.*

2 We use **look like?** to talk about someone's appearance:
A: **What** does Julie **look like?**
B: *She's tall with brown hair.*

We can also use **like** with **taste, feel, sound,** and **smell:**
A: **What** does that **taste like?**
B: *It **tastes like** cheese.*

A: *What is this material?*
B: *I don't know. It **looks like** wool but it **feels like** cotton.*

3 We can also use **like**, with the question word **Who** and in statements, to mean 'similar to':
A: **Who's** Julie **like** – her father or her mother?
B: *She's **like** her mother.* (= She is similar to her mother.)
*Rio de Janeiro is **like** Buenos Aires.* (= Rio is similar to Buenos Aires.)

4 The word **like** in **What's she like?** is a preposition; it is not the verb **like**. Here is an example of **like** used as a verb:
A: *What music does Julie **like?***
B: *She **likes** rock music.*

5 We usually use **How?**, not **What ... like?**, when we ask about someone's health or temporary state:
A: **How's** your brother today?
B: *He's feeling much better.*
A: **How** was your boss today?
B: *He was very friendly today!*

Practice

A Use the words in brackets ( ) to make a question that goes with the answer.
Use *is/are* or *look*. Sometimes more than one answer is possible.

▶ (What/Sally/like)
A: What is Sally like .... ? ~ B: She's clever, but she's a bit boring.

▶ (What/Jane/like)
A: What does Jane look like .... ? ~ B: She's quite short and has dark hair.

1 (What/Peter/like)
A: .... ? ~ B: He's not a very interesting person.

2 (What/Anna's parents/like)
A: .... ? ~ B: They're very generous.

3 (What/Tom/like)
A: .... ? ~ B: He's very tall, and he has blond hair.

4 (What/Eva/like)
A: .... ? ~ B: She's tall and strong.

5 (What/Bob and Tom/like)
A: .... ? ~ B: They're very amusing.

6 (What/Susan/like)
A: .... ? ~ B: She's tall and slim, and she wears glasses.

B Read the following descriptions.

> Kiwis are a round, brown fruit with a rough skin. They have almost no smell, but they are sweet, with a flavour similar to strawberries.
> A double bass is a musical instrument. It is the largest member of the violin family. It has a deep sound.

Now for each of the answers, write a question about kiwis or a double bass, using *look/sound/taste/smell/feel* + *like*.

QUESTION	ANSWER
▶ *What do kiwis look like* ....?	~ They're round and brown.
1 ....?	~ It has a deep sound.
2 ....?	~ They don't really have a smell.
3 ....?	~ They have a flavour like strawberries.
4 ....?	~ Like a very big violin.
5 ....?	~ They are rough to the touch.

C Use the words in brackets ( ) to write a question with the preposition *like* or the verb *like*. Add any other necessary words.

▶ (What music/you/like)
   A: *What music do you like* ....? ~ B: I like rock music.
▶ (What/Julie/like)
   A: *What is Julie like* ....? ~ B: She is very amusing.
1 (Who/your sister/like)
   A: ....? ~ B: She likes a boy in her class.
2 (What/Paul's brothers/like)
   A: ....? ~ B: They think they're clever, but I don't.
3 (What/Jane/like/for breakfast)
   A: ....? ~ B: She likes toast and marmalade.
4 (Who/you/like)
   A: ....? ~ B: I'm like my mother.
5 (What/Mary's husband/like)
   A: ....? ~ B: He is rather boring. He's not like her.

D Write questions with *What ... like?* (for things that are permanent) or *How ... ?* (for health or temporary situations). Use a form of *be* and the other words in brackets ( ).

▶ (be/Atlanta) *What is Atlanta like* .... ? ~ It's a very modern city.
▶ (be/Mike/yesterday) *How was Mike yesterday* .. ? ~ He felt a lot better.
1 (be/John's flat) .... ? ~ It's very big, and it has a wonderful view over the city.
2 (be/your boss/yesterday) .... ? ~ He was tired but friendly.
3 (be/a squash racquet) .... ? ~ It's similar to a tennis racquet, but lighter.
4 (be/your sister) .... ? ~ She's very well, thank you.
5 (be/Portugal) .... ? ~ It's very interesting. There are lots of things to see.

34 **Who** and **what**: subject and object

1 Compare these examples:

Ann: | SUBJECT | *Who* | *told you?*
Mary: *James told me.*

This is a subject question.

Ann: | OBJECT | *Who* | *did you tell?*
Mary: *I told Bill.*

This is an object question.

2 Compare subject and object questions with **who**:

In the sentence *Who told you?* **Who** is the subject. Here is another example:

Ann: | SUBJECT | *Who* | *wrote Hamlet?*
(= **Somebody** wrote Hamlet. Who?)
Mary: *Shakespeare wrote Hamlet.*

When **who** is the subject, the order of the words is the same as in a statement:

SUBJECT	
Who	*is going to come with me?*
Who	*lives in that old house?*
Who	*wants some more coffee?*

In the sentence *Who did you tell?* **Who** is the object. Here is another example:

Ann: | OBJECT | *Who* | *did you* **meet** *last night?*
(= You met **somebody**. Who?)
Mary: *I met a couple of friends.*

When **who** is the object, we use an auxiliary (**be**, **do**, **have**, etc.) before the subject:

OBJECT	
Who	*are you going to invite?*
Who	*did Laura ask for help?*
Who	*have you told about this?*

3 Compare subject and object questions with **what**:

| SUBJECT | |
| *What* | *is in this dish?* |
(= **Something** is in it. What?)

| OBJECT | |
| *What* | *did you buy at the shops?* |
(= You bought **something**. What?)

Practice

A Write questions beginning with *Who* or *What* from the sentences in brackets ( ).

▶ (Eric met **somebody**.)   <u>Who did Eric meet?</u>
▶ (**Somebody** ate the last piece of cake.)   <u>Who ate the last piece of cake?</u>
1 (**Somebody** wants some more coffee.)   ....
2 (**Something** happened at the end of the story.)   ....
3 (**Somebody** is going to pay the bill.)   ....
4 (He had **something** for breakfast.)   ....
5 (Their letter said **something**.)   ....
6 (**Somebody** knows the answer to my question.)   ....
7 (They saw **something**.)   ....
8 (She is phoning **somebody**.)   ....

B Use the 'full' answers to write questions using *Who* or *What*. (We usually use the short, <u>underlined</u> answers when we reply to a question.)

QUESTIONS	ANSWERS
► <u>Who were you talking to on the phone</u> ?	~ (I was talking to) <u>Elizabeth</u> (on the phone).
► <u>What was the result of the game</u> ?	~ (The result of the game was) <u>2–0 to Italy</u>.
1 .... ?	~ <u>Anita and Frank</u> (went on the trip).
2 .... ?	~ <u>I'm not sure</u> (what's happening in this film).
3 .... ?	~ (I'm going to phone) <u>Jane</u>.
4 .... ?	~ (I watched) <u>that new comedy programme</u> (on TV last night).
5 .... ?	~ <u>John</u> (sent these flowers).
6 .... ?	~ (I bought) <u>a book</u> (in that shop).
7 .... ?	~ <u>Some good news</u> (has made Tom so happy).

C Read this story and then complete the questions.

> Two days ago Robert took his driving test. He failed it. Afterwards he met his friend Philip. He told Philip that he had failed his test. Then he said, 'Don't tell anyone. It's a secret.' Philip said, 'OK, I won't tell anyone.' Later that day, Philip met Linda for coffee and he said, 'Robert failed his driving test.' Linda laughed. 'Poor Robert,' she said.

QUESTIONS	ANSWERS
► (What/Robert/do/two days ago?) <u>What did Robert do two days ago?</u>	~ He took his driving test.
1 (What/happen?)	~ He failed it.
2 (Who/take/his/driving test?)	~ Robert.
3 (What/Robert/fail?)	~ His driving test.
4 (What/Robert/say/to Philip?)	~ He said, 'Don't tell anyone.'
6 (Who/meet/Linda/for coffee?)	~ Philip.

D Complete the questions for the following answers. Use the words in brackets ( ).

► (Oswald, kill) Who <u>did Oswald kill</u> ?	~ He killed President Kennedy.
► (Kennedy, kill) <u>Who killed Kennedy</u> ?	~ Oswald killed Kennedy.
1 (the Nobel Prize, win) Who .... for Physics in 1909?	~ Marconi.
2 (Marconi, invent) What .... ?	~ Short-wave radio.
3 (Everest, climb) Who .... with Hillary?	~ Sherpa Tensing.
4 (Prince Charles, marry) Who .... ?	~ He married Diana.
5 (Hiroshima, destroy) What .... ?	~ An atomic bomb.
6 (Churchill, smoke) What .... ?	~ Cigars.

35 Whose is this? ~ It's John's.

1 **'s and '**
We use the apostrophe (') to talk about possession:
> *This is Mike's house.* (= The house belongs to Mike.)

Here are the rules:

▶ Singular noun (e.g. **Mary**) + **'s**:
*Where is **Tom's** bike?*

▶ Irregular plural noun (e.g. **men**) + **'s**:
*Have you got the **children's** books?*

▶ Regular plural noun (e.g. **teachers**) + **'**:
*We have eight children. This is the **boys'** bedroom, and this is the **girls'** bedroom.*

2 We use the apostrophe for people, but not normally for things. We use **of** for things:
> *The **boys'** room.* (NOT ~~The room of the boys.~~)
> *The end **of** the film.* (NOT ~~The film's end.~~)

We say:
> *I'm going to the **newsagent's**, the **baker's**, the **butcher's** …*
because we mean 'the newsagent's shop/the baker's shop/the butcher's shop'.

3 We use **whose** to ask about possession:

> A: **Whose car** is that? (= Who does that car belong to?)
> B: *It's **John's**.* (= It belongs to John.)
> A: **Whose shoes** are those?
> B: *They're **mine**.* (= They belong to me.)

The word **whose** does not change:
> *Whose book is that?*
> *Whose books are those?*

We often use **this, that, these** and **those** (see Unit 52) in our questions. We often use **mine, yours, his**, etc. (see Unit 57) in our answers:

> *Whose watch is that?*   ~ *It's **Steven's**.*
>   ~ *It's **his**.*
>
> (We don't need to say: *It's Steven's watch.*)

4 **Whose** sounds the same as **who's** but it is different in meaning:
> *Whose coat is this?* (= Who does this coat belong to?)
> *Who's coming?* (= Who is coming?)
> *Who's finished?* (= Who has finished?)

Practice

A Complete these questions and answers. Use *Whose* and the words in brackets ( ) in each question. Use *It's* or *They're* in each answer.

QUESTIONS		ANSWERS	
▶ (books/be) Whose books are .... those?		~ They're .... Mike's.	
▶ (car/be) Whose car is .... that?		~ It's .... hers.	
1 (pens/be) .... those?		~ .... mine.	
2 (umbrella/be) .... that?		~ .... Paul's.	
3 (house/be) .... that?		~ .... Steven King's.	
4 (clothes/be) .... those?		~ .... his.	
5 (records/be) .... those?		~ .... Carl's.	
6 (bike/be) .... that?		~ .... Christine's.	
7 (painting/be) .... that?		~ .... John's.	
8 (bag/be) .... that?		~ .... hers.	
9 (apple/be) .... that?		~ .... Sheila's.	
10 (motorbike/be) .... that?		~ .... my grandfather's.	
11 (taxi/be) .... that?		~ .... ours.	
12 (jackets/be) .... those?		~ .... the tennis players'.	

B Rewrite each sentence using an apostrophe ('). Use *This is* or *These are*.

► This umbrella belongs to Sue.   <u>This is Sue's umbrella.</u>

► These books belong to the students.   <u>These are the students' books.</u>

1 These keys belong to Peter.   ....

2 This football belongs to the boys.   ....

3 This house belongs to my teacher.   ....

4 These bikes belong to my sisters.   ....

5 This room belongs to the children.   ....

6 This chair belongs to the manager.   ....

7 These suitcases belong to Mark.   ....

8 These bags belong to the women.   ....

9 This radio belongs to Joan.   ....

C Put the names of shops in the gaps in this conversation. Use the words in the box, as in the example.

fishmonger	chemist	hairdresser	tobacconist
greengrocer	butcher	newsagent	~~baker~~

Mike: Have we got everything we need for the weekend?

Anne: I hope so. I went to the (►) baker's .... for some bread. Then I went to the bank. After that, I bought some apples at the (1)............... , and some cough medicine at the (2)............... .

Mike: Did you get any meat?

Anne: Yes. I went to the (3)............... and bought some beef. I also got some fish at the (4)............... . What did you get?

Mike: Well, I had a cup of coffee and a piece of cake, and then I bought a newspaper at the (5)............... . Then I went to the (6)............... for some cigars.

Anne: Did you get any milk or sugar or tea?

Mike: No, I'm sorry. I forgot. But I did go to the (7)............... for a haircut. Do you like it?

D Put *Who's* or *Whose* in the gaps in these sentences.

► <u>Who's</u> ..... finished their homework?

► <u>Whose</u> .... flat are you staying in?

1 .... going to the cinema tonight?

2 .... watch is that.

3 .... got an answer to question number three?

4 .... playing football in the park on Sunday?

5 .... house is near to the railway station?

6 .... bags are these?

7 .... chair is that?

8 .... been to France this year?

36 Question tags

1 A question tag is a short question
(e.g. **isn't it?**, **haven't we?**) that we can add
at the end of a statement:
Henry: *We've met before, **haven't we?***
Jeff: *Yes, we have.*

2 Look at this part of a conversation:
Anna: *Sandra is Swiss.*
David: *No, she's French, **isn't she?***
(= I thought she was French, but am I
wrong?)

When tag questions really are questions, like
David's, the voice goes up at the end.

But when tag questions are not really
questions, the voice goes down at the end:

*That was a boring programme, **wasn't it?***
(= I think that was a boring programme.)

3 Note that the verb we use in the tag depends
on the verb used in the statement:

	VERB	+ TAG
be:	*You're French,*	*aren't you?*
verb:	*He **plays** golf,*	*doesn't he?*
auxiliary verb:	*It **has** arrived,*	*hasn't it?*

Thus, most verbs use **do/does**, while **be** and
auxiliary verbs use the same verb in the
question tag.

4 A positive statement has a negative tag:

POSITIVE	+ NEGATIVE
I'm right,	*aren't I?*
	(NOT *am't I?*)
You're 18,	*aren't you?*
They're getting tired,	*aren't they?*
They were friendly,	*weren't they?*
He lives in France	*doesn't he?*
You speak Spanish,	*don't you?*
You passed your exams,	*didn't you?*
She has left,	*hasn't she?*
You can drive,	*can't you?*
The bus will come soon,	*won't it?*

5 A negative statement has a positive tag:

NEGATIVE	+ POSITIVE
It isn't very cheap,	*is it?*
We aren't going to be late,	*are we?*
She wasn't angry,	*was she?*
You don't like this,	*do you?*
She didn't win,	*did she?*
She hasn't visited Ireland,	*has she?*
She can't drive,	*can she?*
It won't rain today,	*will it?*

Practice

A Complete the conversation by putting in question tags.

Tim: We haven't met before, (▶) *have we* ?

Jo: No, I've just arrived in this country.

Tim: You come from Australia, (1) ?

Jo: Yes, from Sydney.

Tim: It's very hot there, (2) ?

Jo: Most of the time, but not always.

Tim: But it never gets very cold, (3) ?

Jo: No, well, not as cold as some places.

Tim: They speak English there, (4) ?

Jo: Yes, that's right.

Tim: You haven't been here long, (5) ?

Jo: No, I only got here two weeks ago.

Tim: You're on holiday, (6) ?

Jo: Yes, I'm travelling around for six months.

B Complete the sentences by putting in question tags.

▶ The programme starts at seven o'clock, *doesn't it*.......... ? ~ Yes, that's right.
1 I can use this ticket on any bus, ... ? ~ Yes, you can.
2 The bill won't be very high, ... ? ~ No, I don't think so.
3 He wasn't very polite, ... ? ~ No, he wasn't.
4 I didn't make a mistake, ... ? ~ No, you didn't.
5 It won't be a difficult thing to do, ... ? ~ No, I don't think so.
6 That was a lovely meal, ... ? ~ Yes, it was delicious.
7 You can't play the piano, ... ? ~ No, I can't.
8 They left last week, ... ? ~ Yes, that's right.

C Complete the conversation with question tags.

Charles: You're going to Helsinki this week, (▶) *aren't you*.......... ?
Marta: Yes, I'm going tomorrow.
Charles: Helsinki is in Finland, (1)...................... ?
Marta: Yes, it's the capital.
Charles: You've been there before, (2)...................... ?
Marta: Yes, two years ago.
Charles: But you can't speak Finnish, (3)...................... ?
Marta: No, I can't.
Charles: But a lot of Finnish people speak English, (4)...................... ?
Marta: Yes.
Charles: Well, I'll see you before you leave, (5)...................... ?
Marta: Yes, I'll see you tonight.

D Complete the sentence with a question tag before each reply.

▶ A: *She comes from Italy, doesn't she?*.......................................
   B: Yes, she comes from Italy.
1 A: You can ....
   B: Yes, I can speak French very well.
2 A: You haven't ....
   B: No, I haven't heard this story.
3 A: You went ....
   B: Yes, I went to Frank's party.
4 A: It isn't ....
   B: No, it isn't very far from here.
5 A: She won't ....
   B: No, she won't be angry.
6 A: You're not ....
   B: No, I'm not going to leave now.
7 A: You'll ....
   B: Yes, I'll be at home tonight.

37 Short answers

1 Look at this example:

QUESTION	+ SHORT ANSWER
Is he at work?	~ **Yes, he is.**
Can I come?	~ **No, you can't.**
Do you like it?	~ **Yes, I do.**
Does she live here?	~ **No, she doesn't.**

We call these 'short answers' because they are not 'full' answers:

Is she sick? { *Yes, she is sick.* (full answer)
{ *Yes, she is.* (short answer)

We use short answers to reply to 'yes/no' questions (see Unit 29):

Are you coming? { *Yes, I am.*
{ *No, I'm not.*

2 We form short answers by not using the main verb from the question:

Have *they gone?* ~ *Yes, they* **have** ~~gone~~.
Did *he go to Paris?* ~ *Yes, he* **did** ~~go~~.
Is *she waiting?* ~ *Yes, she* **is** ~~waiting~~.

When the main verb is **be**, we use **be**:

Are you tired? ~ *Yes, I* **am**.

When we answer **No**, we use a negative verb:

Will *they win?* ~ *No, they* **won't**.
Did *Paul come?* ~ *No, he* **didn't**.
Are *you cold?* ~ *No, I'm* **not**.

We never use positive short forms in short answers:

Are you tired? ~ *Yes, I am.* (NOT ~~Yes, I'm.~~)
Is he happy? ~ *Yes, he is.* (NOT ~~Yes, he's.~~)

3 We can also use short answers to reply 'yes' or 'no' to statements:

STATEMENT	+ REPLY
He's working hard.	~ *Yes, he is.*
She's at work.	~ *No, she isn't.*
She loves films.	~ *Yes, she does.*

Note that with Present Simple or Past Simple verbs, we use **do, does** or **did** in the reply:

She loves films. ~ *Yes, she* **does**.

He liked the book. ~ *Yes, he* **did**.

4 When we write, we normally put a 'comma' (,) after **Yes** or **No** in short answers:

He lives in London. ~ **No,** *he doesn't.*

Practice

A Make short answers by putting in a 'full stop' (.) and a line (—).

QUESTIONS

▶ Can you come tonight?
1 Will you see Ted tomorrow?
2 Have you finished your breakfast?
3 Do you drive to work?
4 Did she come yesterday?
5 Were you tired after the game?
6 Can she sing well?
7 Did Tom have a holiday?
8 Is she studying French?
9 Do you play golf?
10 Did you buy a new table?
11 Are you thirsty?
12 Has Jane been to Mexico before?

ANSWERS

~ Yes, I can. ~~come tonight.~~
~ Yes, I will see Ted tomorrow.
~ No, I haven't finished my breakfast.
~ Yes, I do drive to work.
~ No, she didn't come yesterday.
~ Yes, I was tired after the game.
~ No, she can't sing well.
~ Yes, he did have a holiday.
~ Yes, she is studying French.
~ No, I don't play golf.
~ Yes, I did buy a new table.
~ No, I'm not thirsty.
~ Yes, she has been there before.

B Write the correct answers to the questions. Use the phrases in the box.

Yes, she did.	No, he doesn't.	No, she wasn't.	Yes, he has.	No, I can't.
Yes, I will.	Yes, they have.	Yes, I do.	No, they aren't.	

▶ Have they all left?   ~ Yes, they have. ....
1 Does Steve work hard?   ~ ....
2 Do you like this music?   ~ ....
3 Are they listening?   ~ ....
4 Did she enjoy her holiday?   ~ ....
5 Was Mary at the concert?   ~ ....
6 Will you phone this weekend?   ~ ....
7 Can you play the guitar?   ~ ....
8 Has he gone to bed?   ~ ....

C Write positive short answers and then negative short answers for the questions.

▶ Was the film good?
{ ~ Yes, it was. ....
{ ~ No, it wasn't. ....

1 Does he enjoy French food?
{ ~ Yes, ...
{ ~ No, ...

2 Can he swim?
{ ~ Yes, ...
{ ~ No, ...

3 Will they return tonight?
{ ~ Yes, ...
{ ~ No, ...

4 Do you want to buy that shirt?
{ ~ Yes, ...
{ ~ No, ...

5 Are they coming in Mike's car?
{ ~Yes, ...
{ ~ No, ...

6 Did you ask Sally to come?
{ ~Yes, ...
{ ~ No, ...

7 Is your headache better?
{ ~Yes, ...
{ ~ No, ...

8 Were the exams difficult?
{ ~Yes, ...
{ ~ No, ...

D Bill always says *Yes*. Tom always says *No*. Write their answers.

                                          Bill: Tom:
▶ Japanese people eat a lot of fish. ~ Yes, they do. .... ~ No, they don't. ......
1 The sun always shines in England. ~ .... ~ ....
2 New York is the capital of America. ~ .... ~ ....
3 Italy will win the next World Cup. ~ .... ~ ....
4 Bananas are delicious.   ~ .... ~ ....
5 Cats can sing beautifully.   ~ .... ~ ....
6 The English speak very slowly.   ~ .... ~ ....

38 So am I, I am too, Neither am I, etc.

1 Look at this:

She is saying that she is also tired.

2 Here are some more examples:

He **was** very angry. ~ So **was I**.

My flat's quite small. ~ So **is mine**.
They **were** waiting. ~ So **was she**.
I'm going to have tea. ~ So **am I**.
Ann **has** finished her work and so **has Mary**.
They've been waiting. ~ So **has she**.
I **work** in an office. ~ So **do I**.
I **enjoyed** the film. ~ So **did I**.
Philip **will** pass the exam and so **will you**.
He **can** drive. ~ So **can she**.

Note:

▶ we use **so** after a positive statement;

▶ the verb we use after **so** depends on the verb used in the positive statement.

3 Instead of **so am I**, we can say **I am too**, with the same meaning. Here are some examples:

I'm tired.~ **I am too**.
We've got a small flat. ~ **We have too**.
I work in an office. ~ **I do too**.
Bill enjoyed the film and **I did too**.
He can drive. ~ **She can too**.

4 We can use expressions like **neither am** I to reply to a negative statement:

I'm not tired. ~ Neither **am I**.
            (= And I'm not tired.)
I haven't seen that film. ~ Neither **have I**.
I don't like this place. ~ Neither **do I**.
I didn't see that play. ~ Neither **did I**.
His sister can't drive and neither **can he**.

5 We can say **I'm not either** to mean the same as **neither am I**:

I'm not tired. ~ **I'm not** either.
            (= And I'm not tired.)
I haven't seen that film. ~ **I haven't** either.
I don't like this place. ~ **I don't** either.
I didn't see that play. ~ **I didn't** either.
His sister can't drive and **he can't** either.

Practice

A **Complete the sentences with** so, too, either **or** neither.

▶ I really enjoyed that meal. ~ So............ did I.

▶ I haven't done the homework. ~ I haven't either........ .

▶ We live in the centre of town. ~ We do too............ .

1 I don't like football. ~ .... do I.

2 I haven't been to America. ~ .... have I.

3 My father works in an office. ~ .... does mine.

4 I haven't read a newspaper today. ~ .... have I.

5 I play a lot of different sports. ~ I do ....

6 I've been working very hard lately. ~ .... have I.

7 Ann will be at the party and .... will Jane.

8 My brother can't speak any foreign languages and .... can my sister.

9 Helen sent me a birthday card and Robin did ....

10 George isn't going to the meeting and I'm not ....

11 Tony arrived late and .... did I.

12 Kathy didn't go to the concert and .... did I.

B Put in the replies, using *so* or *neither* and the words in brackets ( ), as in the examples.

QUESTIONS	ANSWERS
▶ I've got a cold. (I)	*So have I.* ....
▶ I haven't got much money. (I)	*Neither have I.* ....
1 We're going to the concert. (we)	....
2 My pen doesn't work. (mine)	....
3 I haven't read today's paper. (I)	....
4 My meal was excellent. (mine)	....
5 I've been ill. (Frank)	....
6 Ron didn't go to the party. (George)	....
7 I can't understand this game. (I)	....
8 I'm not working tomorrow. (I)	....
9 Ruth passed the exam. (John)	....
10 I've eaten enough. (I)	....
11 I'm going to see that film. (we)	....
12 My car is very old. (mine)	....

C Look at the information in the table about four people and complete the sentences using *so, too, either* or *neither*.

	JULIA	ROBERT	SANDRA	PAUL
Lives in:	New York	Chicago	New York	Los Angeles
Speaks:	Spanish	French	Spanish	French
Drives?	Yes	No	No	Yes
Likes:	reading	travelling	travelling	reading
Plays:	basketball	basketball	tennis	tennis

▶ Julia lives in New York and Sandra *does too* ....
▶ Julia lives in New York and *so does* .... Sandra.
1 Robert doesn't live in New York and .... Paul.
2 Robert doesn't live in New York and Paul ....
3 Julia speaks Spanish and .... Sandra.
4 Julia speaks Spanish and Sandra ....
5 Robert can't speak Spanish and .... Paul.
6 Robert can't speak Spanish and Paul ....
7 Julia can drive and Paul ....
8 Robert can't drive and .... Sandra.
9 Julia has passed her driving test and .... Paul.
10 Robert likes travelling and .... Sandra.
11 Julia likes reading and Paul ....
12 Julia plays basketball and .... Robert.
13 Sandra doesn't play basketball and .... Paul.

Test D: Sentences and questions

A A policeman is asking Philip some questions. Put the questions in the right order and with correct punctuation, and complete the short answers.

Policeman: get/you/did/sir/home/your/before/wife,

(►) <u>Did you get home before your wife, Sir</u> ....?

Philip: Yes, (►) <u>I did</u> .... Half an hour before.

Policeman: normally/the/home/take/do/bus/you

(1)...?

Philip: No, (2)........................ . I normally walk. But it was raining yesterday.

Policeman: I see. Shall we sit down, sir?

Philip: Of course. I'll make you some tea.

Policeman: wife/soon/is/home/coming/your

(3)...?

Philip: Yes, (4)........................ . Just like yesterday.

Policeman: by/travel/she/bus/does

(5)...?

Philip: No, (6)........................ . She runs.

Policeman: Runs? Even in the rain, sir?

Philip: That's right. She likes to exercise.

Policeman: she/was/yesterday/tired

(7)...?

Philip: Yes, (8)........................ . Sometimes she runs too fast.

Policeman: If she was running and you were on the bus, who was driving your car when it crashed, then?

Philip: I've no idea, officer. Do you take sugar in your tea?

B Brian is going to ask people in Manchester about their lives and attitudes. Write the first word in each question to complete his questionnaire.

► <u>When</u> .... do you usually go to bed?

► <u>Do</u> .... you play sports?

1 .... many brothers and sisters have you got?

2 .... was your childhood like?

3 .... do you talk to, if you need financial advice?

4 .... you do your shopping in the town centre?

5 .... much exercise do you take?

6 .... type of washing powder do you use?

7 .... do you enjoy doing on Saturday nights?

8 .... do English people eat so little fish?

9 .... your neighbours speak to you?

10 .... you born in Manchester?

11 .... is your favourite TV programme?

12 .... washes the dishes in your house?

13 .... you go on holiday in the UK or abroad this year?

14 .... is football so popular in Manchester?

C Joan and her husband agree on everything. Finish Joan's sentences, using *neither* or *so*.

'He won't eat anything yellow, and (▶) neither will I .... We enjoy walking sometimes, but he prefers sitting in the garden and (1)........................ . I can play the piano, and (2)........................ , so we play together in the evenings. He has been to Egypt, and (3)........................ , but we both went there before we met. I don't like long films on the TV, and (4)........................ . We always fall asleep before the end. He had a very lonely childhood, I'm afraid, and (5)........................ . I'll never forget the first time we met, and (6)........................ . We were in a music shop and he began playing my favourite song on the piano. He hasn't stopped playing, and (7)........................ !'

D Penny has bought a new second-hand yacht. Greg is asking her about it. Complete his questions with three words, using *how* each time.

Greg: It looks fantastic! (▶) How long is it?
Penny: Twenty metres. I'm going to sail to the Greek islands next month.
Greg: That sounds nice. (1)........................ that?
Penny: I'm not sure. About a thousand kilometres.
Greg: It looks fairly new. (2)........................ it?
Penny: Six and a half years. But the last owner didn't use it much. He was too busy working.
Greg: I would use it every weekend, if it was mine. (3)........................ you going to use it?
Penny: At least once a month, for long weekends.
Greg: (4)........................ you go?
Penny: Just to France, I think. Are you any good at sailing?
Greg: I am actually. But I'm better at standing on the deck in the sun. By the way, (5)........................ it cost?
Penny: I can't tell you. I don't want to remember!

E Put the correct question tag at the end of each line.

John: That was an interesting play, (▶) wasn't it .... ?
Paul: You didn't like the main actor, (1)........................ ?
John: Not exactly. He's in that TV programme, (2)........................ ?
Paul: I think so. He plays the boy's father, (3)........................ ?
John: That's right. I couldn't hear him tonight. He hasn't got a very loud voice, (4)........................ ?
Paul: No, not at all. You just can't hear actors these days, (5)........................ ?
John: That's because they work in TV, (6)........................ ?
Paul: I suppose so. More money. He won't earn so much tonight, (7)........................ ?
John: He was terrible, so he shouldn't earn so much tonight, (8)........................ ?
Paul: No. You're right. He wasn't great, (9)........................ ?
John: Anyway, you didn't pay very much for the tickets, (10)........................ ?
Paul: I can't remember. They were free, (11)........................ ?
John: That's OK, then, (12)........................ ?

39 Ability: **can, can't, could, couldn't**

1 We form sentences with **can** like this:

can + INFINITIVE
I can ski.

POSITIVE
I/He/She/It/We/You/They **can ski.**

NEGATIVE	FULL FORM	SHORT FORM
I/He/She/It/You (etc.)	**cannot ski.**	**can't ski.**

QUESTIONS
Can I/he/she/it/you (etc.) **ski?**

In spoken English **cannot** is possible, but we normally use **can't**:
  *He **can't** swim.*

For short answers (*Can you swim? ~ No, I can't*), see Unit 37.

2 We use **can** and **can't** to talk about things we are able to do <u>generally</u>.
  *She **can speak** Japanese.* (= She is able to speak Japanese.)
  *He **can't ski**.* (= He isn't able to ski.)

We also use **can** and **can't** to talk about things we are able to do <u>at the moment</u>:
  *I **can see** the moon.* (= I am able to see it now.)

3 We form sentences with **could** like this:

could + INFINITIVE
I could swim.

POSITIVE
I/he/she/it/we/you/they **could ski.**

NEGATIVE	FULL FORM	SHORT FORM
I/he/you (etc.)	**could not ski**	**couldn't ski.**

We use **could** to talk about things we were able to do <u>generally</u> in the past:

  *I **could run** 100 metres in 12 seconds when I was young.*
  *Susan **could read** when she was three years old.*

4 We do not normally use **could** for something that happened on a particular occasion in the past. We use **was able to** or **managed to**:
  *The boat was in difficulties, but in the end it **managed to** reach the port.* (OR... *it was **able to** reach ...*; NOT ... *it could reach* ...)

5 When we talk about a person's ability to do something in the future, we use **will be able** to.
  *The baby **will be able to** talk soon.*

Practice

A Complete the sentences with *can, can't* or *couldn't* and the verbs in brackets ( ).

▶ You don't have to shout. I <u>can hear</u>............ (hear) you very well.

▶ I <u>couldn't watch</u>...... (watch) that programme last night because I had to go out.

1 He .... (play) last week because he was injured.

2 He eats in restaurants all the time because he .... (cook).

3 I .... (give) you a lift in my car because it isn't working at the moment.

4 I didn't have a good seat in the theatre, so I .... (see) the stage very well.

5 John doesn't need a calculator. He .... (do) very difficult sums in his head.

6 She's very good at music. She .... (play) three instruments.

7 I .... (find) my address book. Have you seen it?

8 He spoke very quickly and I .... (understand) anything he said.

9 We .... (go) on the trip because we .... (afford) it. It was very expensive.

10 I .... (do) any more work because I was very tired, so I stopped.

11 I'm afraid that I .... (talk) to you now. I'm in a hurry. I have to be at work in five minutes.

3 Use the words in brackets ( ) to complete each sentence, with *can*, *can't*, *could* or *couldn't*.

▶ Sarah phoned Jane yesterday. (They/not/talk/for a long time, because Jane had to go out.)
They couldn't talk for a long time, because Jane had to go out. ....

1 Grandma needs her glasses. (She/not/see/anything without her glasses.)
She ....

2 Mary won her race. (She was so tired after the race that she/not/stand up.)
She ....

3 (Last year, Robert/beat/his younger brother at chess.) But he can't beat him now.
Last year, ...

4 John and Anna have a wonderful view from their hotel room. (They/see/the whole of the city.)
They ....

C Complete these sentences using *managed to* or the correct form of *be able to*.

▶ I _was able to/managed to_.. get the last ticket for the concert.

1 After waiting for a long time, we .... go into the museum.

2 They .... buy a new carpet yesterday.

3 I .... eat three plates of pasta in the restaurant last night!

4 Our friends .... visit us tomorrow afternoon.

5 She .... have a long holiday next year.

6 We .... ski in Scotland last weekend.

D Look at this table and complete the sentences using *can*, *could*, or *will be able to*.

	LAST YEAR	NOW	HOPES FOR THE FUTURE
Joy	swim 100 metres	swim 1000 metres	swim for her club team
Mark	type 15 words per minute	type 30 words per minute	work as a secretary
Anne	speak only a little French	speak French quite well	work as an interpreter
Carol	only cook omelettes	cook quite well	work as a chef
Tom	only play the piano	play the piano and the violin	be a professional musician
Susan	ride a bike	drive a car	drive a racing car

▶ Last year Joy _could swim 100 metres_.... . Now, _she can swim 1000 metres_ .

▶ At the moment Anne _can speak French_.......... quite well, and if she studies hard, perhaps _she'll be able to work_...... as an interpreter.

1 Last year Mark .... Now, ...

2 Last year Anne .... Now, ...

3 At the moment Carol .... , and if she works hard, perhaps

....

4 Last year Tom .... Now, ... , and if he studies hard, perhaps ....

5 Last year Susan .... Now, ... , and she hopes that one day ....

40 Can/Could I? May I? Can/Could you?

1 We form questions with **can**, **may** and **could** like this:

QUESTIONS		
Can		
May	} I/he/she/it/we (etc.)	**wait?**
Could		

2 We use **can**, **may** and **could** to ask for things:

Can etc.	+ I/we +	**have**	...?
Can	I	**have**	*a coffee?*

Could we **have** *two tickets, please?*
Can I **have** *some sugar?*

3 We use **can**, **may** or **could** to ask for permission. **Could I** and **May I** are more formal and polite than **Can I**:

Can/May/Could	+ I/we +	INFINITIVE ...?
May	I	*see*	*her?*

Could we **look** *at your map, please?*
Can I **borrow** *your tennis racquet, please?*

We use **can** or **may** to give permission:
You **can** *leave your bag here.* (OR ... *may leave ...*)

If we talk about what is allowed in general, rather than by a particular person, we use **can**:
People **can** *drive on the roads when they are seventeen.*

But official notices often use **may**:
BAGS MAY BE LEFT HERE.

4 We use **Can you**, **Could you** and **Would you** (but not ~~May you~~) when we ask someone to do something. **Could** and **would** are more formal and polite than **can**.

Can/Could/Would	+ you +	INFINITIVE	...?
Could	you	*help*	*me?*

A: *I'm cold.* **Can** *you* **close** *the window?*
B: *Yes, of course.*

Practice

A Put the words in brackets ( ) in the right order to make questions.

▶ (have – a return ticket to York – could – please – I – ?)
   Could I have a return ticket to York, please?
   ....

1 (please – I – may – a glass of orange juice – have – ?)
   ....

2 (we – listen to your new CD – can – ?)
   ....

3 (your mobile – please – use – I – can – ?)
   ....

4 (may – borrow – your camera tomorrow – I – ?)
   ....

5 (please – the menu – pass – you – could – ?)
   ....

6 (can – this letter for me – you – post – ?)
   ....

B Ask for permission. Use the words in brackets ( ) and the words in the box.

| use your photocopier | ~~use your dictionary~~ | close the window |
| borrow your pen | turn on the TV | |

▶ SITUATION: You want to find the meaning of a word.
(may I) _May I use your dictionary?_ ....

1 SITUATION: You want to write down a telephone number.
(can I) ....

2 SITUATION: You want to watch a programme.
(can I … please) ....

3 SITUATION: You're feeling cold.
(may I) ....

4 SITUATION: You need a photocopy of a letter.
(may I … please) ....

C Ask people to do things. Use the words in brackets ( ) and the phrases in the box.

| ~~buy me a magazine~~ | tell me the time | make me a sandwich |
| tell me the way to Buckingham Palace | carry one of these cases | |

▶ PROBLEM: You're sick. You're in bed. You're bored.
(can you … please) _Can you buy me a magazine, please?_ ....

1 PROBLEM: Your suitcases are very heavy.
(could you) ....

2 PROBLEM: You're lost in London.
(could you … please) ....

3 PROBLEM: You've forgotten to put your watch on.
(can you) ....

4 PROBLEM: You're hungry. You're very tired.
(can you … please) ....

D Choose the right word from the words in brackets ( ), and put it in the gap.

▶ _Could_ .... (May/Could) you give me one of these forms, please?

1 In the street:
Excuse me, officer, ... (could/may) you tell me how to
get to the station?

2 At a railway station:
A: Let's have our sandwiches here.
B: .... (Couldn't/Can't) you read? Look at the notice; it says:
'FOOD .... (MAY/COULD) NOT BE EATEN IN THIS WAITING ROOM.'

3 A: .... (Could/May) you phone Jenny about tomorrow's meeting?
B: I .... (may not/can't/couldn't) phone her because she has lost her mobile.

4 A: .... (May/Could) someone help me?
B: What .... (may/can) I do to help you?
A: We need to move the chairs and to clean this room. Can you help?
B: I'm afraid I .... (may not/can't) move the chairs because of my bad back.

41 Must, mustn't

1 We use must with an infinitive (**do**, **go**, **work**, etc.):

$$You \quad must \quad \boxed{\text{INFINITIVE} \atop work} \quad harder.$$

Don't use **to** before the infinitive:
NOT ~~You must to work harder.~~

The form of **must** is the same for all persons:

> I/you/he/she/it/we/they **must leave** soon.

2 We use **must** in rules, to say that an action is necessary:

> All visitors **must go** to reception when they arrive.

We use **You must …** to give somebody an order:

> Your work is poor – **you must try** harder.
> **You must finish** this work tomorrow.

We use **I/We must …** to say that we think it is necessary or important that we do something:

> I'm getting tired. **I must go** home now.
> **We must get** a new car soon.

3 We also use **You must …** to strongly recommend or offer something:

> **You must read** this book; it's fantastic!
> **You must come** for lunch at our house.

4 The negative form of **must** is **mustn't** or **must not**:

> **You mustn't park** here – it's not allowed.
> NOT ~~You mustn't to park here.~~

5 We use **You mustn't …** (or **You must not**) to say that it is necessary that somebody does NOT do something:

> **You mustn't smoke** in here.
> **You mustn't make** this mistake again.

We use **I/We mustn't …** (or **must not**) to say that we think it is necessary that we do NOT do something:

> **I mustn't forget** her birthday again.
> **We mustn't be** late for the meeting.

6 Notice that we can use **must** and **mustn't** (NOT ~~will must~~) to talk about the future:

> I must phone Harry tomorrow.
> (NOT ~~I will must phone …~~)

To talk about what was necessary in the past, we cannot use **must**; we use a form of **have to** (see Unit 42).

We don't generally use **must** in a question form. We use **have to** (see Unit 42).

Practice

A The 'Hotel Strict' is not a very nice hotel. It has a lot of rules. Read the list of rules, and change each one into a sentence using *must* or *must not*.

> **Notice to guests**
> Leave your key at reception when you go out.
> Vacate your room by 9 a.m. on the day you leave.
> Return to the hotel before 10 o'clock every night.
> Do not take food into your room.
> Pay for your room when you arrive.
> Do not smoke in the restaurant.

▶ _You must leave_ .... your key at reception when you go out.

1 You .... food into your room.

2 .... for your room when you arrive.

3 .... your room by 9 a.m. on the day you leave.

4 .... in the restaurant.

5 .... to the hotel before 10 o'clock every night.

B Look at this table of instructions for students in a school. Use the table to make sentences with *must* or *mustn't*.

	Yes	No
Attend all classes.	✓	
Take school books home with you.		✓
Make a noise in the corridors.		✓
Write in school books.		✓
Arrive for lessons on time.	✓	
Bring your own pens and paper.	✓	

► <u>You must attend</u>............ all classes.
1 .... school books home with you.
2 .... a noise in the corridors.
3 .... in school books.
4 .... for lessons on time.
5 .... your own pens and paper.

C Henry wants to make some changes in his life. Look at the pictures and make sentences using the phrases in the box with *must* or *mustn't*.

study in the evening	run every morning	~~dress smartly~~	watch TV all day
~~smoke~~	visit my grandmother	sleep in the afternoon	dance all night

► <u>I mustn't smoke.</u> ► <u>I must dress smartly.</u>  1..................... 2.....................

3..................... 4..................... 5..................... 6.....................

D Rewrite the sentences in brackets ( ) using *must* or *mustn't/must not*.

► (Have some of this fish. It's wonderful.)
You <u>must have some of this fish.</u>... . It's wonderful.
1 (Don't tell lies. It's bad.)
You .... It's bad.
2 (Passengers: Do not open the door while the train is moving.)
Passengers .... while the train is moving.
3 (Come for dinner with us one evening next week!)
You .... one evening next week!
4 (All staff: show identity cards when you enter the building.)
All staff .... when they enter the building.
5 (It's bad for you to eat so much unhealthy food.)
You .... so much unhealthy food.
6 (Follow the instructions when using this machine.)
You .... when using this machine.

42 Have to

1 The Present Simple forms of **have to** are:

POSITIVE and NEGATIVE

I/you/we/they { have / don't have }
He/she/it { has / doesn't have } to go.

QUESTIONS

Do I/you/we/they
Does he/she/it } have to go?

2 We use **have to** to talk about things that are necessary because of rules that other people oblige us to follow:
> My brother **has to travel** a lot in his job.
> (It is required by his employer.)
> We **have to pay** the rent every month.
> (It is required by the landlord.)

To talk about things that WE think are necessary, we usually use **must** (see Unit 43).

3 We also use **have to** for things that are necessary because of the circumstances:
> I **have to get** a bus to school. (It is the only way I can travel there.)
> She **has to live** on a small income. (She only receives a small amount of money to pay for what she needs.)

4 We use **don't have to** to say that something is NOT necessary.

> We **don't have to hurry**; we're early.
> (= It's not necessary to hurry. We have plenty of time.)
> I **don't have to get** up early on Sunday.
> (I can stay in bed if I want.)

5 We can use **have got to** with the same meaning as **have to** to talk about something that is necessary at one particular time (but not in general):
> I **have to/I've got to make** a phone call now.
> You **don't have to/haven't got to do** this immediately.

6 The past form of **have to** is **had to**:
> I **had to do** a lot of work yesterday.
> (See Unit 48.)

7 The future form of **have to** is **will have to**:
> He'll **have to look** for another job.
> We **won't have to get** tickets in advance.
> **Will** they **have to get** visas?

Note that we cannot use **have got to** in past or future forms:
> Yesterday I **had to work** hard. (NOT ~~I had got to work hard.~~)

8 We can use the Present Simple of **have to** to talk about the future:
> I **have to do** some shopping tomorrow.
> Do you **have to work** next weekend?

Practice

A Look at this table about different jobs and use the information to complete the sentences, using *have to* or *don't have to*.

	Shop assistants	Bank clerks	Doctors	Teachers
deal with the public	✓	✓	✓	✗
be polite to people	✓	✓	✗	✗
work with money	✓	✓	✗	✗
wear uniforms	✓	✗	✓	✗

▶ Shop assistants <u>have to deal</u> with the public.
1 Teachers .... to people.
2 Bank clerks .... to people.
3 Bank clerks .... with money.
4 Doctors .... with money.

5   Shop assistants often .... uniforms.
6   Teachers .... uniforms.

B Complete the sentences using the correct forms of *have to* or *have got to* and the words in brackets ( ). Be careful to use the correct tense.

▶   I have to leave .... (I/leave) now; I've got an appointment at the dentist's.

▶   Did you have to study .... (you/study) literature when you were at school?

▶   You haven't got to come .... (You/not/come) with me now if you don't want to.

1   .... (I/not/work) hard because the job was very easy.

2   .... (I/do) this work now, or can I do it tomorrow?

3   .... (I/run) to school because I was late.

4   .... (I/go) to an important meeting yesterday.

5   .... (you/show) your passports when you reached the border?

6   .... (I/pay) in cash next week or can I give you a cheque?

7   I want to be an airline pilot. What qualifications .... (you/have) to be a pilot?

8   .... (You/not/decide) today. You can tell me tomorrow.

9   I arrived late yesterday because .... (I/wait) a long time for a bus.

10 A: .... (you/work) every weekend?
    B: No, I don't; but .... (I/work) last weekend.

C Complete the conversations, using the correct forms of *have to* or *have got to*.

A: (Good morning, I'd like to buy a travel card. What/I/do?)
   (▶) Good morning. I'd like to buy a travel card. What do I have to do? ....

B: (You/fill/in an application form.)
   (1)...

A: (I/give/you/a photograph?)
   (2)...

B: (No, you/not/give/me anything, except the money for the card!)
   (3)...

Dad: (What/you/do/at school today?)
       (▶) What did you have to do at school today?

Geoff: (We/do/some/English tests.)
       (4)...

Dad: (How many questions/you/answer?)
       (5)...

Geoff: (We/answer/about forty grammar questions.)
       (6)...
       (I/think/about them very carefully.)
       (7)...

Dad: (you/write/a composition?)
       (8)...

Geoff: (No, but we/do/one next week.)
       (9)...

43 Must/have to, mustn't/don't have to

1 We use **must** when the speaker thinks it is necessary or important to do an action:
> *You **must** go.* (= It is important that you go.)

We make negatives, questions and short answers like this:
> *You **mustn't** go.*
> *__Must__ you go?* ~ *Yes, I **must**.*

2 We use **have to** to talk about an action that is necessary because of rules or laws, or because someone obliges us to do it:
> *Doctors sometimes **have to work** on Sunday.* (It is in the rules of their work.)

We make negatives, questions and short answers with a form of **do**:
> *Teachers **don't have to work** on Sunday.*
> *Do you **have to work** today?* ~ *No, I **don't**.*

3 POSITIVE
In positive sentences we can often use **must** and **have to** with little difference in meaning, because many things are important both because we think so and because there are rules:
> *You **must work** hard in order to succeed* (OR *... you **have to work** ...*).

4 NEGATIVE
Note the difference in meaning between **mustn't** and **don't have to**.

In negative sentences we often use **mustn't** to say that something is against the rules, or against the law:
> *You **mustn't smoke** on buses.* (Smoking is against the rules.)
> *In football you **mustn't touch** the ball with your hands.* (Touching the ball is against the rules.)

We use **don't have to** to say that people are not obliged to do something:
> *In Britain, people **don't have to carry** a passport with them.* (= People are not obliged to carry one.)
> *Nowadays pupils **do not have to learn** Latin at school.* (= They are not obliged to learn it.)

5 QUESTIONS
In questions we usually use **do/does ... have to** (NOT ~~must~~) to ask if something is obligatory or important:
> ***Does** Michael **have to get** up early tomorrow?*
> ***Do** we **have to wait** here?*

Practice

A The Stanton Squash Club has decided that it is important for all club members to do these things:

wear sports shoes and clean clothes   have a shower   pay before you play   finish on time

But these things are **not allowed**:

disturb other players   eat or drink outside the bar   take club balls home

Put *have to*, *don't have to* or *mustn't* in the gaps.

▶ You _don't have to_ wear white clothes, but you _have to_ wear sports shoes.
▶ You _mustn't_ disturb other players, but you _don't have to_ be silent.
1 You .... finish on time, but you .... start on time.
2 You .... play with club balls, but if you do, you .... take them home.
3 You .... eat or drink outside the bar, but you .... buy your food in the bar if you don't want to.
4 You .... have a shower, and you .... wear clean clothes.

B Look at the signs and complete the sentences with *don't have to* or *mustn't*.

ANTIQUES
Please feel free to come in.
(No eating inside.)

▶ You _don't have to_ go in.
▶ You _mustn't_ eat inside.

Entry possible
30 minutes
before the concert.
No late arrivals
allowed.

1 .... arrive half an hour early.
2 You .... arrive late.

All vehicles – **slow**.
Drivers of large
vehicles, wait for
guard before crossing.

3 Small vehicles .... wait.
4 Drivers of large vehicles .... cross alone.

STUDENTS!
Please be quiet –
4th-year exam
in progress.

5 Students .... make a noise.
6 Third-year students .... take the exam.

LIBRARY
No talking.
Please leave books
on tables.

7 You .... talk in the library.
8 You .... put the books back on the shelves.

SWIMMING POOL
Free swim today.
No eating.
No drinking.

9 Swimmers .... pay today.
10 Swimmers .... eat or drink by the pool.

C Put the words in the box in the gaps. Don't add any other words.

Does she	have to	has	she has	must	mustn't	~~have~~	does she

Mark: We (▶) _have_ to get up early tomorrow.
Bob: Why?
Mark: Have you forgotten? Angela (1)............... to move to a new flat tomorrow, and I
     promised we would help her.
Bob: (2)............... have to move out by a particular time?
Mark: No, there's no rush. She doesn't (3)............... leave her old flat before the
     afternoon, but there are lots of things that (4)............... to pack, so we
     (5)............... get there fairly early.
Bob: Why (6)............... have to move, by the way?
Mark: She said that I (7)............... tell you because she wants to tell you herself, when
     she sees you tomorrow.

44 Must, can't, may, might, could

1 We use **must**, **can't**, **may** and **could** with an infinitive (e.g. be, go, come, earn):

> | INFINITIVE |
> *They **must*** | ***earn*** | *a lot.*

2 CERTAINTY | *She **must be** rich.* |

Look at this example with **must**: *Jane got top marks in her exams. She **must be** very clever.* (= From what we know, we can be certain that Jane is very clever.)

We use **must** to say we are certain:
> *The Greens have two houses and two cars. They **must earn** a lot of money.*
> (= We can be sure that the Greens earn a lot of money.)
> A: *There's someone outside in an orange car.*
> B: *It **must be** Susan. She's the only person I know with an orange car.*

3 IMPOSSIBILITY | *She **can't be** poor.* |

Look at this example with **can't**:
> *Mark studied hard for his exams, but he got poor marks; he **can't be** very clever.*
> (= From what we know, we can guess that Mark is **not** very clever.)

We use **can't** to talk about impossibility:
> *The Browns both have part-time jobs; they **can't earn** much money.* (= We can guess that the Browns do **not** earn a lot of money.)
> A: *There's someone at the door. I think it's Bill.*
> B: *It **can't be** Bill. He's in Australia.*

4 POSSIBILITY

> *She* $\begin{Bmatrix} may \\ might \\ could \end{Bmatrix}$ *be in the garden.*

Look at this example with **may**:
> A: *Eve's not in her room. Where is she?*
> B: *She **may be** in the garden.* (= From what we know, **perhaps** she **is** in the garden.)

We use **may**, **might** and **could** for something that is possible but not certain, now or in the future:
> *My sister **might come** tomorrow.* (= From what we know, perhaps she **will** come.)

Now look at this example with **may not**:
> A: *I've phoned Jill, but there's no answer.*
> B: *She **may not** be at home.* (OR *She **might not be** …*) (= Perhaps she is not at home.)

Could not is not possible here.

Practice

A Complete the sentences using *must* or *can't* and one of the verbs from the box.

| be | belong | ~~speak~~ | come | spend | have | like | live | want | remember |

- ▶ Anna lived in America for three years, so she <u>must speak</u>. English.
- ▶ Tom's brother doesn't know anything about medicine, so he <u>can't be</u>...... a doctor.
- 1 Jane has an incredible number of CDs. She .... music a lot.
- 2 Peter doesn't speak German, so he .... from Germany.
- 3 This jacket .... to Janet because it's not her size.
- 4 That man .... around here because he doesn't know any of the street names.
- 5 Jack .... a lot of clothes. He wears something different every day.
- 6 Sam's grandmother is over 80 years old, so she .... the Second World War.
- 7 You've got ten cats already. You .... to get another one.
- 8 Susan buys a new dress every day. She .... a lot of money on clothes.

B Someone has robbed a bank. The police are sure that the criminal is one of these men. Look at the pictures and complete the sentences using *can't be*, *could be* or *must be*.

▶ A witness says that the robber had short hair. If that's true, then it <u>can't be</u> Drake or Rogers, but it <u>could be</u> Hall.

▶ A witness says that the robber had glasses. If that's true, then it <u>can't be</u> Brown or Drake. It <u>must be</u> either Hall or Rogers or Smith.

1 A witness says that the robber had black hair. If that's true, then it .... Hall, but it .... Brown.

2 A witness says that the robber had a moustache. If that's true, then it .... Rogers but it .... Drake or Brown.

3 A witness says that the robber didn't have a beard. If that's true, then it .... Drake or Brown but it .... Hall or Smith.

4 A witness says that the robber had a moustache, but no beard. If that's true, then it .... Drake or Rogers. It .... Hall.

5 A witness says that the robber had black hair and wore glasses. If that's true, then it .... Rogers. It .... Hall.

6 And if what everyone says is true, then it ....

C Complete the dialogues with *must*, *can't* or *might* and one of the phrases in the box.

cost a lot of money	be a soldier	work long hours	go to Portugal
come this weekend	take much interest	also be at the shops	be at the gym

▶ Ruth: I think Ann's brother is in the army.
  James: He <u>can't be a soldier</u> ; he's only 15.

1 Bob: What are you going to do next summer?
  Susan: I don't know. We .... , but it's not certain yet.

2 Fred: Mike's new flat is all electric – kitchen, heating, everything.
  Peter: That .... in electricity bills.

3 Sam: Is Mary coming to see us this week?
  Sally: It depends on her work. She .... if she finishes the project that she's doing.

4 Carol: Have Brian and Kim got any children?
  Tom: Yes, they have two children, but they .... in them, because they never talk about them.

5 Andrew: Do you see your new neighbours very much?
  Sarah: No, they .... , because they are hardly ever at home.

6 Paul: Fred's gone out, hasn't he? Where has he gone?
  Ann: I don't know. He .... or he ....

45 Should, shouldn't

1 We use **should** with an infinitive (**do, go**, etc.):

I *should* INFINITIVE do *some work tonight.*

The form of **should** is the same for all persons:

I/you/he/she/it/we/they **should go.**

2 The negative form is **shouldn't**:
*You **shouldn't** sit in the sun all day.*
*They **shouldn't** spend so much money.*

3 We use **I should** or **we should** to say what is a good thing for us to do:
*I **should** go home. It's midnight.*
*We **should** invite them for a meal.*

We use **I** or **we shouldn't** to say that something is a bad thing for us to do:
*I **shouldn't** spend so much money.*

We use **you should/shouldn't** to give advice:
*You **should** look for a better job.*
*You **shouldn't** drive so fast.*

Should is not as strong as **must** or **have to.** Compare:
*You **should** eat more fruit.* (It's a good idea.)
*'You **must** eat more fruit,' said the doctor.* (It's very important).

4 We use the question form **should I/we ...?** to ask for advice:

*What **should** I say to Helen?*
*I need a new passport. Where **should** I go?*

5 We can say **I think we should, I don't think you should,** etc. to give an opinion:

I don't think you should believe everything he says.

We do not usually say:
I think you shouldn't ...

6 We can use **do you think I should ...?** to ask for advice:
*He hasn't replied to my email. **Do you think I should** phone him?*
*What **do you think I should** give Tom for his birthday?*

Practice

A Complete the sentences, using *should* or *shouldn't* and the words in brackets ( ).

► You shouldn't work .... (You/work) so hard. Have a holiday.
► I enjoyed that film. We should go .... (We/go) to the cinema more often.
1 .... (You/park) here. It's not allowed.
2 What .... (I/cook) for dinner tonight?
3 .... (You/wear) a coat. It's cold outside.
4 .... (You/smoke). It's bad for you.
5 .... (We/arrive) at the airport two hours before the flight.
6 .... (I/pay) now or later?
7 Do you think .... (I/apply) for this job?
8 What do you think .... (I/write) in this space on the form?
9 .... (I/eat) any more cake. I've already eaten too much.
10 This food is terrible. .... (We/complain) to the manager.
11 Which shirt do you think .... (I/buy)?

3 Henry is cooking a meal. Give him some useful advice. Use *you should* or *you shouldn't* and the notes in the box.

> Don't leave the meat in the oven for more than one hour.
> Cut the onions as small as possible.
> Use fresh herbs and fresh vegetables.
> Don't put in too much salt and pepper.
> Wait until the water boils before you put the vegetables into it.
> Heat the oven before you put the meat in.
> Cut the meat into four equal slices.

► _You shouldn't leave_ .... the meat in the oven for more than one hour.

1 .... the onions as small as possible.

2 .... fresh herbs and fresh vegetables.

3 .... in too much salt and pepper.

4 .... until the water boils before you put the vegetables into it.

5 .... the oven before you put the meat in.

6 .... the meat into four equal slices.

C Write this conversation between Brian and Keith using the words in brackets ( ). Put in *do* or *should* where required.

Brian: (I want to buy a motorbike. What/you/think/I/do?)

(►) _I want to buy a motorbike. What do you think I should do?_ ....

Keith: (You/look/at the advertisements in the papers.)

(►) _You should look at the advertisements in the papers._ ....

Brian: (Which papers/I/get?)

(1)...

Keith: (I think/you/buy/the local newspapers.)

(2)...

Brian: (What/you/think/I/do/before I buy a bike?)

(3)...

Keith: (I/not/think/you/decide/too quickly.)

(4)...

(You/check/the condition of the bike.)

(5)...

(You/ask/somebody who knows about bikes to look at the bike for you.)

(6)...

(You/not/buy/one simply because it looks nice!)

(7)...

(You/be/very careful.)

(8)...

46 Should, ought to, had better

1 We use **should**, **ought to** and **had better** with an infinitive (e.g. **be**, **go**, **ask**, **wait**):

	INFINITIVE
I should	*go.*
You ought to	*ask.*
We had better	*wait.*

2 We use both **should** and **ought to** to ask for or to give advice, to say what is the correct or best thing to do:

> A: *I've got toothache. What should I do?*
> (= What is the best thing for me to do?)
> B: *You should go to the dentist's.*
> (= The best thing for you to do is to go to the dentist's.)

When we are talking about a duty or a law, we usually use **ought to**:

> A: *I saw a robbery. What should I do?*
> B: *You ought to report it to the police.*
> (= It is a person's duty to report it.)

On the other hand, when we are giving a personal opinion, we usually use **should**:

> B: *I think you should forget about it.*

We use **should** much more than **ought to** in negatives and questions:

> *I shouldn't go.* (OR *I ought not to go.*)
> *Should I go?* (OR *Ought I to go?*)

3 We can also use **had better** to give advice, to say what is the best thing to do:

> *There'll be a lot of traffic tomorrow. We had* (OR *We'd*) *better leave early.*
> *I had* (OR *I'd*) *better ask the doctor about the pain in my stomach.*

Note that **had** is a past form, but it does not refer to past time here; we use it to talk about present or future time.

We only use **had better** to give advice about a particular thing; when we give general advice, we use **should** or **ought to**:

> *When people are in trouble, they should go to the police.* (NOT … ~~they had better go to the police.~~)

The negative is **had better not**:

> *They had better not be late.*

Practice

A Use *should* or *shouldn't* and one of the phrases from the box in each dialogue.

call an ambulance	~~report it to the police~~	move the person yourself
drive home in her car	touch anything	~~do anything about it~~
~~decide for herself~~	give you a new cup	make him do lots of sport
borrow money	leave everything where it is	ask someone to take her
let him eat so much		

▶ A: There is a house near my home where I often hear a child crying.
  B: You *should report it to the police* .

▶ A: My daughter wants to marry a sailor. What should I do about it?
  B: In my opinion, *you shouldn't do anything about it* .
    Your daughter *should decide for herself* .

1 A: If someone has a serious accident, what's the right thing to do?
  B: Well, you .... It's not a good idea to move an
    injured person. Instead, you .... to take the person
    to hospital.

2 A: Last Saturday I bought some coffee cups but one of the handles was broken.
      What can I expect the shop to do?
   B: They ....
3 A: My son is 12 years old and he's already very fat.
   B: Well, it's important not to eat too much, so you ....
      Also, you ....
4 A: If you come home and see that you've been robbed, what's the best thing to do?
   B: Well, you .... You
      .... and call the police.
5 A: Mary can't work because she's feeling sick. How can she get home?
   B: Well, she .... She
      .... home.
6 People .... if they can't pay it back.

B Use the sentences in brackets ( ) to write a reply with *had better* in the following dialogues.

▶ A: I've got a headache.
   B: (You should go and lie down.) You'd better go and lie down. ....
1 A: The children want to play in the kitchen.
   B: (Well, they should clear everything away when they finish.)
      Well, ... when they finish.
2 A: I think it's going to rain.
   B: (Yes, we ought to take our umbrellas.) Yes, ...
3 A: I'm going to go to bed now. We have to get up very early tomorrow.
   B: (Yes, I should go to bed early too.) Yes, ...

C Complete the second part of the dialogue using the correct form of the word in brackets ( ). Put *to* or *not* in the correct place if necessary.

▶ A: Should Henry stay in bed?
   B: No, the doctor said he _shouldn't_.... (should) stay in bed.
1 A: Can we move that cupboard?
   B: No, it's very delicate, so you .... (ought) leave it where it is.
2 A: Should we change these notices?
   B: No, the show is still on, so we .... (should) change them until next week.
3 A: You'd better tell the boss about the accident immediately.
   B: No, she's in a bad mod. I .... (had better) tell her until tomorrow.
4 A: Does the doctor say it's all right for Mrs Bradley to work?
   B: Yes, but she must be careful. She .... (ought) lift anything heavy, for example
5 A: Can they come before dinner?
   B: No, we haven't got enough food, so they .... (had better) come after dinner.

47 Need, needn't, needn't have

1 We use the verb **need** to talk about things that we must do. We use **to** + infinitive (e.g. **to do, to go**) after **need**:

	to + INFINITIVE	
I need	*to go*	*to the dentist's.*

After **he/she/it** we use **needs**:
*Mary/she **needs to buy** some white paint.*

We make negatives, questions and short answers with a form of **do**:
*You **don't need to go** to the doctor's.*
*Mary **doesn't need to buy** any green paint.*
A: *Do you **need to go** to the dentist's?*
B: *Yes, I **do**./No, I **don't**.*
A: *Does Mary **need to buy** any brushes?*
B: *Yes, she **does**./No, she **doesn't**.*

2 We can also use **need** to talk about things that we must get. Here we use an object after need:

	OBJECT
*Mary **needs***	*some white paint.*
*I **don't need***	*a new car.*
*Does Peter **need***	*any help?*

3 To talk about what we do not need to do, we can use **needn't**. We use an infinitive (e.g. **go, buy**) after **needn't**. **Needn't** has the same meaning as **don't/doesn't need to**:

	INFINITIVE	

*You **needn't** go to the shops. We have enough food.*
(OR *You **don't need to go** to the shops.*)
*Mary **needn't buy** any paint.*
(OR *Mary **doesn't need to buy** any paint.*)

We cannot use **needn't** before an object (e.g. your coat); we must use **don't need**:
*You **don't need** your coat. It's not cold outside.*
(NOT ~~You **needn't** your coat.~~)

4 We can use **needed to** for past time:
*They **needed to clean** everything before they started to paint.*

The negative past simple form is **didn't need to.**
*The room wasn't dirty so they **didn't need to clean it** before they started to paint it.*
(= It was not necessary to clean the room so we didn't clean it.)

We use **needn't have** + past participle to talk about something that **was** done although it wasn't necessary:
*We **needn't have lit** the fire, because it was a warm evening.* (= We lit the fire, but it was not necessary to light it.)
*You **needn't have bought** any bread, Jim. There is plenty in the cupboard.*
(= You bought some bread, but it was not necessary.)

Practice

A **From the statements in brackets ( ), make a question and a short answer, like those in the examples.**

▶ (Tom needs to take some warm clothes.) <u>Does Tom need to take</u>
<u>some warm clothes</u> ? ~ Yes, <u>he does</u> .

▶ (She doesn't need to study hard.) <u>Does she need to study hard</u> ? ~ No, <u>she doesn't</u> .

1 (Fred needs a ladder.) .... ? ~ Yes, ...

2 (We don't need to go to the shops.) .... ? ~ No, ...

3 (John doesn't need to leave before lunch.) .... ? ~ No, ...

4 (They need to check the train times.) .... ? ~ Yes, ...

3 Change each sentence in brackets ( ) into a negative sentence with *needn't*, where possible. If not possible, write a negative sentence with *doesn't/don't need*.

▶ (Jane needs to pay Jim today.) Jane needn't pay Jim today.

▶ (The car needs new tyres.) The car doesn't need new tyres.

1 (We need a lot of red paper.) ....

2 (Mark needs to get everything ready today.) ....

3 (Mary needs to leave at six o'clock.) ....

4 (Ann needs a new bag.) ....

C When there are exams or competitions at Brightside School, the school provides certain things for all the students, but there are other things that the school does not provide. Look at the table.

Examinations	The school provides:	The school doesn't provide:
art exams	paint	brushes
maths exams	rubbers	pens and pencils
drawing exams	paper	rulers and pencils
tennis competitions	balls	racquets
football competitions	shirts	shorts and boots

Use the information in the table to write sentences with *need to bring* or *needn't bring*.

▶ (art exams/paint) For art exams, students needn't bring paint.

▶ (tennis competitions/racquets) For tennis competitions, students need to bring racquets.

1 (maths exams/pens and pencils) ....

2 (football competitions/shirts) ....

3 (drawing exams/paper) ....

4 (art exams/brushes) ....

5 (tennis competitions/balls) ....

6 (football competitions/shorts and boots) ....

7 (maths exams/rubbers) ....

8 (drawing exams/rulers and pencils) ....

D Rewrite the sentences using *didn't need* or *needn't have* + the correct form.

▶ The programmes didn't cost us anything. We didn't pay for them.
  We didn't have to pay .... for the programmes.

▶ You took your umbrella yesterday but it didn't rain.
  You needn't have taken .... your umbrella yesterday.

1 Jill paid for her holiday in advance, but it wasn't necessary.
  Jill .... for her holiday in advance.

2 My sister spoke to Sally yesterday, so I didn't phone her.
  I .... Sally because my sister had spoken to her.

3 We bought extra food but now John and Mary can't come.
  We .... extra food because John and Mary can't come.

4 Why did you work during the weekend? We don't have to finish until next week.
  You .... during the weekend.

5 I didn't take my passport with me because an identity card was enough.
  I .... my passport with me.

48 Had to do/go, should have done/gone

1 Look at this example:

*Jane **had to wait** an hour for a bus.*

Had to wait means that Jane waited because no bus came for an hour.

We use **had to** to talk about something that someone did because it was necessary.

If someone did not do something because it was not necessary, we use **didn't have to**:
*I **didn't have to work** last Saturday. (= I didn't work because it was not necessary.)*

The question form is **did … have to**:
*Did you **have to work** last Saturday?*

2 Now consider this situation:

> Pam's job includes working on Saturday. Last Saturday she was ill, so she didn't work:
> *Pam **should have gone** to work last Saturday, but she was ill. So she stayed at home.*

We use **should have** (**done/gone**, etc.) to say that something which did not happen was the correct or best action. We can also use **should have** to criticize someone. Look at this example:

> Peter, a farm worker, didn't close a gate, and the cows got into the wrong field:
> *Peter **should have closed** the gate.*

We use **shouldn't have** (**done/gone**, etc.) to say that something which did happen was not the correct action:
*I **shouldn't have got** angry with Jane.*
(= I got angry with Jane, but it was not a good thing to do.)
*Peter **shouldn't have left** the gate open.*

Practice

A Complete the dialogues with *had to*, or *did … have to* and the words in brackets.

▶ Jim: When you had that stomach trouble, <u>did you have to</u> .... (you) go into hospital?

Joan: No, <u>I didn't have to</u> .... (not) go into hospital, but <u>I had to</u> .... stay in bed for a week.

1 Alan: Was there a translation in the exam?

Jane: No, we .... (not) translate anything, but we .... write three essays.

2 Ann: I was very busy yesterday.

Bill: What .... (you) do?

Ann: I .... prepare everything for today's meeting.

3 Ken: .... (you) wear uniform when you were at school?

Jean: Yes, and we .... make sure it was always neat and tidy, as well.

4 Tom: What .... (you) do to get your international driving licence?

Tina: I .... show the police my national driving licence, but I .... (not) take another driving test.

5 Mark: Our children enjoyed their holiday at the summer camp.

Mary: .... (they) help at mealtimes?

Mark: Well, they .... (not) make the food, but they .... (help) with the washing-up.

Complete the sentences with *should have* or *shouldn't have* for these situations.

▶ Philip didn't take his medicine. Later he got very ill.
Philip *should have taken* .... his medicine.

▶ Sara drove her car when she was tired and she had an accident.
Sara *should have driven* .... her car when she was tired.

1 Tony didn't buy any sugar so he couldn't make a cake.
Tony .... some sugar.

2 Sally had a cold but she still went to the cinema. Later she had to stay in bed.
Sally .... to the cinema.

3 Ted ate a lot of apples. Later he had stomach ache.
Ted .... so many apples.

4 Lucy didn't lock the door to her flat when she went to buy a newspaper. While she was away, someone stole her television.
Lucy .... the door when she went out.

5 Mary borrowed Tom's camera without asking him.
Mary .... Tom's camera without asking him.

Here is the work plan for the Information Office at Heathrow Airport for last weekend. If someone did not in fact work, there is a comment.

SATURDAY		SUNDAY	
On duty	Comments	On duty	Comments
Jenny	✓	Colin	✓
Brian	ill	Mary	✓
Joan	ill	Derek	ill
Daniel	✓	Carol	ill

From the information in the table, write complete sentences using *had to*, *didn't have to*, or *should have* and the words in brackets.

▶ (Jenny/Saturday) *Jenny had to work on Saturday.* ....
▶ (Colin/Saturday) *Colin didn't have to work on Saturday.* ....
▶ (Carol/Sunday) *Carol should have worked on Sunday* .... but she was ill.
1 (Colin/Sunday) ....
2 (Joan/Sunday) ....
3 (Derek/Sunday) .... but he was ill.
4 (Mary/Saturday) ....
5 (Brian/Saturday) .... but he was ill.
6 (Daniel/Saturday) ....
7 (Joan/Saturday) .... but she was ill.
8 (Derek/Saturday) ....

Test E: Modal verbs

A **Chris is going to Carstairs College in Scotland. Miranda is already studying there. Cross out the modal verb forms that are wrong.**

Chris: (►)Can I/~~Do I can~~ ask you a few questions about Carstairs?
Miranda: Of course. (1) You should/You ought to get as much information as possible before you go.
Chris: Do (2) I must/I have to wear a uniform?
Miranda: No, but (3) you must/you have dress smartly. You can't wear jeans.
Chris: (4) Should I/Had I take my laptop computer with me?
Miranda: No, (5) you don't ought/you don't need to! You have to write all your essays by hand!
Chris: What? Will (6) I be possible/I be able to use email?
Miranda: No, I'm afraid not. Carstairs is very old-fashioned. Anyway, when are you leaving?
Chris: (7) I managed/I could to get a ticket for the train this evening. (8) I should/I must have reserved a seat, though. (9) I can/I may have to stand all the way to Scotland.
Miranda: (10) Should I better/Had I better give you a ring later and see how things are going?
Chris: Sure. Can I use my mobile phone at college?
Miranda: Yes, don't worry. But (11) you need/you must switch it off during the school day.
Chris: OK. Can you give me any more advice?
Miranda: Yes. (12) You must/You ought visit the lake near the college. It's beautiful!

B **Paula is emailing Sarah. The numbered words in the box are missing from the text. Put one number only in the text at the right place.**

> (1) able (2) have (3) to (4) should (5) managed (6) needn't (7) ought (8) couldn't (9) had

I've had a terrible day! I (►) $\overset{4}{\wedge}$ have got up early, but I couldn't get out of bed! It was too late to go by bus, so I to get a taxi. Luckily, I to find one quite quickly. Of course, when we arrived outside the office, I didn't have any money, so I pay the driver. Anyway, I was to borrow some from the receptionist. I've paid her back already, but do you think I to give her a present as well? My boss was waiting for me in her office. I should arrived at nine o'clock, and I was half an hour late. I have taken a taxi at all, though! She told me the company was closing, so I had find a new job!

C **Mr and Mrs Buck are deciding what to take with them on holiday. Rewrite the sentences, using the word in brackets ( ).**

Mrs Buck: It's not necessary to take the tent. (need)
(►) *We don't need to take the tent.*..
We're not going camping again!
Mr Buck: The hotels will be full, possibly. (might)
(1) The ....
Mrs Buck: Then it will be necessary to sleep in the car. (have)
(2) Then we ....
Mr Buck: Well, I think we've got everything we need. What's in that paper bag?
Mrs Buck: I'm sure it's the sun cream we got in Brighton. (must)
(3) It ....

Mr Buck:	It wasn't necessary to buy it. (needn't)
	(4) We ....
Mrs Buck:	Is it a good idea to take it with us this time? (Should)
	(5) .... ?
Mrs Buck:	It's not possible for us to make the sun shine. (can't)
	(6) We.. ?
Mr Buck:	The sun's always shining when you're with me, Margaret!
Mrs Buck:	Are you feeling OK, George? Maybe you should have a rest. (better)
	(7)..

D Michael is about to give a presentation. Use the words in the box to finish it.

> don't need to / should have / better start / ~~Can you~~ / could you pass / got to finish /
> mustn't forget / might not / should really / Do I need to use

'(▶) *Can you* .... hear me at the back of the hall? (1)......................... the
microphone? Oh dear, it isn't working! You (2)....................... move to the front if you
can. Excuse me, (3)........................ this information around? Thank you. Have I brought
enough copies? I haven't? I'm so sorry. Sir, I can see you don't have a seat, but you
(4)........................ write anything in my presentation. I'll put everything on my website. I
(5)........................ to give you the address at the end. Now, I've (6)........................ in
thirty minutes, so we'd (7)........................ . I'm sorry, Madam, but you
(8)........................ be able to see the screen unless you move forward. Anyway, I
(9)........................ started five minutes ago. Right, where are my notes?'

E Four friends are in a café. If the underlined modal verb forms are wrong, correct
them. If they are right, put a tick (✓).

Tim:	Is that your phone ringing, John?
John:	Yes. It <u>can be</u> (▶) *must be* .... Dave. He said he would ring about now. No,
	wait a moment, it <u>can't be</u> (▶) ✓...................... Dave. That's not his number. I
	wonder who it is.
Phil:	You'll <u>have to</u> (1)........................ answer it if you want to know! Who's that by
	the window, Tim? Is it Alice?
Tim:	It <u>needn't be</u> (2)........................ She's in New York. She <u>must</u>
	(3)........................ go there on business last Monday.
Phil:	Then it <u>must be</u> (4)........................ her sister or something.
John:	That was someone called Louise on the phone. I don't know her ...
Phil:	But she <u>should have</u> (5)........................ your number!
John:	... and she says she's in the café with us. By the window.
Tim:	Really? Well, she <u>could be</u> (6)........................ the girl who looks like Alice.
John:	<u>Shall I</u> (7)........................ speak to her?
Phil:	You <u>don't ought</u> (8)........................ to, because she's coming over now.
Lois:	Hi, John. I'm Alice's cousin. She gave me your number.
John:	Have a seat. <u>Can I</u> (9)........................ get you a coffee?

49 Articles (1): **a**, **an** or **the**

1 Compare **a** and **an**:

We use **a** before words which begin with consonants (**b, c, d, f, g, h, j, k, l** …): *a doctor a big car a girl* We also use **a** before **u** when it sounds like the word 'you'; and before **eu**: *university (sound: 'you'): a university* *a European city*	We use **an** before words which begin with vowels (**a, e, i, o, u**): *an apple an interesting film* We also use **an** before words that begin with a silent **h**. Compare **hour** and **house**: *hour (sound: 'our'): an hour* *house: a house*

2 Compare **a/an** and **the**:

Mary: *I bought a CD player and a TV yesterday.*   ~ Joe: *Was the CD player expensive?*

We usually use **a/an** with a noun to talk about a person or thing for the first time: *a CD player*	We use **the** when we talk about the person or thing again: *the CD player* (= the one that Mary bought)

3 There are some special uses of **a/an** and **the**:

▶ We use **a/an** with prices, frequency and speeds: *It costs £2 a litre.* *I drink about three cups of coffee a day.* *You're driving at ninety miles an hour!* ▶ We use **a/an** before **hundred, thousand, million**: *a hundred people a thousand days* ▶ We use **a/an** for talking about jobs: *I'm a bank manager.*	▶ We use **the** when there is only one of something: *May I turn on the TV?* (There is only one TV in the room.) *Where's Mary? ~ She's in the kitchen.* (There is only one kitchen in the house.) ▶ We use **the** with musical instruments: *I play the guitar. Jane plays the violin.*

Practice

A Put *a* or *an* in the gaps.

- ▶ I bought *a*...... new car yesterday.
- ▶ It's *an*..... old film.

1 She's reading .... interesting book.
2 They've got .... house in Spain.
3 It's .... cheap restaurant.
4 He's .... Italian businessman.

5 The journey took .... hour.
6 We've lost .... black cat.
7 I want to buy .... umbrella.
8 It was .... difficult exam.

B Now finish the sentences using *a* or *an* and the correct phrase from the box.

European country	Indian river	~~American director~~	university town
Japanese city	English airport	German car	

- ▶ Steven Spielberg *is an American director.* ....
- 1 Tokyo is ....
- 2 Heathrow is ....
- 3 The Ganges is ....

4 Oxford is ....

5 A Mercedes is ....

6 Spain is ....

C Ian Brent wants to take out an insurance policy. An agent from the insurance company, Mr Cox, is asking him questions. Put *a*, *an* or *the* in the gaps in these conversations.

Mr Cox: Hello, my name is Mike Cox. I am from (►) *an* .... insurance company. I have (►) *a* .... form with some questions. Your name is Ian Brent. Do you have (1) .... middle name?

Mr Brent: Yes, my full name is Ian Stanley Brent.

Mr Cox: All right. Now, where do you live, Mr Brent?

Mr Brent: I live in (2) .... house in Peckham.

Mr Cox: Peckham, I see. And what is your job?

Mr Brent: I'm (3) .... scientist. I work for (4) .... government.

Mr Cox: Do you work in (5) .... laboratory or in (6) .... office?

Mr Brent: I work in (7) .... small office in (8) .... centre of London.

Mr Cox: And how do you get to (9) .... office from Peckham?

Mr Brent: I usually take (10) .... underground.

Mr Cox: What is your salary, Mr Brent?

Mr Brent: Well, I earn almost £35,000 (11) .... year.

Mr Cox: Now, your family. You're married, aren't you?

Mr Brent: Yes, and we have two children, (12) .... girl and (13) .... boy. (14) .... girl is sixteen and (15) .... boy is fourteen.

Mr Cox: Fine. And you want to take out (16) .... insurance policy for £100,000. Is that right?

Mr Brent: Yes, that's right.

Mr Cox: Well, that's all. Can you sign (17) .... form here at (18) .... bottom? Thank you.

D There are some mistakes in these sentences. Put a tick (✓) if you think the <u>underlined</u> word is correct. Cross it out and change it if you think it's wrong.

► I'm not sure what she does, but I think she's *a* ✓.... doctor.

► I saw ~~the~~ *a* ...... thousand different things when I was on holiday.

1 Be careful! That perfume costs £100 <u>a</u> .... bottle.

2 We must invite him to the party. He plays <u>a</u> .... piano and <u>a</u> .... guitar.

3 A: What does John do?

   B: I'm not sure, but I think he is <u>the</u> .... teacher in a school.

4 She likes to drive at <u>the</u> .... hundred miles an hour.

5 I play <u>the</u> .... violin in an orchestra. They pay me £80 <u>the</u> .... day!

6 I've got <u>the</u> .... hundred jobs to do before we leave.

7 A: Is my handbag in the living-room?

   B: No, it isn't. I saw it in <u>a</u> .... kitchen.

50 Articles (2): **a/an**, **the** or no article

1 We use **a/an** with singular nouns:
  *He was reading **a book**.*
  *I saw **an interesting film** yesterday.*

2 Look at this example:
  *When I arrived, John was reading **a book**.*

  We use **a/an** when it isn't necessary to make clear which particular thing we are talking about. There are lots of books; John was reading one of them.

  We use **a/an** to talk about people's jobs:
  *Jim is **an engineer**. (= There are lots of engineers; Jim is one.)*

  We use **a/an** to describe things or people:
  *They have **a beautiful house**. (= There are lots of beautiful houses; they have one.)*
  *John is **an old friend** of mine.*

3 We use **the** with singular or plural nouns:
  the book   **the books**

  We can use **the** with uncountable nouns (e.g. **music, water, food, education**):
  *The **water** is in the fridge.*

  Note:
  ► uncountable nouns do not have a plural (NOT ~~two musics, three waters~~).

  ► we do not use **a/an** with uncountable nouns (NOT ~~a music, a water~~).
  (See Unit 53.)

4 We use **the** when it is clear which person or thing we are talking about:
  *Jean was reading **a book**. She closed **the book**. (= She closed the book that she was reading.)*
  *Anna likes music, but she doesn't like **the music** that John plays.*
  *Mike's gone to **the shops**. (= the local shops)*
  *She's in **the kitchen**. (= the kitchen in this house)*
  *I must go to **the bank**. (= my bank, where I keep my money)*
  the centre/the station/the airport (in a city)
  the River Thames (There is only one.)
  the government in my country

5 We do not use **the** before plural nouns (e.g. **vegetables**) or uncountable nouns (e.g. **education, music**) when we are talking about something in general:
  *Do you like **vegetables**? (= any vegetables)*
  *I think **education** is very important.*

6 We do not use **a** or **the** before names of languages, meal names, the names of cities, most countries and most streets, and the names of airports, stations, single mountains or lakes:
  *She speaks **Spanish**.*
  *She lives in **Amsterdam** in **Holland**. (But we say **the** U.S.A., **the** United Kingdom.)*
  *What time will **lunch** be?*
  *from **Heathrow Airport** to **Oxford Street***

Practice

A **Put *a*, *an* or *the* into the gaps if they are required. Leave the gaps empty if nothing is required.**

  ► I want to put some money into my bank account, so I'm going to <u>the</u>............ bank this afternoon. It's in Midland Street.
  1 I had .... sandwich for .... lunch today.
  2 We flew to .... Dublin Airport in .... Ireland.
  3 It was .... long flight, but eventually we arrived in .... U.S.A.
  4 I'm trying to learn .... Japanese. I'm having .... lesson tomorrow.
  5 He made .... angry speech against .... government.
  6 She is .... famous actress and she is appearing in .... popular TV series.
  7 They live in .... Paris in .... area near to .... River Seine.
  8 They've bought .... small flat in .... Park Street.

3 Complete the sentences by putting in *a*, *an* or *the* if required. Leave the gap empty if nothing is required. (Note that the following words in this exercise are uncountable nouns: *music*, *fuel*, *education*, *fish*, *food*, *coffee*, *exercise*.)

► She read _the_ letters that had arrived that morning.
1 It was a nice day, so we had …….. lunch in …….. garden of my house.
2 I'm just going to …….. shops. I'll be back in a few minutes.
3 We phoned for …….. taxi to take us to …….. airport.
4 I like listening to …….. music when I come home.
5 Without …….. fuel, …….. cars don't work.
6 John was at home. He was reading …….. magazine in …….. living-room.
7 His parents believe that …….. education is a very important thing.
8 Jane doesn't like …….. fish; she never eats it.
9 After …….. dinner, I washed …….. plates and glasses.
10 Did you like …….. food at …….. party yesterday?
11 A: Where's …….. coffee?
   B: It's in …….. cupboard next to …….. sink.
12 Doctors say that …….. exercise is good for everybody.

C Complete this conversation by putting in *a*, *an* or *the* if required. Leave the gap empty if nothing is required.

Mike: Is Maria (►) _a_ student at your college?
Rosie: No, she's (1)…….. old friend of mine. We were at school together.
Mike: What does she do now?
Rosie: She's (2)…….. computer programmer. She's not English, you know. She comes
        from (3)…….. Brazil, but she's living in (4)…….. U.S.A. at the moment.
Mike: Has she got (5)…….. job there?
Rosie: Yes, she's working for (6)…….. big company there.
Mike: Do you send (7)…….. emails to each other?
Rosie: Yes, and I had (8)…….. long email from her yesterday.
Mike: What did she say in (9)…….. email?
Rosie: She said that she was living in (10)…….. nice apartment in (11)…….. centre of
        (12)…….. Chicago.

D Complete the story by putting *a*, *an* or *the* into the gaps.

Yesterday I was sitting on (►) _the_ 6 o'clock train when I saw (1)…….. strange man walking along the platform. He came into the carriage of (2)…….. train where I was sitting, and he sat in the seat opposite mine. He opened (3)…….. newspaper and started reading it. On (4)…….. front page of (5)…….. newspaper, there was (6)…….. picture of (7)…….. bank robber. The words under (8)…….. picture were: 'Wanted by the police'. It was (9)…….. same man!

51 Plural nouns; **one** and **ones**

1 We normally form plural nouns by adding -s:

SINGULAR		PLURAL
a cup	→	some cups
one student	→	three students
the cat	→	the cats

2 **one** and **ones**
Sometimes we use **one** instead of repeating a singular noun:

*I'm going to buy **a drink**. Would you like **one**?*
*Our **house** is the **one** with the red door.*

Or, we use **ones** instead of a plural noun:

*Shall I buy the red **apples** or the green **ones**?*
*These **biscuits** are cheaper than those **ones**.*

3 We often use **Which one** ...? and **Which ones** ...? in questions:

Shop assistant: ***Which one** would you like, the black dress or the pink one?*
Mary: *I'd like the black one, please.*

Jim: *I like the black and white photographs. **Which ones** do you like? The black and white ones or the colour ones?*
Susan: *I prefer the colour ones.*

4 But we form some plural nouns differently:

man	→ men		+ -es		
woman	→ women		bus	→	buses
child	→ children		kiss	→	kisses
person	→ people		wish	→	wishes
foot	→ feet		watch	→	watches
tooth	→ teeth		match	→	matches
sheep	→ sheep		box	→	boxes
mouse	→ mice		potato	→	potatoes
fish	→ fish		tomato	→	tomatoes
-y	→ -ies		-f/-fe	→	-ves
family	→ families		loaf	→	loaves
city	→ cities		wife	→	wives
country	→ countries		knife	→	knives

(For more information on plural nouns, see Appendix 1 on page 242.)

Practice

A Put in plural nouns to describe the pictures.

▶

Some *boxes*

1 Some ....

2 Two ....

3 Some ....

4  Three ....

5  Some ....

6  Some ....

7 Four ....

8 Some ....

9  Some ....

10 Two ....

11  Two ....

B Tick (✓) the correct plural forms and cross out the wrong ones.

► knives ✓   tooths   matches   wishs
► matchs   citys   cities   men
  countries   potatoes   teeth   familys
  wishes   tomatos   mouses   wifes
  wives   potatos   countrys   tomatoes
  mans   mice   knifes   families

C Rewrite the sentence in brackets ( ), replacing one of the words with *one* or *ones*.

► He's just bought a new suit.
  (It's a blue suit.) It's a blue one.
► A: Who is your favourite actor?
  B: (The actor that I like best is Joe Late.) The one that I like best is Joe Late.
1 I'm going to buy an orange juice.
  (Would you like an orange juice?) ....
2 The chocolate cakes are popular.
  (But the strawberry cakes are nicer.) ....
3 A: Which house do you like?
  B: (I like the house with the red door.) ....
4 I bought a blue carpet last time.
  (This time I want a green carpet.) ....
5 English is a difficult language.
  (There isn't an easy language.) ....
6 A: Where did you put the photos?
  B: (Do you mean the photos that we took in Turkey?) ....
  ....

D Eric and Ellen are buying things for their new apartment. Complete the dialogue with *one* or *ones*.

Ellen: Here's the china department. We need some cups.
Eric: Do we want large (►) ones .... or small (1)............... ?
Ellen: Small (2)............... are best.
Eric: But I like tea in a large cup.
Ellen: OK, put six small cups and a large (3)............... in the basket.
Eric: What about a teapot? There's a metal (4)............... and a nice china
          (5)............... . Which (6)............... do you like?
Ellen: I prefer the china (7)............... .
Eric: It's similar to the little cups but it's not like my big (8)............... .
Ellen: Well, it doesn't have to be exactly the same. Now, we also need knives.
Eric: Can't we use the (9)............... that my mother gave us?
Ellen: Well, I suppose the big (10)............... for bread is all right, but we certainly
          need some little (11)............... for vegetables and a sharp (12)...............
          for meat.
Eric: All right. Where are the knives?

52 This, that, these, those

1 Look at these examples:
   This exercise is difficult.
   These are very expensive!
   What is that?
   Did you eat those sandwiches?

2 Here are the singular and plural forms:

SINGULAR		PLURAL
this car	→	these cars
that car	→	those cars

We use **this, that, these, those** with nouns (e.g. painting, apple):
   I like this painting.
   Those apples are delicious.

We use **this, that, these, those** without a noun, when the meaning is clear. For example:

A student has just finished his homework, and he says to his friend:
   That was easy! (*That* = the homework)

Mike meets his mother at the station. He picks up her suitcases, and he says:
   These are heavy! (*These* = the cases)

3 We use **this** and **these** for things which are near to us, and **that** and **those** for things which are not near. Look at these pictures:

4 Things which are happening now are near to us in time, so we use **this** and **these**:
   John (at a concert):
   Some of these songs are beautiful.

Things which are finished are not near to us, so we use **that** or **those**:
   John (after leaving the concert):
   Some of those songs were beautiful.

Practice

A Put *this* or *these* in the gaps.

▶ I'd like to buy .this........... book, please. How much is it?
1 Could you tell me where .... bus goes, please?
2 .... questions are difficult. Could you help me?
3 .... sandwiches are mine. Yours are on the table.
4 .... is wonderful! I love a hot bath after work.
5 Have you got some cheaper pens? .... are very expensive.

Put *that* or *those* in the gaps.

6 Look at .... clouds. I'm sure it's going to rain.
7 Did you enjoy .... film? I thought it was boring.
8 Let's cross the road. .... taxi is free.
9 .... flats are all very expensive, because they're in the centre of town.
10 .... was beautiful! I was so hungry.

B Look at this picture.

You are at the greengrocer's. Ask how much the fruit and vegetables are.
Use *How much ...?* and *these* or *those*.

▶ How much are those cucumbers? ....

▶ How much are these oranges? ....

1 ....

2 ....

3 ....

4 ....

5 ....

6 ....

7 ....

8 ....

C Put *this*, *that*, *these* or *those* in the gaps in these dialogues.

Jim: It's very pleasant to sit here on (▶) this.......... terrace in the middle of
(1)............... mountains.

Ann: Yes, and the food is good. (2)............... grapes are delicious.

Jim: Delicious, yes, but (3)............... one's bad. What are (4)............... people
over there eating?

Ann: Oh, (5)............... is fondue. It's made with cheese. You see, they take one of
(6)............... little pieces of bread and then dip it in (7)............... pot with
the cheese in it.

Jim: We can try (8)............... if we come again.

Ann: All the local restaurants serve it. So if we don't come back here, we can have it
at (9)............... little restaurant in the village.

Jim: Yes, but in the village you don't have (10)............... wonderful view of the
mountains.

53 Countable and uncountable nouns

1 Most nouns have singular and plural forms:

> **house/houses**   **dog/dogs**   **man/men**

We call these nouns countable nouns, because we can count them:

> **one house**   **two dogs**   **three men**

We can use **a**, **some** and **the** with countable nouns:

	SINGULAR	PLURAL
a:	a house	–
some:	–	**some** houses
the:	the house	the houses

2 Some nouns have only one form:

> **water**   **bread**   **petrol**
> **golf**   **tennis** **rain**

We call these uncountable nouns, because we cannot count them.

Look at this picture:

rain (uncountable)   cars (countable)

We do not use **a** or **one, two, three**, etc. before uncountable nouns, but we can use **some** or **the**:

a:	*We need to buy **bread** and **sugar**.*
some:	*Let's stop the car. We need **some** petrol.*
the:	*Look at **the** rain!*

3 Here is a list of common uncountable nouns, and some of the words we use in front of them:

a { glass / bottle } of { water / milk }   a cup of { tea / coffee }

a spoonful of { sugar / coffee }

a { slice / piece } of { cake / bread / toast / cheese }

a piece of { information / luggage / news / advice / homework }

some { money / petrol / snow }

We can use **some** with all these words. We also use **grams, kilos, litres**, etc. in shops:
*Can I have two **litres of milk**, please?*

4 Some nouns can be countable or uncountable:

UNCOUNTABLE:
*I like **tea**.*
*Her **hair** is red.*
*I haven't got **time**.*
*I always have **sugar** in my tea.*

COUNTABLE:
*I'll have **two teas**, please.* (= cups of tea)
*There's **a hair** in my tea.*
*We had **a good time**.*
*Three **sugars** in my tea, please.*

Practice

A Put a circle around the uncountable nouns below.

house	cat	cheese	car	coat	snow	lemon
advice	clock	table	tea	ball	museum	apple
painting	petrol	news	cigar	teacher	film	rain
holiday	office	bed	pen	sugar	homework	watch
tennis	doctor	cinema	luggage	chair	banana	information
cup	coffee	shoe	shirt	money	exam	hour
city	park	toast	sock	nose	water	school
bread	book	jumper	cloud	milk	bike	television

B Put the correct word in the following sentences.

▶ (slice, piece, cup) I'd like a ~~cup~~.......... of coffee, please.
1 (glass, slice, spoonful) Would you like a .... of cheese on your toast?
2 (pieces, cups, bottles) My father gave me two .... of advice.
3 (slice, bottle, piece) Could you buy a .... of milk at the shops?
4 (spoonful, piece, cup) That was a difficult .... of homework!
5 (glass, piece, slice) Would you give me a .... of water, please?
6 (slices, cups, pieces) How many .... of luggage do you have?
7 (spoonfuls, glasses, cups) I normally take three .... of sugar in my tea.
8 (pieces, slices, litres) I've just put forty .... of petrol in the car.
9 (piece, slice, glass) I need a .... of information.
10 (piece, kilo, slice) I'd like half a .... of coffee, please.

C Put a tick (✓) if the sentence is correct, and a cross (✗) if it is incorrect.

▶ We live in a flat. ✓......
1 The car needs a petrol. ....
2 She takes a milk in her tea. ....
3 Mary likes tea; I prefer coffee. ....
4 He's got some new CDs. ....
5 Two glasses of water. ....
6 A table and two chairs. ....
7 Give me two toasts. ....
8 A snow comes in winter. ....
9 Give me some cup of tea. ....
10 Tim doesn't eat meat. ....

▶ I have some moneys. ✗......
11 Two coffees, please. ....
12 Please buy some sugar. ....
13 Two kilos of a bread. ....
14 We have two homeworks. ....
15 I need some information. ....
16 We need some bananas. ....
17 Have we got a butter? ....
18 I like some egg for breakfast. ....
19 I can see some young women. ....
20 Can you see the moon? ....

D Put one word from the box in each gap in the following dialogues.

| a (x2)   bottle   cartons   cup (x2)   pieces   slice (x2)   some (x4)   the (x4)   two (x2) |

▶ My father has .~~a~~............ motorbike.
1 After school I have a .... of bread with .... butter on it.
2 Tom has got three .... of luggage.
3 Sue always has a .... of coffee after lunch.
4 For this experiment we need a glass .... with .... water in it.
5 We want .... coffees, please – one white and one black.
6 We must stop at a garage and put .... petrol in .... car.
7 How much is .... bottle of Coke at .... supermarket.
8 There are two .... of milk in .... fridge.
9 Can I have a .... of tea and a .... of cake, please.
10 There are .... hairs in .... bath. Both are long and blond.

54 A, some, any, no

1 Look at these pictures:

a pen   some pens   some food   no food

2 We use **a** with singular countable nouns
(e.g. **pen, car, friend**):
*I bought **a pen** yesterday.*
*Do you have **a car**?*
*He doesn't have **a friend**.*

(For countable and uncountable nouns,
see Unit 53.)

3 We use **some** or **any** with plural countable
nouns (**pens, friends, books**):
*I bought **some** new pens yesterday.*
*John doesn't have **any** friends.*
*Do you have **any** books about Africa?*

4 We use **some** or **any** with uncountable nouns
(e.g. **money, information, advice, news,
music, coffee, milk, toast, bread, food,
water, snow**):
*I haven't got **any** money.*
*Did the teacher give you **any** advice?*
*I would like **some** coffee, please.*

5 POSITIVE
We normally use **some** in positive sentences:
*She took **some** photos.*
*I'd like **some** information, please.*

But we sometimes use **any** like this:
*You can leave at **any** time.* (= It doesn't
matter when you leave.)
*Take **any** book.* (= It doesn't matter which
book you take.)

6 NEGATIVE
We usually use **any** in negative sentences:
*I didn't see **any** good films last year.*
*We haven't got **any** food.*

We sometimes use **no**, instead of **not … any**:
*I'm sorry, there are **no** buses to the museum.*
*The shops are shut, and we've got **no** food.*

7 QUESTIONS
We use **any** in questions:
*Do you speak **any** Russian?*

But we use **some** in requests:
*Can you give me **some** information?*

We also use **some** when we offer something:
*Would you like **some** coffee?*

Practice

A Put the words in brackets ( ) in the correct order to make sentences.

▶ A: Can I help you, sir?
B: <u>Yes, please. I'd like to buy some furniture for my living-room.</u>
(to buy – for my living – room. – furniture – I'd – some – like)

1 A: Shall we go into town this afternoon?
B: Why? ....
(shops open today. – any – There – aren't)

2 A: ....
(Can I – cheese, please? – some – have)
B: Of course. How much would you like?

3 A: ....
(any – in Cambridge? – museums – Are there)
B: I don't know. We can find out at the Tourist Information Centre.

4 A: I'd like to go to Bristol, please.
   B: Certainly, madam. ....
   (any – You – train from platform 9. – can take)
5 A: I'd love to go to South America.
   B: Really? ....
   (you speak – Spanish? – Do – any)
6 A: I'm hungry! We haven't eaten all day. Look at that wonderful restaurant!
   B: Wait a moment! ....
   (money – with us. – We haven't – any – brought)

B **Make the following statements negative. Use *not ... any*.**

   ▶ We've got some photos of our holiday.
      We haven't got any photos of our holiday. ....
   1 She gave me some advice.
      ....
   2 There are some good films at the cinema this week.
      ....
   3 You'll find some cake in the cupboard.
      ....
   4 Maria had some heavy luggage with her at the airport.
      ....
   5 There are some letters for you today.
      ....
   6 We saw some snow on the mountains this morning.
      ....

C **Tom and Tina are writing a shopping list. Complete the dialogue with *a*, *some*, *any* or *no*.**

   Tom: We haven't got (▶) *any* .... eggs so we need to buy (▶) *some* ....
   Tina: No, no. There are (1) .... in the fridge, but there's (2) .... cheese.
   Tom: OK, cheese. Now, we've got (3) .... fruit in the sitting room but we haven't
          got enough for the weekend so we need to buy (4) .... more. What else?
   Tina: We want to have (5) .... salad for lunch, I think.
   Tom: Yes, of course. So we need (6) .... lettuce. Oh, and (7) ....
          tomatoes because there aren't (8) .... in the kitchen.
   Tina: We must buy (9) .... bottle of oil as well.
   Tom: OK, and I want to buy (10) .... newspaper because there's (11) ....
          football match on TV this afternoon but I don't know what time it starts.
   Tina: But there are (12) .... football matches today because the weather is so
          bad. We can go and see (13) .... film instead.
   Tom: Oh, all right. Anyway, are there (14) .... more things to put on the list?
   Tina: No, I think that's everything. I hope you've got (15) .... money because
          I haven't got (16) ....
   Tina: OK. Put (17) .... coat on and get (18) .... shopping bag and
          we're ready.

55 I and me (subject and object pronouns)

1 Look at this:

SUBJECT	+VERB +	OBJECT
Mary	saw	Peter and Paul.
She	saw	**them.**

Note that we can use **she** (subject pronoun) instead of **Mary**, and **them** (object pronoun) instead of **Peter** and **Paul**.

2 Here are the subject and object pronouns:

		SUBJECT		OBJECT
Singular	1	I	9	me
	2	you	10	you
	3	he	11	him
	4	she	12	her
	5	it	13	it
Plural	6	we	14	us
	7	you	15	you
	8	they	16	them

We must always have a subject in English:
***They** are coming.* (NOT ~~Are coming.~~)

3 Look at the subject and object pronouns (1–16) in this conversation:

A: *I (1) saw Sheila yesterday, but **she** (4) didn't see **me** (9).*

B: *Are **you** (2) going to see **her** (12) tomorrow?*
A: *No, I'm meeting Steve. **We** (6) 're playing golf.*
B: ***You** (7) 're both beginners! **It** (5) isn't an easy game. I played **it** (13) last year and I was terrible!*
A: *Why don't you come with **us** (14)? We can help **you** (10).*
B: *I would like to play with **you** (15) both tomorrow, but my brother is leaving in the afternoon. **He** (3) is catching the two o'clock train, and we're taking **him** (11) to the station. He's spending a month with our aunt and uncle. **They** (8) live in Scotland. I stayed with **them** (16) last year.*

4 We use **it** for things and for the weather, time, days, dates, distances, and for animals:
*I'm studying economics. **It**'s a difficult subject.*
It's hot today.
It's four o'clock.
It's Tuesday. It's the third of April.
It's 200 miles to York.
*Look at that bird! **It**'s eating the bread.*

Practice

A Write these sentences using subject and object pronouns instead of the <u>underlined</u> words.

▶ <u>John and I</u> saw Peter yesterday. He bought <u>John and me</u> a cup of coffee.
  We saw Peter yesterday. He bought us a cup of coffee.

1 <u>David and Mike</u> are arriving today. I'm meeting <u>David and Mike</u> at the station.

....

2 I'm looking for Mary. Have you seen <u>Mary</u>? <u>Mary</u> isn't at home.

....

3 <u>John and I</u> saw a film called *The Tiger* yesterday. Have you seen <u>The Tiger</u>?

....

4 Come to the swimming pool with <u>Joanna and me</u>. <u>Joanna and I</u> are leaving now.

....

5 <u>George and Jane</u> are meeting <u>Paul</u> today. Paul is having lunch with <u>George and Jane</u>.

....

6 There's Jack! <u>Jack's</u> got a heavy suitcase. Shall we help <u>Jack</u>?

....

3 Look at the pictures and put pronouns in the gaps.

▶ .I..... saw _him_..., but _he_..... didn't see _me_.... . ▶

1 .... saw ...., but .... didn't see ....

2 .... saw ...., but .... didn't see ....

3 .... saw ...., but .... didn't see ....

4 .... saw ...., but .... didn't see ....

5 .... saw ...., but .... didn't see ....

6 .... saw ...., but .... didn't see ....

7 .... saw ...., but .... didn't see ....

I   him

1

I   her

2

she   it

3

we   you

4

they   him

5

it   them

6

you   us

7

I   you

C James is talking about himself and his family. Put subject pronouns (*I, you*, etc.) in the gaps.

Hi! (▶).I.............. am James and (1)................ live in Australia. (2)................ 've got two brothers. (3)................ 're called Pete and Mike. My mother works at the hospital. (4)................ is a doctor. My father works in a sports shop. (5)................ works very hard. The shop makes a lot of money, and (6)................ 's always full of people.

Now put object pronouns (*me, you*, etc.) in the gaps.

On Saturdays I work for my father. I help (7)................ in the shop, and he gives (8)................ some money. On Sundays we go to the beach. We have two dogs, and we take (9)................ with us. We also take a ball and they play with (10)................ on the beach while we swim in the sea.

Now put object or subject pronouns in the gaps.

At the moment I'm at university. I'm studying business. (11)................ 's an interesting subject. Two of my schoolfriends are at university with (12)................ . Our teachers are good but (13)................ give (14)................ a lot of work to do. Next week (15)................ are all taking our first exams. I want to get good marks in (16)................ .

56 There or it/they

1 Look at these sentences:
> *There is a big market near the river; **it is** very good for fruit and meat.*
> *There are two buses on Sunday; **they** both go to the station.*

We use **there is/are** when we talk about something for the first time in a conversation, and when we say where it is or when it is. We do not use **there** to talk about the same thing again; we use singular **it** (here meaning 'the big market') or plural **they** (here meaning 'the two buses'). Here are some more examples:
> *There are two schools here; **they** are both new.*
> *There's a good programme on Sunday; **it** gives all the sports news.*

2 We use **there** with different forms of **be**:
> *There weren't any CDs thirty years ago.*
> A: *Have there been any problems this year?*
> B: *Yes, there have.*
> *There used to be a park here.* (= There was a park here but it isn't here now.)
> *There may be some eggs in the fridge.* (= It is possible that there are some eggs …)

3 We also use **there is/are** etc. to talk about the number of people or things in a place. Look at these questions and answers:
> A: *How many people **were there** at your party?*
> B: *There were about twelve.* (NOT ~~We were about twelve.~~)
> A: *Are there many restaurants here?*
> B: *Yes, there must be ten or more.* (NOT ~~They must be ten.~~)

We can use **of us**, **of them**, etc. after the number:
> *There were about twelve **of us**.*

4 For the weather, we use **it** with a verb or adjective, but **there** with a noun:

> **it + verb:** It *rained/snowed* a lot last winter.
> **it + adjective:** It was *foggy/sunny/windy/cloudy*.
> **there + noun:** There was a lot of *fog/cloud*.

5 Notice these examples with **it takes**:
> *It takes seven years to become a doctor.*
> A: *How long **does it take** to make bread?*
> B: *It takes several hours (to make bread).*

These sentences describe the time that is necessary to do something.

Practice

A Put in *there is*, *there are*, *it is* or *they are*.

▶ *There are* .... two cinemas in our town; *they are* both near my flat.

1 .... one train on Sundays; .... an express train.

2 .... two national holidays this month, and .... both on a Friday.

3 .... several trees in our garden, but .... not very tall.

4 .... a big lake in the park; .... very deep.

B Write answers to the questions using *there were ... of* and the words in brackets ( ).

▶ A: How many people were there at your party?
   B: (twenty/us) *There were twenty of us.*

1 A: How many of you were there in the car?
   B: (five/us) ....

2 A: How many sailors were there in the boat?
   B: (six/them) ....

3 A: How many people were there at the supper?
   B: (twelve/us) ....

C Rewrite the sentences using the words in brackets ( ) and *it* or *there*.

▶ There's a lot of snow in December.
(snows a lot) .It snows a lot in December...

▶ It's quite cloudy this morning.
(quite a lot of cloud) There's quite a lot of cloud this morning........................

1 There's a lot of rain in April.
(rains a lot) ....

2 It's foggy on the motorway this morning.
(fog on the motorway) ....

3 There are a lot of clouds in the mountains.
(very cloudy) ....

4 It's very windy on the west coast.
(a lot of wind) ....

D Use *there* and the words in the box to complete the sentences. Use each word in the box once.

have been	is	may be	used to be	was	will be

▶ There is .... an accident on this road almost every day.
1 Last year .... a terrible fire at that factory.
2 Next Monday at 7 p.m. .... a meeting of the committee.
3 When I was young, ... a lot more cinemas than there are now.
4 Since 1900 .... two world wars.
5 .... a late-night bus, but I'm not sure if there is.

E Look at the times needed to prepare certain foods, then write a statement or a question and answer.

bake bread	– about three hours
prepare a salad	– about ten minutes
cook a stew	– about two hours
cook an omelette	– a few minutes
boil an egg	– about three minutes
make tea	– about five minutes.
make a cake	– about an hour.

▶ It takes about three minutes to boil ....an egg.
▶ A: How long does it take to prepare a salad .... ?
  B: It takes about ten minutes ....
1 It .... an omelette.
2 A: How long .... tea?
  B:.. .
3 It .... bread.
4 A: How long .... stew?
  B:.. .
5 It .... cake.

57 My, your; mine, yours

1 Look at these sentences:
This car belongs to me.
It's my car.   It's mine.

2 Now look at this table:

OBJECT PRONOUN	POSSESSIVE ADJECTIVE	POSSESSIVE PRONOUN
me	my	mine
you	your	yours
him	his	his
her	her	hers
it	its	its
us	our	ours
you	your	yours
them	their	theirs

3 **my, your,** etc.

▶ We use **my, your,** etc. with nouns:
my book   his hands   their house

▶ We say:
Tony and his wife. (NOT ... ~~her wife.~~)
Sara and her husband.
(NOT ... ~~his husband.~~)

▶ We use possessive adjectives with parts of the body:
Her hair is red. My hands are cold.

4 **mine, yours,** etc.

▶ We use **mine, yours,** etc. instead of **my book, your keys,** etc:
My flat is in the centre of town. Where's yours? (*yours* = your flat)

▶ We often use possessive pronouns in comparative sentences:
Our cat is smaller than theirs.
(*theirs* = their cat)
Your house is older than mine.
(*mine* = my house)

▶ We use **a/some + noun + of + possessive pronoun** to talk about one of a number of people or things:
I went to the club with a friend of mine.
(= one of my friends)

5 We do not use **a/an** or **the** with possessive adjectives or pronouns:
It's ~~a~~ my bag. They're ~~the~~ ours.

6 **'s or s'**

▶ We use **'s** with singular nouns or names:
When is the team's next game?
I went to Sam's house.

▶ We use **s'** with plural nouns that end with **s**:
She borrowed her parents' car.

▶ We use **'s** with plural nouns that do not end with **s**:
Many people's jobs are difficult.

▶ Remember that **its** and **it's** are different:
I've got a new dog. Its name is Pluto.
(*Its* = possessive adjective)
It's cold today. (*It's* = It is)

(See also Unit 35.)

Practice

A Put possessive adjectives (*my, your,* etc.) and possessive pronouns (*mine, yours,* etc.) in the gaps.

▶ This car belongs to me. This is my........... car. It's mine........... .
1 That ticket belongs to you. That's .... ticket. It's ....
2 These shoes belong to her. These are .... shoes. They're ....
3 This house belongs to them. This is .... house. It's ....
4 These cups belong to us. These are .... cups. They're ....
5 Those books belong to him. Those are .... books. They're ....
6 That bag belongs to me. That's .... bag. It's ....
7 This key belongs to her. This is .... key. It's ....
8 That boat belongs to them. That's .... boat. It's ....
9 Those coats belong to us. Those are .... coats. They're ....

10 These pens belong to me. These are .... pens. They're ....
11 That watch belongs to him. That's .... watch. It's ....
12 These photos belong to you. These are .... photos. They're ....

B **Look at the pictures and then complete the sentences.**
   Use *my*, *your*, etc. and *mine*, *yours*, etc.

me   you   him

us   them   her

► Those are <u>his</u>............ keys.
1 That book is ....
2 These pens are ....
3 That's .... money.
4 This bike is ....
5 That ruler is ....

6 This is .... car.
7 Those are .... sandwiches.
8 Is this bag .... ?
9 Those photos are ....
10 This is .... camera.
11 Is this .... watch?

C **If the <u>underlined</u> words are correct, put a tick (✓). If they are wrong, write**
   the correct words.

► Look at the sky! <u>Its</u> going to rain.   It's ....
► Is that Erica's car?   ✓ ....
1 Those photos on the table are <u>the mine</u>.   ....
2 I met <u>a friend of me</u> at the shops.   ....
3 The <u>childrens'</u> toys were on the floor.   ....
4 I can't do this exercise. <u>Its</u> very difficult. ....
5 I like all of that <u>writers'</u> books.   ....
6 <u>People's</u> opinions often change.   ....
7 The <u>workers'</u> wages are very low so they are very unhappy. ....
8 They were talking about the <u>world's</u> problems. ....
9 Shall we give the cat <u>it's</u> food?   ....
10 She stayed with <u>some relatives of hers</u> in Spain. ....

D **Replace the words in brackets ( ) with possessive pronouns (*mine*, *yours*, etc.).**

► My car is faster than (your car).   yours.........
1 Her house is bigger than (my house).   ....
2 Your watch is more expensive than (his watch).   ....
3 My exams are more difficult than (their exams).   ....
4 Their garden is more beautiful than (our garden).   ....
5 Your son is younger than (her son).   ....
6 My husband is stronger than (your husband).   ....
7 Her job is harder than (his job).   ....

58 **Myself, yourself**, etc.; **each other**

1 Look at this table:

SUBJECT PRONOUNS	OBJECT PRONOUNS	REFLEXIVE PRONOUNS
I	me	myself
you (*singular*)	you	yourself
he	him	himself
she	her	herself
it	it	itself
we	us	ourselves
you (*plural*)	you	yourselves
they	them	themselves

2 Compare:

(i)

Jenny made Jo a cup of coffee.
(= Jenny made the coffee for Jo.)

(ii)

*Jenny made **herself** a cup of coffee.*
(= Jenny made the coffee for herself.)

We use **myself, yourself, herself**, etc. to refer to the subject:

SUBJECT
Be careful. **You** *might hurt* **yourself**.

*I bought **myself** a new shirt.*
*He taught **himself** to swim.*
*They enjoyed **themselves** at the concert.*

3 We also use **myself, yourself**, etc. to emphasize that the subject did the action, not another person:
*He built the whole house **himself**.*
(= He built it alone; nobody helped him.)

4 We use **each other** like this:
Tom and Sue were talking to each other.
(= Tom was talking to Sue, and Sue was talking to Tom.)
*We like **each other** very much.*
(= I like her and she likes me.)

Compare **themselves** and **each other**:
*Alan and Ruth took these photographs **themselves**.* (= They took them, not another person.)
*Alan and Ruth took photographs of **each other**.* (= Alan took a photograph of Ruth, and Ruth took a photograph of Alan.)

Practice

A Fill the gaps with *myself, yourself*, etc.

▶ I cooked <u>myself</u> a meal and then I watched television.

1 I'm sure he'll enjoy .... on his trip.
2 I cut .... while I was preparing the vegetables.
3 We amused .... by playing cards while we were waiting for the plane.
4 She put the plates on the table and told them to help .... to the food.
5 Tom hurt .... when he was playing football.
6 Alan cooked .... a snack when he got home.

B Complete the sentences with the correct verb tenses and *myself, yourself*, etc. in the correct place.

▶ (Be careful with that knife or you/cut/.)
Be careful with that knife or <u>you'll cut yourself</u> .

1 (It was a very nice trip and we/enjoy/very much.)
It was a very nice trip and we ....

2 (I/burn/while I was taking the dish out of the oven.)
   I .... while I was taking the dish out of the oven.
3 (He didn't have lessons. He/teach/.)
   He didn't have lessons. ....
4 (I think I/buy/a new coat tomorrow.)
   .... a new coat tomorrow.
5 (She/make/a sandwich and ate it in the kitchen.)
   .... and ate it in the kitchen.

C Fill the gaps with *myself*, *yourself*, etc.

▶ Did you paint the room _yourself_...... ? ~ Yes, it took me three days to do it.
1 If you won't help me, I'll have to do it all ....
2 She makes all her clothes ....
3 The students organized the concert ....
4 We painted the whole house ....
5 He typed the letter .... and then he posted it.

D Complete the sentences with the correct verb tenses and *myself*, *yourself*, etc. Put *myself*, *yourself*, etc. at the end of the sentence.

▶ (She is a very successful singer. She/write/all her songs/.)
   She is a very successful singer. _She writes all her songs herself._............................
1 Could you post this letter for me? ~ (No, I'm sorry, I won't have time. You/have/to post it/.)
   No, I'm sorry, I won't have time. ....
2 (Nobody helped us, so we/carry/all our luggage/.)
   Nobody helped us, so ....
3 (This is an excellent photograph./you/take it/?)
   This is an excellent photograph. ....
4 (She was wearing a dress that she/make/.)
   She was wearing a dress that ....
5 (I hope you like the present. I/choose/it/.)
   I hope you like the present. ....
6 (Do you like this meal? I/invent/the recipe/.)
   Do you like this meal? ....

E Fill the gaps with *each other*, *ourselves*, *yourselves* or *themselves*.

▶ They spent the whole evening arguing with _each other_.......... .
▶ Their house is very beautiful; they designed it themselves.
1 Mary met John in April, but they didn't see .... again until July.
2 They're not friends; in fact, they don't like .... at all.
3 Don't ask me to help you. You must do it ....
4 We didn't buy it .... A friend bought it for us.
5 I could hear two people shouting at ....
6 We're working in the same office now, so Ron and I see .... every day.

59 Direct and indirect objects

1 Look at this example:

(i) *She gave **her brother** the newspaper.*
(ii) *She gave the newspaper **to her brother.***

In both sentences **a newspaper** is the thing which is given, and **her brother** is the person who receives it.

2 Here are other sentences like (i):

	+ PERSON (indirect object)	+ THING (direct object)
*She **gave***	*her brother*	*a shirt.*
*He **sent***	*me*	*a letter.*
*I **showed***	*him*	*my passport.*
*Jane **lent***	*Frank*	*some money.*
*I'll **offer***	*her*	*a job.*
*I'll **cook***	*them*	*a meal.*
*I **fetched***	*her*	*a plate.*
*I'll **get***	*you*	*a magazine.*
*I'll **buy***	*you*	*a coffee.*

3 Here are some other sentences like (ii):
*She gave the newspaper **to her brother.***

	+ THING (direct object)	+ PERSON (to + object)
*She **gave***	*a shirt*	*to her brother.*
*I **sent***	*postcards*	*to my friends.*
*I **showed***	*my card*	*to the clerk.*
*She **lent***	*some money*	*to her friend.*
*He **offered***	*the chocolates*	*to the others.*

Note that we use **to** + object after these verbs which express the idea of giving or showing something to somebody:
give, send, show, lend, offer

But we use **for** + object after verbs which express the idea of doing something for another person:
cook, fetch, buy, get (= 'fetch' or 'buy')

	+ THING (direct object)	+ PERSON (for + object)
*We **cooked***	*a meal*	*for everybody.*
*He **fetched***	*the newspaper*	*for his father.*
*I'll **get***	*your book*	*for you.*
*She **bought***	*some toys*	*for them.*

Practice

A Put these words into the right order to make sentences. Do not add any words.

▶ (He – lent – his car – Mark – .)
<u>He lent Mark his car.</u> ....

1 (a cigarette – Jim – She offered – .)
....

2 (Mary – his holiday photographs – He showed – .)
....

3 (them – an invitation – Have you sent – ?)
....

4 (a birthday present – Did you buy – her – ?)
....

5 (I – some of my CDs – a friend – gave – .)
....

6 (When you go to the post office, – some stamps – me – could you get – ?)
....

B Now write the sentences from Exercise A again, but using *to* or *for*.

▶ He lent *his car to Mark.* ....

1 She offered ....

2 He showed ....

3 Have you sent ....

4 Did you buy ....

5 I gave ....

6 When you go to the post office, could you get ....

C Write sentences, putting the words in brackets ( ) in the correct place.

▶ She wrote a letter. (me) *She wrote me a letter.* ....

1 They sent an invitation. (us) ....

2 Sheila gave a present. (to Mike) ....

3 I made a sandwich. (her) ....

4 Tom bought a newspaper. (for Sally) ....

5 My uncle sold his camera. (me) ....

6 She left a message. (for you) ....

7 Mary sent some flowers. (them) ....

8 Did you take the money? (to the bank) ....

D Tim and Lucy went to a restaurant last night for a meal. Make sentences about what happened while they were there. Write two sentences. Use the words in brackets ( ).

▶ (The waiter/give/the menu)
  (her) *The waiter gave her the menu.* ....
  (to Lucy) *The waiter gave the menu to Lucy.* ....

1 (The waiter/fetch/some wine)
  (them) ....
  (for them) ....

2 (The waiter/show/the bottle)
  (him) ....
  (to Tim) ....

3 (The chef/cook/a special meal)
  (them) ....
  (for them) ....

4 (The waiter/give/the bill)
  (Tim) ....
  (to Tim) ....

5 (Lucy/lend/some money, because he didn't have enough to pay the bill)
  (Tim) ....
  (to Tim) ....

60 Much, many; how much/many; more

1 Look at these examples with **much** and **many**:

*There weren't **many** people in the restaurant.*

*I don't have **much** money.*

We use **much** and **many** to talk about quantity.

We normally use **much** and **many** in negative sentences:

A: *I'm so hungry.*
B: *I'm sorry, I don't have **much** food in the house. Shall we go out to a restaurant?*
*I haven't bought **many** CDs this year.*

We also use **much** and **many** in questions:

*Do **many** tourists come here?*
*Is there **much** snow in the mountains?*

We can use **how much** and **how many** in questions:

*How **much** luggage have you got?*
*How **many** times have you been to London?*

2 We also use **more** to talk about quantity:

*John did two exams yesterday and he is doing two **more** exams today.*
*We have some food, but we will need **more** food for the party tonight.*
Shall we go to the shops?

We often say **some more** or **any more**:

A: *Would you like **some more** toast?*
B: *No, thanks. I don't want **any more**. But could I have **some more** orange juice?*

3 We use:

▶ **much** with uncountable nouns:
much food   much luggage   much snow
much time   much money
(For uncountable nouns, see Unit 53.)

▶ **many** with plural nouns:
many things   many books   many CDs
many people   many tourists   many times

▶ **more** with uncountable and plural nouns:
more toast/juice   more glasses

▶ **much/many/more** without a noun:
*How **much** did that coat cost?*
A: *That cake was delicious.*
B: *Would you like some **more** (cake)?*

Practice

A If the sentences are correct put a tick (✓). If they are incorrect, put a cross (✗).

▶ I don't have much food in the house.   ✓......
▶ I don't have many food in the house.   ✗......
1 We don't have many information about this machine.   ....
2 We must buy some more apples.   ....
3 How much people can you see?   ....
4 Older students have more exams.   ....
5 Is there many news this week?   ....
6 We don't have much white wine.   ....
7 Do you have many luggage?   ....
8 Pam doesn't earn much money.   ....

3 Write *much* or *many* in front of these nouns.

▶ How much. money? ▶ How many. films? ▶ Not many. people.
1 How .... snow? 8 How .... buses? 15 How .... information?
2 How .... tables? 9 How .... books? 16 How .... toast?
3 How .... cats? 10 How .... food? 17 Not .... news.
4 How .... petrol? 11 How .... cups? 18 Not .... exams.
5 How .... advice? 12 How .... watches? 19 Not .... luggage.
6 How .... cigars? 13 How .... homework? 20 Not .... children.
7 How .... sugar? 14 How .... times? 21 Not .... museums.

C Complete the dialogues using *much*, *many*, *more*, *how much* or *how many*.

▶ A: How many......... CDs has your sister got?
  B: She hasn't got many......... . I've got more......... than she has.
1 A: Is there .... cheese in the fridge?
  B: No, and there aren't .... eggs, either.
2 A: .... money do you earn?
  B: Not .... , but I earn .... than my brother.
3 A: Do you have .... homework?
  B: Yes, because there aren't .... days before the exams.
4 A: .... food do we need?
  B: We haven't got .... vegetables, so we need to buy some ....
5 A: Is there .... luggage in the coach?
  B: There aren't .... big suitcases, but there are a lot of small ones.
6 A: .... toast do you want? .... pieces?
  B: Two please, and without .... butter.
7 A: .... spoonfuls of sugar do you take?
  B: No sugar thank you. I don't usually eat .... sugar.

D Put in *many*, *much* or *more*.

Steve: What did you do on Sunday?
Jenny: I had a terrible day. I met a friend at the airport, because he said he had a lot
       of luggage, and he wanted some help. But his plane was two hours late, and
       he didn't have (▶) much......... luggage! What about you?
Steve: I went into town to buy some books. I spent £50!
Jenny: How (1)............... books did you buy?
Steve: Only three! In fact, I want to buy some (2)............... books tomorrow.
Jenny: I don't have (3)............... time to read at the moment. We're so busy at the office.
Steve: How (4)............... hours a day do you work?
Jenny: I do eight hours at the office, and then I do two (5)............... hours at home!
Steve: Do you get (6)............... money for that?
Jenny: No, I don't get much, but I enjoy the work.
Steve: Why don't you ask your boss for some (7)............... money?
Jenny: I don't have (8)............... opportunities. She's always in America on business.
Steve: I see. Listen, do you want some (9)............... advice?
Jenny: OK.
Steve: Look for a new job!

61 A lot of, lots of, a little, a few

1 Look at this example with **a lot of**:

*She's got **a lot of** luggage.*
(**a lot of** = a big amount or number)

We use **lots of** with the same meaning:
*She's got **lots of** luggage.*

In spoken English, we usually use **a lot of/lots of** in positive sentences:
*There's **a lot of/lots of** information in this book.*
(NOT ~~There's much information in this book.~~)
*I bought **a lot of/lots of** new books today.*
(NOT ~~I bought many new books today.~~)
A lot of/Lots of students work in the holidays.

But in written English, we often use **much** and **many** in positive sentences:
*There are big problems in **many** parts of the world.*

2 We use **a lot of/lots of**:

▶ with uncountable nouns:
a lot of luggage   lots of information

▶ with plural nouns:
a lot of books   lots of students

3 Use a singular verb with an uncountable noun:
*There **is** a lot of **information** in this book.*
(NOT ...are...)

Use a plural verb with a plural noun:
*A lot of **students work**. (NOT ...~~works~~.)*

4 Look at these examples with **a few** and **a little**:

*She has **a few** bags.*
*She has **a little** luggage.*
(**a few** and **a little** = a small number or amount)

We can use **a few** and **a little** with **more**:
*Would you like **a little more** coffee?*
*I should have had **a few more** hours' sleep.*

5 We use:

▶ **a little** with uncountable nouns:
*I have **a little money**, but I don't have much.*

▶ **a few** with plural nouns:
*Can you wait **a few minutes**, John?*

We can use **a few** and **a little** without a noun:
A: *Have you got any money?*
B: *Sorry. I only have **a little** (money).*
A: *How many of his albums have you got?*
B: *I'm not sure exactly. **A few** (albums).*

6 Here are some common uncountable nouns:

coffee	milk	cheese	information
water	bread	money	advice
sugar	news	luggage	homework

Practice

A Write the second line of these dialogues using the words in brackets ( ). Put in *a lot of* or *lots of* in the right place.

▶ A: Are you going to the cinema tonight?
   B: (No, I have homework to do.) No, I have a lot of/lots of homework to do.

1 A: Are you hungry?
   B: (No, I ate cake in town.) ....

2 A: Do you want some help?
   B: (Yes, please. I have luggage.) ....

3 A: Did you enjoy the party?
   B: (Yes, I met interesting people.) ....

4 A: Can you pay for our plane tickets?
   B: (Yes, I have money at the moment.) ....

5 A: Is Bill coming?
   B: (No, he isn't. He has things to do.) ....

6 A: Did she help you?
   B: (Yes, she gave me good advice.) ....

B What do you see in the pictures? Write your answers. Use *a lot of/lots of*, *a few* or *a little*.

▶ *a few pens* ....

1 ....

2 ....

3 ....

4 ....

5 ....

6 ....

7 ....

C A friend is visiting you. Rewrite the questions you ask your friend, using *a few* or *a little* instead of *some*.

▶ Would you like some coffee? *Would you like a little coffee?* ....
1 Would you like some biscuits? ....
2 Shall I make you some sandwiches? ....
3 Would you like some cheese? ....
4 Can I bring you some cake? ....
5 Would you like some milk in your coffee? ....
6 Would you like some more sugar in your coffee? ....

D In these sentences, tick (✓) the <u>underlined</u> words if they are right. Rewrite them if they are wrong.

▶ There <u>is</u> *are*............. a lot of tall buildings in New York.
▶ I bought <u>a few</u> ✓.............. presents today.
1 A lot of people <u>travels</u> .... to work by car.
2 She only has <u>a little</u> .... luggage with her.
3 We need <u>a little</u> .... tomatoes for this meal.
4 There <u>are</u> .... a lot of news on TV in Britain.
5 My father gave me <u>a little</u> .... advice before I went to university.
6 Could you give me <u>a few</u> .... water, please?
7 <u>Lots of</u> .... children use computers in school.
8 Are you hungry? Shall I make you <u>a little</u> .... sandwiches?

62 Something, anybody, nothing, etc.

1 **something/anything** = a thing
somebody/anybody = a person
someone/anyone = a person
somewhere/anywhere = a place

2 We usually use **something, somebody, someone** and **somewhere** in positive sentences:
Something is burning. (= I can smell burning. I don't know what is burning.)
*I'm going to have **something** to eat.* (= I'm going to eat; I don't know what I'm going to eat.)
Somebody told me that it was a good film. (= A person told me it was a good film. I can't remember who told me.)
*She lives **somewhere** in the north.*

3 We usually use **anything, anybody, anyone** and **anywhere** in negative sentences, and in questions:
*I didn't know **anyone** at the party.* (= There were no people at the party who I knew.)
*I couldn't find my bag **anywhere**.*
(= I couldn't find my bag in any place.)
*Did you understand **anything** she said?*

4 **nothing** = not anything
nobody/no one = not anybody/not anyone
nowhere = not anywhere

We use **nothing, nobody, no one** and **nowhere** before or after positive verbs:

Nothing makes Joe unhappy. (= There isn't anything that makes Joe unhappy.)
*There's **nothing** I want to watch on TV.*
Nobody was there when I arrived.
*There is **nowhere** that I would prefer to live than here.* (= There isn't anywhere …)

5 **everything** = all things
everybody/everyone = all people
everywhere = all places

We use **everything, everybody, everyone** and **everywhere** before or after positive verbs:
Everyone likes music.
*I've done **everything** I can.*

6 Note that we use a singular verb after all these words:
*Nothing **is** wrong.*
*Everyone **was** friendly.*

7 We can use **else** after **something, anybody, nowhere, everyone,** etc.:
*Let's talk about **something else**.*
(= Let's talk about a different subject.)
*I didn't tell **anybody else**.*
(= I didn't tell another person.)
*There is **nowhere else** I can look for it.*

8 We can also use an adjective (e.g. **wrong, nice**) after **something, anything,** etc.:
*Have I said **something wrong**?*

Practice

A Put in the correct word from the box in each gap.

anything	nobody	everything	somebody (x2)	somewhere
nothing	everywhere	something	anyone	everyone

▶ She didn't say _anything_ about her job when I spoke to her
1 .... phoned you today, but he didn't tell me his name.
2 I'm sure you'll find it .... in the house if you keep looking.
3 I had to go to the cinema on my own because I couldn't find .... to go with me.
4 She said that .... was fine and she was very happy.
5 Can I speak to you for a moment? I want to discuss .... with you.
6 Unfortunately, I couldn't help. There was .... I could do about the problem.

7 I looked .... but I couldn't find it.
8 She married .... she met when she was a student.
9 .... was out of the office so there was .... to answer the phone.

B Choose the correct verb form in brackets ( ).

▶ I'm afraid I _don't know_.......... (know/don't know) anything about this subject.
▶ I rang the doorbell but nobody _was_.................. (was/wasn't) in.
1 I asked a lot of people, but nobody .... (knew/didn't know) the answer.
2 I .... (have seen/haven't seen) anything so lovely before in my life!
3 I .... (ate/didn't eat) anything for lunch yesterday.
4 Nothing interesting .... (has happened/hasn't happened) since the last time I spoke to you.
5 He loves football. Nothing else .... (is/isn't) important to him.
6 She .... (said/didn't say) anything about her plans for the future.

C Change each of these sentences into a sentence with the same meaning. Use the word in brackets ( ) with the <u>underlined</u> adjective or with *else*.

▶ A <u>strange</u> thing happened yesterday. (something)
   Something strange........ happened yesterday.
▶ Let's listen to some different music. (something)
   Let's listen to _something else_.............. .
1 Is there an <u>interesting</u> programme on TV tonight? (anything)
   Is there .... on TV tonight?
2 You won't find better food in any other place. (anywhere)
   You won't find better food ....
3 Is there a <u>cheap</u> place we can go for lunch? (anywhere)
   Is there .... we can go for lunch?
4 Let's sit in a different place. (somewhere)
   Let's sit ....
5 I'd like a <u>hot</u> drink. (something)
   I'd like .... to drink.

D Put the right form of a word beginning with *some-*, *any-*, *no-* or *every-* into the conversation.

Dennis: Have you read (▶) _anything_..... interesting lately?
Sarah: Yes, (1)................ lent me a novel last week and I really enjoyed it.
Dennis: What was it about?
Sarah: It was about (2)................ who goes to visit Australia. She likes to go (3)................ alone. While she's travelling around on her own, (4)................ terrible happens to her. She loses (5)................ – including her passport and all her money. She doesn't know (6)................ who can help her, and she's got (7)................ to stay.
Dennis: What happens then?
Sarah: I'm not going to tell you (8)................ else! You should read the book yourself.
Dennis: It sounds like a very depressing book! I'd prefer to read (9)................ funny.
Sarah: No, read it. It's great fun. And (10)................ wonderful happens at the end.

63 Every/each; one/another/other/others

1 We use **every** and **each** to talk about all people or things in a group or series. In many contexts, both **every** and **each** are correct:

> *The letter has been sent to **every/each** member of staff.*
> *We checked **every/each** item before we sent it.*

We use **every/each** + singular noun + singular verb:

> *Every/Each student has to fill in this form.*

We can use **each** (but not **every**) + **of** + **the/possessive** + **plural noun**:

> *I put **each of the documents** into the correct place.*

We can use **each** (but not **every**) on its own as a subject or between a subject and a main verb:

> *Tickets are now available and **each** costs the same.*
> *Tickets (will) **each** cost the same.*

2 Sometimes we can only use **every**; at other times we can only use **each**. We use **every** to talk about a group or series of people or things in general, with the meaning 'all of them':

> *Every ticket had been sold.*

We use **each** to talk about all individual things or people in a group or series:

> *Each ticket costs £20.*

3 We use **one** + **of** + **the/possessive** + **plural noun** to talk about one person or thing when there are several or many:

> *One of the students in my class was off sick today.*
> *He is staying with **one of his relatives**.*

We can use **one** + singular noun:

> *One flight leaves at five p.m. and the other is at nine.*

We can use **one** + singular verb:

> *There are two flights. **One leaves** at five p.m and the other leaves at nine.*

(See also Unit 51.)

4 We use **another** + singular noun with the meanings 'one more' or 'a different one':

> *Would you like **another drink**?*
> *Let's go to **another restaurant** for a change.*

Notice that we do not use **another** with **one** and a singular noun (NOT ~~another one drink~~).

Notice also that we do not use **another** with a plural noun (NOT ~~I met another people~~).

5 We use **the/possessive/quantifier** + **other** + **plural noun** with the meanings 'different ones' or 'ones that have not been mentioned':

> *The other hotels were more expensive.*
> *Ray agreed with me but **my other friends** said I was wrong.*
> *For **all other enquiries**, phone this number.*

We use **the/possessive** + **other** + **singular noun** with the meaning 'the one that has not already been mentioned':

> *One of his sisters lives in France and **his/the other sister** lives in Australia.*

We use **the other (one)** to talk about a person or thing that has not already been mentioned:

> *He's got two homes – one is in London and **the other (one)** is in Florida.*

6 We use **others** with the meaning 'other people or things':

> *Some people like sport and **others** aren't interested in it at all.*

We use **the others** with the meaning 'the other people or things (in a set or group)':

> *We arrived first and **the others** came later.*

Practice

A Decide whether the <u>underlined</u> parts of these sentences are correct or not. Put a tick (✓) next to the sentences that are correct and rewrite the underlined parts of the sentences that are not correct.

▶ I've told every of my friends about this. *each of my friends* ....

▶ Each room has its own private bathroom. ✓ ....

1 Every house in the street is exactly the same. ....

2 Each assignment on the course have to be completed on time. ....

3 Each candidate for the job was interviewed separately. ....

4 We couldn't park because every car park were full. ....

5 We each paid £5 towards the cost of the food. ....

6 There are three tests and every lasts for one hour. ....

3 Complete these questions, using *another*, *other* or *others*.

▶ Could I ask you *another* ...... question?

1 What time is the .... flight that day?

2 What will the .... say when I tell them about this?

3 Do you know any .... clubs that are as good as this one?

4 Will you have .... chance to take the exam?

5 Could we change our meeting to .... date?

C Complete this article about a film star, using *one*, *another*, *other* or *others*.

Walter Richards had a remarkably successful film career. (▶) *One* .... reason for
his success was that he had such a relaxed acting style that he never really seemed to be
acting. (1) .... reason was of course his good looks. No (2) .... actor
looked quite like him and his image was used on posters and all sorts of other goods. In a
film career spanning sixty years, he won two Oscars and many (3) .... awards. He
first came to fame playing an ambitious musician in *The Path To Glory* and he played a
similar character in (4) .... film shortly afterwards – *High Hat*. (5) .... roles
quickly followed and he was soon a household name. Many people felt that, although he
made over 100 films, most of the (6) .... weren't as good as the first two.
Nevertheless, he continued to have a highly successful career, and was working on
(7) .... film when he died, aged eighty-five.

D Complete these dialogues, using *one*, *another*, *other*, *the other*, *others* or *the others*.

▶ A: All their flights are fully booked.
B: Well, we'll have to phone *another* .... airline. Lots of airlines fly there.

1 A: Do you like this writer?
B: I'm not sure. I really enjoyed one of her books but I haven't enjoyed any of
.... books she's written.

2 A: Have you been to any .... cities in Britain apart from London?
B: Yes, on my .... visit to this country last year, I went to Birmingham.

3 A: Are you on your own?
B: Yes, but .... are on their way. They'll be here soon.

4 A: Is the company you work for big?
B: It has two main offices. .... office is in Lisbon and ....
is in Paris.

5 A: Can we make a decision now?
B: No, I think we should have .... discussion about the subject later.

64 All, most, some, none

1 We use

> all/most/some + NOUN (e.g. **most cities**)

to talk about things or people in general:
> *She thinks that **all sports** are boring.*
> (= She thinks that every sport is boring.)
> ***Most cities** have a lot of shops.*
> (= Almost every city has a lot of shops.)
> *In **some countries** life is very hard.*
> (= In a number of countries in the world,
> but not all or most …)

We do not say **all/most/some + of + noun**:
> ***Most people** take exams during their lives.*
> (NOT ~~Most of people~~ …)

2 We can also use **all** with **morning/afternoon/
evening/night/day/week/year** (e.g. **all
afternoon**) to mean 'the whole', 'from the
beginning to the end of':

> *They've been working hard **all day**.*
> *I waited for the phone call **all morning**.*

3 We use

> all/most } + of + the/my/her + NOUN
> some/none
> (e.g. **all of my books**)

to talk about particular things or people:
> *He spent **all of his money**.*
> *Most of **my friends** are interested in sport.*
> *I knew **some of the people** at the party.*
> ***None of the shops** were open.*

Notice that we use a positive verb with **none**.
We can leave out **of** after **all** (but not after
most, some, none):
> *He spent **all his money**.*

4 We can use

> all/most/some/none + of + it/them

when we have already mentioned the noun
that **it** or **them** refers to:
> *It was lovely food, but I couldn't eat **all of it**.*
> (**it** = the food)
> *I phoned a number of hotels, but **most of
> them** were full.* (**them** = the hotels)
> *That cake looks nice. Can I have **some of it**?*
> (**it** = the cake)

Practice

A Look at these exam results for four people and complete the sentences, using *all of*,
some of, *most of* or *none of*. Sometimes you will need *the* (e.g. *some of the*).

STUDENT	EXAM 1	EXAM 2	EXAM 3	EXAM 4	EXAM 5	EXAM 6
Alice	PASS	PASS	FAIL	PASS	PASS	PASS
Bill	PASS	PASS	PASS	PASS	PASS	PASS
Carol	FAIL	PASS	PASS	PASS	FAIL	FAIL
David	FAIL	FAIL	FAIL	FAIL	FAIL	FAIL

▶ Alice passed *most of the* exams.

1 Bill passed .... exams.

2 Bill failed .... them.

3 Carol passed .... exams.

4 Carol passed .... them.

5 Carol failed .... them.

6 David passed .... them.

7 David passed .... exams.

8 David failed .... exams.

3 Complete the sentences by putting in the correct words from the box.

all	all the	none of the	some	some of the

- ▶ _All_ European children have to go to school.
- ▶ The classroom is empty because _some of the_ children are outside.
- 1 We can't buy anything today because .... shops are closed.
- 2 We like that restaurant. .... food is expensive, but everything is very good.
- 3 .... people say he's the best tennis player in the world, but I don't agree.
- 4 That's a terrible shop. .... assistants are very helpful.
- 5 Bill's very lazy. He reads the newspaper .... morning.
- 6 .... phones here are working. Has anyone got a mobile?
- 7 It's a wonderful trip. You have .... day to see the sights.
- 8 IMPORTANT NOTICE: .... passengers must have a valid ticket.
- 9 If .... students can answer the teacher's questions, she explains the point again.
- 10 We can't sit down. .... chairs are wet.
- 11 .... cars use petrol and others use diesel.
- 12 This light works .... time, but not always.

C Write full sentences using *all*, *most*, *some* or *none*. Use *them* or *it* when possible and include *of* or *the* if necessary.

- ▶ 100% – sports – physical and – 20% – dangerous.
  All sports are physical and some of them are dangerous.
- ▶ 80% – Hepworth's art – abstract and – 25% – difficult to understand
  Most of Hepworth's art is abstract and some of it is difficult to understand.
- 1 80% – professional footballers – well off and – 20% – very rich.

  ....

- 2 80% – sea – very salty and – 0% – fresh water.

  ....

- 3 30% – pop music – very pleasant but – 20% – terrible.

  ....

- 4 75% – Indian food – spicy and – 15% – very spicy.

  ....

- 5 100% – my relatives – slim and – 0% – very tall.

  ....

- 6 75% – my friends – students but – 0% – very clever.

  ....

- 7 80% – Nepal – mountainous and – 0% – flat.

  ....

- 8 75% – the Earth – inhabited but – 10% – desert.

  ....

Test F: Articles, nouns, pronouns, etc.

A This is an advertisement in a music shop. In the numbered lines cross out one or two of the words *a*, *an* or *the*.

▶ It's ~~a~~ time to change your life!
1 Would you like to learn to play the a piano?
2 All you need is half a an hour a day and a the simple book!
3 What's the name of the a book? Bob Bryant's Big Piano Book
4 The friends are great, but the music will be your partner forever!
   Don't just stand there! Buy this book today!
5 You'll also get the a free CD of piano music from around a the world!

B Bill and Sheila are going on holiday with their children, Penny and Dan. Put the correct words from the box in the spaces, but note that you do not need one of the words.

everywhere	anybody	someone	everyone
~~anywhere~~	somewhere	nothing	nobody

Bill: Has anyone seen the big blue beach ball? I can't find it (▶) anywhere..... .
Penny: Have you looked in the cupboard under the stairs?
Bill: Yes, there's (1)................ there. Only a box.
Penny: And did you look in the box?
Bill: Of course. I've looked (2)................ .
Penny: Well, it must be (3)................ .
Dan: Come on, (4)................ , let's help Dad find the blue beach ball!
Sheila: But (5)................ could find it last year, or the year before.
Bill: Surely (6)................ has seen it?
Penny: Do you know what I think? I think we've never had a blue beach ball.

C Read this text about the British Museum. Put *a*, *an*, *the* or nothing in the gaps.

Cathy: Have you been to (▶) the.... British Museum yet?
Alice: I don't even know where it is, I'm afraid.
Cathy   It's in (1)........ street near Tottenham Court Road.
Alice: What's the name of (2)........ street?
Cathy: Russell Street. The mummies from Ancient Egypt are on (3)........ ground floor.
Alice: I'd love to see (4)........ Egyptian mummy. People say that when kings died, the ancient Egyptians gave them (5)........ food and (6)........ water to take to the next world.
Cathy: That's right. And have you heard about the Elgin Marbles?
Alice: Yes. They were part of (7)........ Parthenon in Athens, and Lord Elgin brought them back to London two hundred years ago. Now they're in the British Museum, but (8)........ Greek Government wants them back in Athens. What do you think about that?
Cathy: I'm not sure. If we send (9)........ Marbles back to (10)........ Greece, we'll have to send everything back in the end, won't we?
Alice: Why not?
Cathy: So all (11)........ paintings by Picasso in museums around the world would go back to Spain?

Alice: Yes. I think it's (12)........ good idea. Everyone would have to travel to (13)........
           countries that made these famous things.

D Two students are in a café, talking about going home to Mexico. If the underlined phrases are correct, put a tick in the space provided. If they're wrong, rewrite them.

Federico: How many sugar do you take in your coffee? (▶) .How much sugar..
Maria: Half a spoonful, please. I only like a little. (▶) ✓.....................
Federico: So, how many bags have you packed? (1).......................
Maria: Two. Why? How many luggage have you got? (2).......................
Federico: Too much. I'll have to post some of it. (3)....................... How much costs it
           to post things? (4)....................... Is it very expensive?
Maria: I don't know. I'm OK at the moment, but I haven't bought some presents yet.
           (5)....................... I'm waiting for my Dad to send me any more money!
           (6).......................
Federico: How many presents are you going to buy, then? (7).......................
Maria: A lot! (8)....................... I've got a big family. What about you?
Federico: Me? I'm only going to get a little things. (9)....................... I've only got a
           little cash left, I'm afraid. Can you give me an advice? (10).......................
Maria: Well, you could get a lot of (11)....................... small presents, I suppose, or
           just a little, big ones. (12).......................
Federico: Do you want some more coffee? I think there's a few more in the pot.
           (13).......................
Maria: No thanks, I haven't got a lot of time. (14)....................... I've had three cups
           already.

E John and Steve used to share a house, but John has just left this morning. Steve is sending him an email. Put the words from the box in the gaps.

| me | mine | one | ones | some | that | them |
| them | there | there's | ~~your~~ | yours | yourself | |

To: ☺ John
Cc:
Subject:
▶ Attachments: none

[Geneva ▼] [12 ▼] **B** _I_ U T [icons]

John
Are you sure that you've taken all (▶) your........... things? I'm sure (1)................ green
football on top of the wardrobe isn't mine, and (2)................ an expensive black fountain
pen on the table which is (3)................ . And did you give (4)................ the book on
fishing, or did you buy it for (5)................? I can't remember. There are (6)................
purple socks with Mickey Mouse on (7)................ . Are those the (8)................ you
bought at the market? Also, (9)................ are no sheets left on your bed. But the sheets
were (10)................ , weren't they? I lent (11)................ to you, and I want them back!
Finally, I'm sure I bought two big cakes yesterday. You haven't taken (12)................ ,
have you?
Steve

65 Adjectives (order)

1 We use adjectives to describe people and things. Here are some examples:

| old | small | friendly | rich | cheap |

Look at these sentences:
*I've bought an **old** table for my kitchen.*
*My home town is **small** and **friendly**.*
*We had lunch in a **cheap** restaurant.*

2 The form of adjectives never changes:
*a **rich** man   a **rich** woman   two **rich** men*

3 We put an adjective before a noun:

	ADJECTIVE + NOUN	
I saw a	beautiful	cat.

We put an adjective after **be**:

	be +	ADJECTIVE
They	are	hungry.

We sometimes use these verbs instead of **be**:

| look | feel | taste | smell | sound |

Here are some examples:
*She **looks** happy.*
*This cheese **tastes** wonderful.*
*I **feel** cold.*

4 When we use two adjectives before a noun, we put in a comma (,):
*He's a **nice, old** man.*

When we use two adjectives without a noun, we use **and**:
*You look **tired** and **hungry**.*

5 When we use more than one adjective, there is a general guide to the correct order:

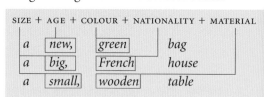

SIZE + AGE + COLOUR + NATIONALITY + MATERIAL

a	new,	green	bag
a	big,	French	house
a	small,	wooden	table

We often use 'materials' as adjectives:
*a **cotton** shirt   a **silver** ring   a **plastic** bag*

6 Here are some common 'nationality' adjectives:

American	German	Portuguese
Australian	Greek	Russian
Chinese	Indian	Turkish
Dutch	Italian	South African
English	Japanese	Spanish
French	Polish	Swedish

Practice

A There are thirteen adjectives in this story. <u>Underline</u> them.

My (►) <u>favourite</u> picture is one of a large, square room by a Dutch artist. An elegant man sits on a wooden bench in a corner. He has a small black dog at his feet. The dog looks sleepy. Through the open window you can see bright sunshine. When I look at this picture I feel warm and happy.

B Put adjectives from the box into the gaps.

| busy | careful | ~~enjoyable~~ | free | good | late | long | old | tall | valuable |

Ladies and gentlemen! This is Covent Garden. We want you to have an (►) enjoyable.... visit so the coach waits here a (1)................ time. We get on it again at twelve o'clock, in the coach park behind the (2)................ tower you can see over there. Covent Garden is in fact an (3)................ market but today it is a place where there is (4)................ entertainment – you don't have to pay to see anything. But be (5)................! Like all (6)................ places, Covent Garden has pickpockets, so look after your money and your (7)................ possessions like cameras. Have a (8)................ time and please don't be (9)................ for the coach.

C Put a verb from the box in each sentence. Use the correct form.

look (x2)	feel	taste	sound (x2)	smell

▶ _Taste_......... these apples. I've already eaten two. They're delicious!
1 That music .... terrible. What group is playing?
2 Those flowers look nice and they .... good too. What are they?
3 I saw Jane yesterday, but I didn't speak to her. She .... tired.
4 Could you close the door, please? I .... cold.
5 That new picture will .... wonderful in your dining room.
6 Do you know where that song comes from? It .... Spanish.

D Look at these sentences. If you think the adjectives are in the wrong order, cross them out and write in the correct order. If you think the order is correct, put a tick (✓) .

▶ She lost a gold small _small gold_........... ring at the disco yesterday night.
▶ I have an old Italian ✓..................... painting in my living room.
1 I'm looking for my cotton green .... shirt and my brown leather
   .... shoes.
2 George has a Spanish modern .... villa near the sea. He goes there
   every summer.
3 I live in an old white .... house near the river. I've got a black large
   .... dog!
4 I had an interesting talk with a Polish young .... student last week.
5 We are having lunch in a big Japanese new .... restaurant in the centre
   of town.
6 I left all my books in a red plastic .... bag on the bus. I was so stupid!

E Choose a name and a nationality from the boxes to complete the sentences.

Names:	Salamanca Alfred Nobel Gérard Depardieu	Vincent van Gogh Sherlock Holmes vodka	A Volkswagen Chang Batman Forever
Nationalities:	Dutch French Spanish	Russian English Swedish	German American Chinese

▶ _Batman Forever_.... is an _American_............. film.
1 .... is a .... car.
2 .... was a .... artist.
3 .... is an .... detective.
4 .... is a .... actor.
5 .... is a .... drink.
6 .... was a .... chemist.
7 .... is a .... surname.
8 .... is a .... city.

66 Adjectives: **-ed** or **-ing**

1 Compare **frightened** and **frightening**:

We can use adjectives that end with **-ed** to describe people's feelings:

We use an adjective that ends with **-ing** (e.g. frightening) to talk about a thing or person that makes us have a feeling:

frightened

frightening

> SUBJECT
> *Ann was very frightened.*

The subject of the sentence (e.g. **Ann**) is the person who has the feeling.

> SUBJECT
> *The ghost was very frightening.*

The subject of the sentence (e.g. **the ghost**) causes the feeling.

2 Here are some more examples to compare:

We are all surprised by the news.
  (= We feel surprised.)
I was very tired at the end of the journey.
  (= I felt tired.)
He was excited by the way the game ended.
I'm interested in your idea.
The students were bored during the lesson.
Were you disappointed by the film?
I wasn't nervous before the exam; I was relaxed.
The children were entertained by three clowns.
*Jack was totally convinced by Ann's
  explanation*

The news is surprising.
  (= The news makes us feel surprised.)
The journey was very tiring.*
  (= The journey made us feel tired.)
The end of the game was exciting.
Your idea is interesting.
The lesson was boring.
Was the film disappointing?
I went for a relaxing walk.
The clowns were very entertaining.
Ann's explanation was totally convincing.

*Note that we can say:
  The journey was very tiring.
  OR:
  It was a very tiring journey.

Practice

A Choose the correct adjective in brackets ( ) to put in the gaps.

▶ It was a terrible play and I was *bored*......... (bored/boring) from start to finish.

1 I'm very .... (excited/exciting) because I'm going to New York tomorrow.

2 Are you .... (surprised/surprising) or were you expecting this news?

3 I'm reading a very .... (interested/interesting) book at the moment.

4 I've had a very .... (tired/tiring) day at work today and I want to go to bed.

5 Most people were .... (surprised/surprising) that he won the championship.

6 I'm .... (bored/boring). Let's go out for a cup of coffee somewhere.

7 Visit our .... (excited/exciting) new shop!

8 His speech was very long and very .... (bored/boring).

B Complete each sentence using the correct word from the box. Use each word once.

bored	interested	surprising	amusing	confused
boring	amused	confusing	surprised	~~interesting~~

▶ Your idea is very interesting... Tell me more about it.

1 He told me a very .... story. I laughed and laughed.

2 This is a terribly .... book. Nothing happens in it.

3 She's .... in politics and often talks about it.

4 The map was .... and I got lost.

5 She was .... because she had nothing to do all day.

6 Everyone else thought it was funny, but she wasn't ....

7 Could you repeat that, please? I'm a bit .... because it was very complicated.

8 It is .... that she failed the exam, because she's a good student.

9 Everyone was .... by the sudden noise.

C Complete the dialogue using the correct word from the box.

bored	boring	confusing	convinced	convincing	disappointed	~~entertained~~
entertaining	frightened	interesting	relaxed	surprised	surprising	

Craig: What sort of films do you like?

Liz: When I go to the cinema, I like to be (▶) entertained............... .

Craig: And what sort of films do you find (1)............................... ?

Liz: Well, I like films that tell a good (2)............................... story. And I mean a story that you can follow, not the sort that goes backwards and forwards in time. I find those very (3)............................... . And I'm (4)............................... . when I watch a horror film. I usually close my eyes when the horror starts.

Craig: Yes, but if the story is too simple, surely you get (5)............................... because you know exactly what's going to happen.

Liz: I don't mean that. If something is intelligible, it's not necessarily (6)............................... . Often good stories have (7)............................... events or endings – things that you can't possibly know at the beginning.

Craig: For me the most important thing is that the actors must be (8)............................... so that you really believe that they are the person they are acting.

Liz: If that's true, I imagine that you are (9)............................... most of the time because, well, for example, Harrison Ford is always Harrison Ford. I'm never (10)............................... that he's somebody else.

Craig: Yes, but it's often not important in his films because they're escapist – if you're feeling tense about work or something, you have a good laugh and you come out feeling (11)............................... and happy with the world.

Liz: I'm (12)............................... that you like his films. Although the special effects are good, the story is always terribly simple.

Craig: He's not my favourite, but his films are not bad.

67 Cardinal and ordinal numbers

1 Look at these examples:
Three students were late.
*She lives on the **third** floor.*

Three is a cardinal number.
Third is an ordinal number.

2 Now look at these tables:

CARDINAL NUMBERS		ORDINAL NUMBERS	
1	one	1st	first
2	two	2nd	second
3	three	3rd	third
4	four	4th	fourth
5	five	5th	fifth
6	six	6th	sixth
7	seven	7th	seventh
8	eight	8th	eighth
9	nine	9th	ninth
10	ten	10th	tenth
11	eleven	11th	eleventh
12	twelve	12th	twelfth
13	thirteen	13th	thirteenth
14	fourteen	14th	fourteenth
15	fifteen	15th	fifteenth
16	sixteen	16th	sixteenth
17	seventeen	17th	seventeenth

18	eighteen	18th	eighteenth
19	nineteen	19th	nineteenth
20	twenty	20th	twentieth
21	twenty-one	21st	twenty-first
22	twenty-two	22nd	twenty-second
30	thirty	30th	thirtieth

3 CARDINALS (40 to 4,000,000)

40 forty	60 sixty	80 eighty
50 fifty	70 seventy	90 ninety

100 a hundred
101 a hundred and one
1,000 a thousand
1,000,000 a million
200 two hundred
210 two hundred and ten
3,000 three thousand
$4,000,000 four million dollars

4 Look at how we say these dates:
13 or 13th June: *The **thirteenth** of June.*
*June the **thirteenth**.*
1994: *Nineteen ninety-four.*
26 or 26th March 1995 (26.3.95):
*The **twenty-sixth** of March, nineteen ninety-five.*

Practice

A Tick (✓) the correct form in each pair. Put a line through the wrong form.

▶	(116)	a hundred sixteen	a hundred and sixteen ✓
1	(49)	fourty-nine	forty-nine
2	(600)	six hundred	six hundreds
3	(4th)	fourth	forth
4	(12th)	twelfth	twelfth
5	($2,000)	two thousand dollars	two thousands dollars
6	(23rd)	twenty-three	twenty-third
7	(78)	eighty-seven	seventy-eight
8	(8th)	eightth	eighth
9	(17)	seventeen	seventeenth
10	(5th)	fiveth	fifth
11	(7,000,000)	seven million	seven millions
12	(9th)	ninth	nineth
13	(30th)	thirteenth	thirtieth
14	(395)	three hundred and ninety-five	three hundred ninety-five

3 Write out the following numbers.

▶ (211) two hundred and eleven

1 (462) ....
2 (20th) ....
3 (1st) ....
4 (12th) ....
5 (9,000,000) ....
6 (310) ....
7 (8th) ....
8 (111) ....

9 (14) ....
10 (2nd) ....
11 (5,000) ....
12 (68) ....
13 (34th) ....
14 (150) ....
15 (3rd) ....
16 (25th) ....
17 (19th) ....

C Look at where these people live in the block of flats. Finish the sentences, as in the example.

▶ John lives in flat forty on the fourth floor.
1 Charles lives in flat ....
2 Maria ....
3 Diana ....
4 Michael ....
5 Peter ....
6 Jane ....
7 Ann ....
8 Oliver ....

Floor 7	○	Flat 72 **PETER**	
Floor 6	○	Flat 61 OLIVER	
Floor 5	○	Flat 54 MICHAEL	Flat 59 ANN
Floor 4	○	Flat 40 **JOHN**	
Floor 3	○	Flat 37 **DIANA**	
Floor 2	○○	Flat 23 CHARLES	Flat 25 JANE
Floor 1	○	Flat 11 **MARIA**	

D Write the dates and years in words in this interview, using the information in brackets ( ).

A: When were you born?
B: I was born on (▶) the thirteenth of October, nineteen seventy-five ... (13.10.75)
A: When did you go to secondary school?
B: In (1)... (1986)
A: And when did you leave secondary school?
B: Seven years later. My final exam was on (2)..................................... (16.6.93)
A: Did you start university in the same year?
B: Yes, on (3).. (29 September)
A: Did you spend three or four years there?
B: Well, I left in (4)... (1997) That's four years.
A: And your first job? When was that?
B: I started work in an office on (5).. (10.1.98)
A: Did you enjoy it? How long did you stay?
B: It was terrible! I left two months later, on (6).................................... (9 March)
A: What did you do then?
B: I went to America. I spent two years in New York. I returned to England in
(7)... (2000)

68 Comparison: (not) as . . . as

1 We use **as + adjective + as** (e.g. **as old as**) to say that two things or people are the same in some way:

The chair is **as expensive as** the table.
You're **as old as** me. (= We are the same age.)

Note that we say **as me/as him/as her/as us/as them**, and not **as I/as he/as she**, etc:
*She's **as strong as** him.* (NOT … ~~as he~~.)
*I'm **as fast as** them.* (NOT … ~~as they~~.)

We use **not as … as** to talk about a difference between two things or people:

The two-star hotel **isn't as big as** the four-star hotel.
*I'm **not as clever as** her.* (= She is cleverer than me.)

2 We can also use **as + adverb + as** (e.g. **as well as**):
*Jean cooks **as well as** Tom.* (= Jean and Tom are both good cooks.)
*He couldn't run **as quickly as** Maria.* (= Maria ran more quickly than him.)

3 We use **as many + plural noun + as** (e.g. **as many friends as**) to say that the numbers of two things are equal:
*Jane has got **as many friends as** Mary.*

We use **not as many … as** to say two things are not equal:
*I don't have **as many books as** you.*

4 We use **as much + uncountable noun + as** (e.g. **as much money as**) to compare two things. Uncountable nouns are words for things that we cannot count, and so they do not have a plural form (e.g. **money, work, luggage, traffic**):
*Helen earns **as much money as** Colin.*
*Jack doesn't do **as much work as** me.*
*They aren't carrying **as much luggage as** us.*

(See also Unit 53.)

Practice

A Complete each sentence so that it means the same as the one above it. Use *as + adjective/adverb + as.*

► Sweden is bigger than Britain.
Britain isn't *as big as Sweden* .

1 The other students learn more quickly than me.
I don't learn .... the other students.

2 You're very angry and I'm very angry also.
I'm .... you.

3 The seats at the front are more expensive than the seats at the back.
The seats at the back aren't .... the seats at the front.

4 Central Park in New York is bigger than Hyde Park in London.
Hyde Park in London isn't .... Central Park in New York.

5 Her last film was very good and her new film is also very good.
Her new film is .... her last film.

6 The other students work harder than him.
He doesn't work .... the other students.

3 Complete the sentences about each picture, using *as ... as* and a word from the box. Use each word once.

long	clean	fast	fresh	tall	big	~~cheap~~	strong	wide	full

Janet   Kathy

Jane
Matthew

High St. Main St.

▶ The carrots aren't *as cheap as*........ the cabbages.
1 The black car is going .... the blue car.
2 The footballers aren't .... the basketball players.
3 Janet's hair is .... Kathy's hair.
4 The car on the left isn't .... the car on the right.
5 The flowers on the right aren't .... the flowers on the left.
6 The big glass isn't .... the little glass.
7 Jane is .... Matthew.
8 High Street isn't .... Main Street.
9 The black book is .... the white book.

C Join each pair of sentences in brackets ( ), using *as much ... as* or *as many ... as*.

▶ (I've got about 50 books. Jack's got about 100.)
  I haven't got *as many books as* Jack.
▶ (You've done a lot of work. I've done a lot of work also.)
  I've done *as much work as* you.
1 (Alan earns a lot of money. Sheila only earns a little.)
  Sheila doesn't earn .... Alan.
2 (George has been to five countries. I've also been to five countries.)
  I've been to .... George.
3 (You've had five jobs. I've only had two.)
  I haven't had .... you.
4 (Tom has a lot of luggage. Jane has a lot of luggage too.)
  Jane has .... Tom.
5 (Mary answered most of the questions. I only answered about half.)
  I didn't answer .... Mary.
6 (Ruth spent £50. I also spent £50.)
  I spent .... Ruth.

69 Too and enough

1 Look at this example:

*The case is **too heavy**. He can't carry it.*

We use **too** to mean 'more than is good or suitable in the situation'.

2 We can use **too** like this:

too + ADJECTIVE:
*I don't want to go out. I'm **too tired**.*

too many + PLURAL NOUN:
*I couldn't find her at the concert because there were **too many people** there.*

too much + UNCOUNTABLE NOUN:
(e.g. **too much work/money/food/noise/salt/information/time/bread**)
*Our teacher gives us **too much work**.*

3 We can use **too** with **to** + **infinitive** to explain why someone cannot do something:
*She's **too young to drive**.* (= She can't drive because she's too young.)

4 Now look at this example:

*This case is **big enough**. I can put all my clothes into it. The small case **isn't big enough**.*

We use **enough** to mean 'as much or as many as we need'. We use **not ... enough** to mean 'less than we need'.

5 We can use **enough** like this:

ADJECTIVE + **enough**:
*Is your room warm **enough**?*

enough + PLURAL NOUN:
*I've got **enough potatoes**, thanks.*

enough + UNCOUNTABLE NOUN:
*I can't talk to you now. I haven't got **enough time**.*

6 We can also use **not ... enough** + **to** + **infinitive** to say why someone cannot do something:
*She **isn't old enough to drive**.* (= She can't drive because she isn't old enough.)

Practice

A Complete the sentences using *too* or *enough* and the word in brackets ( ).

▶ I can't eat this soup because it's *too hot* .... (hot).
▶ We couldn't buy the tickets because we didn't have *enough money* ...... (money).
▶ We didn't buy the car because it wasn't *big enough* .... (big).
1 I couldn't see her because it was .... (dark).
2 I can't decide what to do because I haven't got .... (information).
3 You can't change the situation now. It's .... (late).
4 Have you had .... (food), or would you like some more?
5 He did badly in the exam because he was .... (nervous).
6 Slow down! You're driving .... (fast).
7 He shouldn't play in the team because he isn't .... (good).
8 I haven't got .... (clothes). I must buy some more.
9 Robert didn't go to work because he didn't feel .... (well).
10 I couldn't lift the suitcase because I wasn't .... (strong).
11 We didn't go swimming because the water was .... (cold).
12 Mary couldn't post all the letters because she didn't have .... (stamps).

3 Complete the sentences using *too much*, *too many* or *enough* and the word in brackets ( ).

▶ I'm not enjoying my job at the moment because they're giving me
  <u>too much work</u>............. (work).

▶ Is your coffee <u>sweet enough</u>............. (sweet)?

1 Shall we have another coffee? Have we got .... (time)?

2 I couldn't finish the exam because there were .... (questions).

3 We didn't go for a walk because it wasn't .... (warm).

4 I couldn't eat the meal because there was .... (salt) in it.

5 Mary passed the test because she answered .... (questions) correctly.

6 I didn't enjoy the party because there were .... (people) there.

7 Is that chair .... (comfortable) or would you like to sit here?

8 George couldn't work because the others were making .... (noise).

9 We can't play that game because we haven't got .... (players).

10 Shall I make some sandwiches? Have we got .... (bread)?

11 Her work isn't very good. She makes .... (mistakes).

C Join each pair of sentences using *too* or *enough* with *to + infinitive* (e.g. *to do*, *to go*).

▶ Clare couldn't sleep. She was too worried.
  <u>Clare was too worried to sleep.</u>...

▶ I can't go on holiday. I haven't got enough money.
  <u>I haven't got enough money to go on holiday.</u>.................................

1 I can't do any more work. I'm too tired.
  ....

2 Judy won't pass the exam. She isn't good enough.
  ....

3 Clive can't play basketball. He's too short.
  ....

4 His girlfriend couldn't go to the party. She was too ill.
  ....

5 David couldn't pay the bill. He didn't have enough money.
  ....

6 Shall we go to the beach? Is it hot enough?
  ....

7 I can't see you tonight. I'm too busy.
  ....

8 I don't want to go home. It's too early.
  ....

9 Chris couldn't repair the car. He didn't have enough tools.
  ....

10 I didn't visit all the museums. I didn't have enough time.
  ....

70 **So** and **such**

We use **so** and **such** to intensify adjectives. Compare:

1 *Helen got all the answers right. She is **so** clever.*
(= She is very clever.)

We use **so** before adjectives that do not have a noun after them, and before adverbs:

	ADJECTIVE
*This tea is **so***	*sweet!*
*Tom's feet are **so***	*big!*

	ADVERB
*They get up **so***	*late.*
*Maria sang **so***	*beautifully!*

*Helen got all the answers right. She is **such a** clever person.* (= She is a very clever person.)

We use **such a/an** before an adjective + singular noun (e.g. **person**). We use **such** before a plural noun (e.g. **feet**) or an uncountable noun (e.g. **food**):

	ADJECTIVE + NOUN
*It was **such an***	*amazing car!*
*He has **such***	*big feet!*
*That was **such***	*excellent food.*

(For uncountable nouns, see Unit 53.)

2 We can use **so** with **many** and **much**:

▶ **so many** + plural noun:
*There were **so many** people in the shop.*

▶ **so much** + uncountable noun:
*We had **so much** work to do.*

We can use **such** with **a lot of**:

▶ **such a lot of** + plural noun:
*There were **such a lot of** people in the shop.*

▶ **such a lot of** + uncountable noun:
*We had **such a lot of** work to do.*

3 Sentences with **so** and **such** can also describe the result of something:

	RESULT
*It was **so** dark*	*that we didn't see him.*
*He arrived **so** late,*	*he missed his plane.*

	RESULT
*It was **such a** dark night*	*that we didn't see him.*
*It was **such a** lovely day,*	*we went to the beach.*

Practice

A Put in *such* or *so*.

▶ Tom is very handsome. He has such........... beautiful eyes.
▶ It was a very pleasant trip because the guide was so............. nice.
1 My birthday was wonderful. I got .... lovely presents.
2 It was difficult to drive because there was .... much snow.
3 I like Tom. He is .... a nice person.
4 We couldn't play tennis because it was .... windy.
5 Jack loves his children. He is .... a wonderful father.
6 Nobody listens to Jane because she says .... silly things.
7 The nurses are wonderful here. They are .... helpful.
8 Look at the stars. They are .... bright tonight.

B Put *such*, *such a* or *such an* in the gaps.

▶ Edinburgh is <u>such a</u>........ wonderful city.
1 Motorbikes are .... dangerous machines.
2 I love skiing. It's .... exciting sport. But it's a dangerous sport, too.
3 My cousin had .... terrible accident. He almost died.
4 I like these new dresses. They have .... pretty colours.
5 We had .... wonderful meal. The food was excellent.
6 Susan Strange is .... interesting writer.

C Use *so*, *such*, *such a* or *such an* to write sentences using the words in brackets ( ).
Put the verbs in the correct tense.

▶ I can't believe that Tom is only thirteen. (He/have/grow/tall)
   <u>He has grown so tall!</u>................................
▶ I never believe those boys. (They/be/always/tell/stupid lies)
   <u>They are always telling such stupid lies!</u>................
1 I enjoy John's cooking. (He/be/wonderful cook)
   ....
2 I can't hear anything. (Those people/be/make/much noise)
   ....
3 Fred won three prizes. (He/be/lucky)
   ....
4 Sara always looks lovely. (She/wear/pretty clothes)
   ....
5 We had three ice-creams. (They/be/delicious)
   ....
6 I don't smoke. (It/be/unhealthy habit)
   ....
7 I enjoyed that test. (It/be/easy)
   ....

D For each sentence, write another sentence with a similar meaning.
Use *so ... that*.

▶ We decided not to phone them because it was very late.
   It was <u>so late that we decided not to phone them.</u>................
1 Sally didn't finish the exam because she worked very slowly.
   She worked ....
2 We didn't buy the camera because it was very expensive.
   The camera was ....
3 Paul didn't go out because he was very tired.
   Paul was ....
4 Peter couldn't see the holes because they were very small.
   The holes were ....
5 I couldn't finish the food because there was too much of it.
   There was ....

71 Comparative adjectives

1 Look at the way we compare things:

£100 per night   £50 per night

*The Plaza Hotel is **cheaper than** the Excelsior.*
*The Excelsior Hotel is **bigger than** the Plaza.*
*The Excelsior is **more expensive than** the Plaza.*
*The Plaza Hotel is **smaller than** the Excelsior.*

2 **Cheaper** and **more expensive** are comparative adjectives. We form them like this:

▶ short adjectives (one syllable):

ADJECTIVE	COMPARATIVE
old	**older**
long	**longer**
nice	**nicer**
new	**newer**
slow	**slower**
fat	**fatter**
hot	**hotter**
big	**bigger**

▶ long adjectives (two syllables or more):

ADJECTIVE	COMPARATIVE
famous	**more famous**
difficult	**more difficult**
careful	**more careful**
expensive	**more expensive**

▶ adjectives ending with -y:

happy	**happier**
hungry	**hungrier**

▶ irregular adjectives:

good	**better**
bad	**worse**

(For more information, see Appendix 4, page 245)

3 To compare things, we use a comparative adjective + **than**:
*Tom is **richer than** Paul.*
*Paris is **more beautiful** than London.*
*My new car is **better than** my old one.*

Practice

A **Write the comparative form of these adjectives.**

▶ cold   <u>colder</u>

1 big   ....
2 careful   ....
3 expensive   ....
4 good   ....
5 fat   ....
6 famous   ....
7 new   ....
8 modern   ....
9 young   ....
10 cheap   ....
11 delicious   ....
12 rich   ....

13 long   ....
14 hungry   ....
15 nice   ....
16 happy   ....
17 difficult   ....
18 old   ....
19 beautiful   ....
20 friendly   ....
21 hot   ....
22 wonderful   ....
23 bad   ....
24 small   ....
25 sad   ....

3 Write comparative sentences about the pictures using *than* and the words in brackets ( ). Use the Present Simple.

Tom   Sam

1 Alaska   Spain

2 Steve   Jane

3 Washington   New York

4 Mary   Mike

5 I   My brother

6 Film Stars   Teachers

7 Peter   Chris

▶ (be/tall)   Tom is taller than Sam.
1 (be/cold)   ....
2 (be/hungry)   ....
3 (be/small)   ....
4 (be/happy)   ....
5 (be/young)   ....
6 (be/rich)   ....
7 (be/friendly) ....

C Look at the information about two boats, the Queen Anne and the King John.

BOATS	LENGTH	AREA	TOP SPEED	YEAR MADE	PRICE
Queen Anne	14 metres	40 metres^2	35 knots	2005	£9,000
King John	9 metres	23 metres^2	30 knots	1997	£3,500

Now put words from the box in the sentences.

King John (x2)	~~bigger~~	slower	is	than
Queen Anne (x2)	longer	expensive	more	

▶ The Queen Anne is *bigger*......... than the King John.
1 The King John is smaller .... the Queen Anne.
2 The Queen Anne is .... modern than the King John.
3 The King John .... older than the Queen Anne.
4 The .... is faster than the ....
5 The Queen Anne is more .... than the King John.
6 The King John is .... than the Queen Anne.
7 The .... is cheaper than the ....
8 The Queen Anne is .... than the King John.

72 Superlative adjectives

1 We use superlatives in the following way:

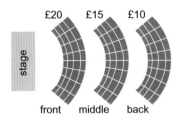

£20 £15 £10

stage

front   middle   back

The most expensive seats are at the front of the theatre.
The cheapest seats are at the back.
The least expensive seats are at the back.
He is the worst player in the team.
It was the happiest day of their lives.

We can use the superlative without a noun:
The seats at the back are the cheapest.

2 Look at these tables:

► short adjectives (one syllable):

ADJECTIVE	SUPERLATIVE
warm	the warmest
tall	the tallest
low	the lowest
big	the biggest
hot	the hottest
wet	the wettest

► long adjectives (two syllables or more):

ADJECTIVE	SUPERLATIVE
famous	the most/least famous
difficult	the most/least difficult
careful	the most/least careful
expensive	the most/least expensive

► adjectives ending with –y:

easy	the easiest
happy	the happiest

► irregular adjectives:

good	the best
bad	the worst

(For more details see Appendix 4, page 245.)

3 We usually use **the** before the superlative:
London is the biggest city in England.
The Taj Mahal is the most beautiful building in the world.

Note that we use **in** (not **of**) for places after the superlative:
… the richest man in Europe. (NOT *… of Europe.*)

We do not always use a noun after a superlative adjective:
George and Mary have three children. Mike is the oldest.
A: *Which table did you buy?*
B: *The most expensive.*

4 We often use the Present Perfect with **ever** after the superlative:
That was the best film I've ever seen.
A: *How was your holiday?*
B: *Fantastic! Iceland is the most beautiful country I've ever visited.*

Practice

A Put the words in brackets ( ) in the right order to make sentences.

► (the world – Antarctica – coldest – is – place – the – in – .)
   Antarctica is the coldest place in the world. ....

1 (city – the – Manchester – in England – is – friendliest – .)
   ....

2 (in New York – expensive – restaurant – The Manhattan – the – is – most – .)
   ....

3 (is – river – the world – the – The Nile – longest – in – .)
   ....

4 (town – most – in Spain – Granada – beautiful – is – the – .)
   ....

5 (painting – The Mona Lisa – the – famous – in – is – most – the world – .)

....

6 (the – Europe – mountain – in – highest – Mont Blanc – is – .)

....

B Complete the sentences using the superlative form of the adjective in brackets ( ):

▶ Anna is _the youngest_ .... (young) person in the class.

1 We stayed in .... (bad) hotel in the whole city.

2 People say that it is .... (funny) film of the year.

3 What is .... (tall) building in the world?

4 Her teachers say that she is .... (good) student in the school.

5 Many people say that Venice is .... (beautiful) city in the world.

C Look at the information about three boats and complete the sentences using the correct superlative form of the adjectives in brackets ( ).

BOATS	LENGTH	TOP SPEED	PRICE
Queen Anne	14 metres	35 knots	£9,000
Red Devil	6 metres	72 knots	£23,000
Jolly Jim	4 metres	28 knots	£6,000

▶ (long)   _The Queen Anne is the longest_ .... boat.

1 (short)   .... boat.

2 (fast)   .... boat.

3 (slow)   .... boat.

4 (expensive)   The Red Devil is .... boat.

5 (expensive)   The Jolly Jim is .... boat.

D Use the words in brackets ( ) to write sentences. Use *the* + superlative, and the Present Perfect + *ever*.

▶ (It's/cold/place/I/visit)   _It's the coldest place I've ever visited._ ....

1 (It's/big/ship/I/see)   ....

2 (He's/rich/man/I/meet)   ....

3 (It's/difficult/exam/I/do)   ....

4 (It's/sad/film/I/see)   ....

5 (She's/happy/person/I/meet)   ....

6 (It's/modern/flat/I/see)   ....

7 (It's/hot/country/I/visit)   ....

8 (It's/small/dog/I/see)   ....

73 Adverbs (1): adjectives and adverbs

1 Here are some adjectives and adverbs:

ADJECTIVE	ADVERB
quick	quickly
careful	carefully
easy	easily

2 Compare adverbs and adjectives:

ADVERBS
We use adverbs to describe how someone or something does an action:
*Peter **plays** the violin **beautifully.***
(***Beautifully** describes how Peter plays.*)

ADJECTIVES
We use adjectives to describe people or things. We use adjectives before nouns, or after **be/seem/get**:
*Look at that **beautiful** violin!*
*That violin is **beautiful.***

3 We form most regular adverbs by adding **-ly** to the adjective:

slow → slowly   bad → badly

*The whole team played very **badly.***

If an adjective ends with **-y**, the adverb ends with **-ily**:

happy → happily   easy → easily

*We solved the problem **easily.***

If an adjective ends with **-ble**, the adverb ends in **-bly**:

comfortable → comfortably

4 Some adverbs are irregular; they do not end with **-ly**:

good → well

*He's a **good** guitar player. (**good** = adjective)*
*He plays the guitar **well.** (**well** = adverb)*

Fast and hard are both adjectives and adverbs:

fast → fast   hard → hard

*Maria is a **fast** learner. (**fast** = adjective)*
*Maria learns **fast.** (**fast** = adverb)*
*James is a **hard** worker. (**hard** = adjective)*
*James works **hard.** (**hard** = adverb)*

5 We form the comparative of regular adverbs with **more** or **less**:

carefully → more/less carefully

*You should do your work **more carefully.***
*She does her work **less carefully** than other people.*

The comparative of **well** is **better**:
*She speaks Arabic **better** than **me.***

The comparatives of **fast** and **hard** are **faster** and **harder**:
*Could you walk **faster**? We're in a hurry.*
*You will have to work **harder** in future.*

6 We form the superlative of regular adverbs with **the most/the least**:

more efficiently → the most efficiently
                   the least efficiently

*In the office, Alan does his work **the most efficiently** and Sally does her work **the least efficiently.***

The superlative of **well** is **the best** and the superlative of **badly** is **the worst**:
*Which member of the team played **the best** and who played **the worst**?*

The superlatives of **fast** and **hard** are **the fastest** and **the hardest**:
*They decided to find out who could run **the fastest.***
*Who works **the hardest** in your class?*

Practice

A Put in the adjective or the adverbs in brackets ( ).

▶ The train was very slow.......... (slow/slowly) and I arrived late.
1 The journey took a long time because the train went very .... (slow/slowly).

2 Mrs Green went .... (quick/quickly) back to her office.
3 I'm afraid I can't give you an .... (immediate/immediately) answer.
4 The work that the builders did for us was very .... (bad/badly).
5 The builders did the work for us very .... (bad/badly).
6 She organized the party very .... (good/well), and everybody enjoyed it.

B Complete the sentences. Put in the adverb form of the adjective in brackets ( ).

▶ She read the message quickly........ (quick).
1 Read the instructions .... (careful).
2 He looked at her .... (angry), but he didn't say anything.
3 She passed all her exams .... (easy).
4 I ran as .... (fast) as I could.
5 He thinks that he did the test .... (bad) and that he'll fail.
6 She was working .... (busy) when I arrived.
7 He was playing .... (happy) when I came into the room.

C Complete the dialogues by putting a suitable adverb into the gaps. Use an adjective from the box to make the adverb.

| slow   fast   hard   good (x2)   ~~easy~~   bad |

▶ A: Were the questions difficult?
   B: No, I answered them easily......... .
1 A: Does she speak English ....?
   B: No, she only knows a few words of English.
2 A: Hurry up! I'm waiting!
   B: Just a minute. I'm coming as .... as I can.
3 A: Did you lose at tennis again?
   B: Yes, I played .... and I lost.
4 A: Have you been working .... today?
   B: No, I've done nothing all day!
5 A: Have you finished that book yet?
   B: No, I always read very .... It takes me a long time to finish a book.

D Put in the comparative or superlative adverb form of the adjective in brackets ( ).

▶ You must do your work more carefully....... (careful) in future.
1 He has run the 100 metres .... (fast) than any other athlete in the world
   this year.
2 Everyone else did the test .... (good) than me, because they'd worked
   .... (hard) than me.
3 You can travel .... (cheap) at certain times of the year.
4 He plays .... (confident) than he did in the past because he has got
   .... (good) at the game.
5 You could eat .... (expensive) if you didn't buy so many takeaways.
6 You will be able to sit .... (comfortable) in this chair.

74 Adverbs (2): adverbs of frequency

1 Look at how often Jane does things in a year:

She has a cup of tea at breakfast.	365
She goes to the cinema.	10
She walks to work.	0
She goes swimming.	52
She goes on holiday.	2

We can say:
> She *always* has a cup of tea at breakfast.
> She *sometimes* goes to the cinema.
> She *never* walks to work.
> She goes swimming *every week*.
> She goes on holiday *twice a year*.

2 We use these adverbs to talk about how often we do things:

always	usually	normally	often
sometimes	rarely	hardly ever	never

We put **always, usually**, etc. after **be** or an auxiliary (e.g. **have, must**):
> He *is always* late.
> I've *often* been to Spain for my holidays.
> You *must never* swim after a big meal.

But we put **always** etc. before main verbs:
> I *usually walk* to work.
> She *hardly ever drinks* coffee.

3 We can compare the meaning of these adverbs like this:

0%	never	100%	always
5%	hardly ever	90%	usually
10%	rarely	80%	normally
30%	sometimes	70%	often

(We usually say the word **often** without pronouncing the letter **t**.)

4 If we want to say exactly how often we do things, we use these expressions:

every ...	once a ...	twice/two times a ...
three times a ...	four times a ...	

We put these expressions at the end of sentences. Here are some examples:
> I run round the park *every day*.
> I play tennis *once a week*.
> She drinks coffee *three times a day*.
> I go skiing *once a year*.
> He drives to London *twice a month*.

Practice

A **Put the words in brackets ( ) in the right place in these sentences.**

▶ I work late at the office.
   (often) I often work late at the office.
1 You must lock the front door when you leave.
   (always) ....
2 Steve and Jill play golf.
   (twice a month) ....
3 I eat a sandwich for lunch.
   (usually) ....
4 I go to jazz concerts at the weekend.
   (sometimes) ....
5 My teacher gives me a lot of homework.
   (every day) ....
6 We see our Mexican friends.
   (hardly ever) ....

7 They go to Morocco for their holidays.

(often) ....

8 Bill and Marie go to the theatre.

(four times a year) ....

9 They are at home in the evening.

(rarely) ....

B Look at the table below, find the correct adverbs from the table in section 3 (opposite), then write sentences comparing Liz and Ken.

		10%	20%	30%	40%	50%	60%	70%	80%	90%	100%
► walk to work	Liz										
	Ken										
1 get up early	Liz										
	Ken										
2 watch TV	Liz										
	Ken										
3 take a taxi	Liz										
	Ken										
4 have supper at home	Liz										
	Ken										

► Liz sometimes walks to work. Ken never walks to work.

1 ....

2 ....

3 ....

4 ....

C Look at the table below about John's activities and write sentences, using the words in brackets ( ) and the Present Simple.

	DAY	WEEK	MONTH	YEAR
swimming		2		
a newspaper	1			
his mother			3	
a shower	2			
abroad				1
sister				3
tennis		4		

► (He/go/swimming/...)   He goes swimming twice a week. ....

1 (He/buy/a newspaper/...) ....

2 (He/phone/his mother/...) ....

3 (He/have/a shower/...)   ....

4 (He/go/abroad/...)   ....

5 (He/visit/his sister/...)   ....

6 (He/play/tennis/...)   ....

75 Adverbs (3): place, direction, sequence

1 We use **here** with the meaning 'in or to this place/the place where the speaker is':
> *I've been living **here** for three years.*
> *Come **here**, I want to speak to you.*

We use **there** with the meaning 'in or to that place/another place, away from where the speaker is':
> *Stay **there**, I'll come and get you.*
> *Go and stand **there**, I'll take a picture of you.*

We also use **there** with the meaning 'in or to a place previously mentioned':
> *I lived in France for a year and I made a lot of friends while I was **there**.*

We often use **over here** and **over there** when we are speaking informally:
> *Come **over here** and sit down.*

2 Some common adverbs describing a place or a movement in a particular direction are:

> **abroad** (= in/to another country), **ahead, away, back, downstairs/upstairs, in/out, inside/outside** (= in or out of a building), **nearby, forward(s)/backward(s)/sideways**

> *Mary is **abroad** but she's coming back soon.*
> *She ran **downstairs** and opened the front door.*
> *He walked **out**, saying that he couldn't stay.*
> *The queue slowly moved **forward(s)**.*

Notice that we use **out** with the meaning 'not at home/work etc. for part of a day or a day' and **away** with the meaning 'not at home/work etc. for more than a day':

> *Mr Butler is **out** at the moment. He'll be back at around twelve o'clock.*
> *Mr Butler is **away** this week. He's at a three-day conference.*

3 We often use these adverbial phrases when giving someone directions to a place:

> **straight on/ahead, turn left/right, on the left/right** (to say where something is), **to the left/right** (for movement), **as far as**

> *Go **straight on**. When you come to the traffic lights, **turn right**. The first road on **the left** is the one you want.*

4 When we talk about a number of actions or events that happen one after the other, we can indicate the order with these adverbs and adverbial phrases:

> **first(ly)/first of all, second(ly), third(ly), etc, last(ly), finally**

Instead of using **secondly**, **thirdly**, etc., we often use these adverbs and adverbial phrases to link actions or events in a sequence:

> **then, next, afterwards, after that**

> *To make this dish, **firstly** you chop some tomatoes, **then** you get some garlic ...*
> *First of all I went to Paris, **after that** I spent some time in Switzerland, **then** I travelled round Germany and **finally** I went to Holland.*

Practice

A Complete the sentences with the correct adverb in brackets ( ).

▶ Joan lived <u>abroad</u> (abroad/away) for several years, mostly in the US.
1 We had to wait .... (out/outside) until the club opened.
2 I'm going .... (out/away) now and I'll be back in about an hour.
3 Fortunately there was a hospital .... (nearby/sideways).
4 I went .... (upstair/upstairs) and looked for the bathroom.
5 The queue of traffic slowly moved .... (forwards/out).
6 We're going .... (out/away) for the weekend.
7 George has gone .... (out/away) until the end of the week.
8 Would you like to live .... (away/abroad)?

3 Complete the directions from the station to Tom's house, using these adverbial phrases:

on the right	turn left	straight ahead	turn right	~~turn right~~

▶ Come out of the station and *turn right*.............. .

1 .... at the first junction.

2 Go .... until you reach the traffic lights.

3 .... into my road.

4 You'll find my house ....

C Look at this sequence of events and put them in the right order. Link the events, using suitable adverbs or adverbial phrases. More than one answer is possible in each gap.

> **How I found an apartment to rent:**
>
> I agreed with the landlord that I would rent it.
> I made a list of apartments I could afford.
> I signed the contract.
> I went to see some of the apartments.
> ~~I looked through the adverts in the local newspaper.~~
> I moved into the apartment.
> I paid the first month's rent as a deposit.
> I decided which apartment to rent.

▶ *First of all/First(ly) I looked through the adverts in the local newspaper.*..........

1 ....

2 ....

3 ....

4 ....

5 ....

6 ....

7 ....

76 Adverb + adjective; noun + noun; etc.

1

It was cold.   *It was **very** cold.*

We can use an adverb (e.g. **very**) before an adjective (e.g. **cold**) to make the adjective stronger. Some common adverbs we use in this way are:

> **very**   **extremely**   **really**

> *We were **very tired** after the trip.*
> *I felt **extremely nervous** before the exam.*
> *I'm **really angry** with you.* (= very angry)

We can also make an adjective weaker with these adverbs:

> **fairly**   **quite**   **rather**

> *Our car is **fairly old**.* (= It's old, but it isn't very old.)
> *The meal was **quite nice**.* (= It was nice but not wonderful.)
> *It was **rather late** when we finally arrived.* (= It was late but not very late.)

2   When we use two adjectives together, we order them like this:

▶ We use 'opinion' adjectives (e.g. **wonderful, nice, pleasant, strange**) before any other adjective (e.g. **new**):

	OPINION	
a	*wonderful*	new product
a	*lovely*	warm day
a	*beautiful*	little cottage
a	*horrible*	green shirt

▶ We use 'size' adjectives (e.g. **big, tall**) before an adjective that gives other information, for example its age (**new, old**), its colour, its shape (**thin, round**):

	SIZE	
a	*big*	new building
a	*small*	red mark
a	*huge*	black cloud
a	*large*	round stone

3   We can use two nouns together. The first noun is like an adjective and gives information about the second noun:

	NOUN	+ NOUN
a	*cardboard*	*box*
a	*cassette*	*recorder*
a	*cheque*	*book*
an	*alarm*	*clock*

Practice

A Complete these sentences using *really* or *quite*.

▶ The film was *really* .... good. I enjoyed it a lot.
1 It's .... cold outside, but not very cold.
2 It isn't a wonderful book, but it's .... good.
3 The tickets were .... expensive – they cost much more than I expected.
4 This programme is .... popular in my country; millions of people watch it.
5 He's .... good at his job, but he sometimes makes bad mistakes.
6 The meal was .... nice, but it wasn't very good.
7 It's .... dangerous to drive so fast in such terrible weather conditions.
8 I'm not a very good tennis player, but I am .... good.
9 They're all .... intelligent students, and they will all pass their exams easily.
10 The company that I work for is .... big, but it's not enormous.

3 Put these words into the correct order.

► (a – town – beautiful – little)   *a beautiful little town* ....

1 (a – day – pleasant – sunny) ....

2 (a – smile – big – nice) ....

3 (a – large – coffee – black) ....

4 (a – old – coat – horrible) ....

5 (a – large – building – white) ....

6 (a – bird – big – grey) ....

7 (a – woman – thin – tall) ....

8 (a – small – car – blue) ....

9 (a – story – little – strange) ....

C Match the words in box A and box B to describe what you can see in each picture.

A			B		
~~table~~	tennis	paper	cup	court	pot
photograph	door	soup	handle	sign	hanger
road	air	music	system	bowl	~~lamp~~
coat	coffee	telephone	book	hostess	album

► *a table lamp* ....   1 ....   2 ....   3 ....

4 ....   5 ....   6 ....   7 ....

8 ....   9 ....   10 ....   11 ....

ADJECTIVES AND ADVERBS • PAGE 165

77 Position of adverbs in a sentence

1 There are three possible positions for adverbs:

- before the subject:
  Sometimes she gets very tired.
- between the subject and the verb:
  I sometimes read biographies.
- between a modal or auxiliary and the main verb:
  I can sometimes play this game very well.
- at the end of a clause or sentence:
  He makes me angry sometimes.

However, not all adverbs can go in all three positions.

2 We use adverbs of certainty (**probably, certainly, definitely**) in these positions:

- between the subject and a positive verb:
  Jane probably knows the answer.
- after a positive auxiliary/modal:
  They'll probably win.
- before a negative auxiliary/modal:
  Jane probably doesn't know the answer.
  They probably won't win.

3 We use adverbs of completeness (**almost, nearly,** etc.) in these positions:

- between the subject and the verb:
  He almost died.
- after an auxiliary/modal:
  I've nearly finished.

4 We use some adverbs that emphasize a statement (**even, just** (= simply), **only, also**) in these positions:

- between the subject and the verb:
  She was rude and she even laughed at me.
  I don't know why, I just like jazz.
- after an auxiliary/modal:
  I can't even understand a word.
  I'm only joking.

Notice that we use **just** before a negative modal or auxiliary:
I just don't understand why it happened.

5 Note that all these adverbs go after **be**:
She is probably at work now.

For the positions of adverbs related to time (**just, already, yet**) see Unit 15.

6 We use **too** and **either** at the end of a sentence. We use **too** after two positive verbs and **either** after two negative verbs:
George earns a lot and he spends a lot too.
I don't like dogs and I'm not keen on cats either. (See also Unit 103.)

7 We usually use adverbs of manner (those that describe how something is done, e.g. **well, badly, quickly, carefully**) in these positions:

- after the verb:
  Please drive carefully.
- after an object:
  I read the letter carefully.

8 We use adverbial phrases of time (e.g. *in the morning, last Saturday, during the holidays*) at the beginning or end of a sentence or clause:
Last Saturday I had a great time.
I had a great time last Saturday.

We usually use other adverbial phrases (e.g. those describing place or manner) after the object:
He put his suitcase on the floor.
She opened the letters with a knife.

9 When there is more than one adverb or adverbial phrase in a sentence, we normally use them in this order:

| manner → place → time |

He was working hard in his office last night.

Practice

A **Write sentences using the adverb in brackets ( ) in the correct place.**

- (probably) They will take the train.   They will probably take the train.
1 (definitely) She comes from Leeds.   ....

2 (nearly) The meal is ready. ....
3 (even) He lent me some money. ....
4 (certainly) She works very hard. ....
5 (only) There were two tickets left. ....

3 These sentences are taken from a newspaper's sports section but they are all incorrect. Rewrite them so that they are correct.

▶ He will play definitely in Saturday's game.
  He will definitely play in Saturday's game. ....

1 Tickets for the game almost have sold out.
  ....

2 They won't probably become champions.
  ....

3 He scored two goals and he created also two goals.
  ....

4 They didn't just play well enough to win.
  ....

5 They won nearly but they were unlucky at the end.
  ....

C These sentences are taken from film reviews. Put the adverbs in brackets ( ) into the correct position in the underlined parts of the sentences.

▶ This film <u>will be</u> a big hit with the public. (definitely)   *will definitely be* ....

1 Many of the characters and events <u>are unbelievable</u>. (almost)   ....

2 This film <u>doesn't create</u> any interest or excitement. (just)   ....

3 The plot isn't very interesting and the performances <u>aren't very good</u>. (either)   ....

4 Although the film <u>was released</u> last week, it has earned a lot of money. (only)   ....

5 This film <u>has attracted</u> a lot of publicity. (certainly)   ....

6 She can act very well <u>and she can sing</u> very well. (also)   ....

D Put the words and phrases in the right order to make sentences.

▶ hard/worked/yesterday
  Susan *worked hard yesterday.* ....

1 all day/have/well/worked
  They ....

2 after lunch/in the sea/swam
  The children ....

3 during the night/rained/heavily
  It ....

4 before supper/did/in my room/my homework
  I ....

5 better/last week/played
  Our team ....

Test G: Adjectives and adverbs

A Put the correct comparative or superlative form of the adjective or adverb in the gaps in this conversation between two neighbours.

Geoff: I'm pretty sure my house is a bit (▶) _bigger_........ (big) than yours.

Pete   Really? I thought mine was (1)................ (big) in the street.

Geoff: Oh. Anyway, my daughter Jo is (2)................ (pretty) girl in her school. They had a beauty contest last week.

Pete: That reminds me. I saw you and Jo pushing your car last week. I must say my car works (3)................ (good) than yours.

Geoff: Really? What's (4)................ (far) you've ever driven? We've crossed America from coast to coast in my car.

Pete: Your wife didn't enjoy the journey, though, did she? You know, I think I've been (5)................ (happy) married than you.

Geoff: I'm not surprised. You've bought your wife (6)................ (expensive) presents in the world, haven't you?

Pete: Well, I've got enough money. I suppose I work (7)................ (hard) than you, don't I, and earn money (8)................ (quick)?

Geoff: I think we'd have a fight if you weren't (9)................ (tall) man in town.

B Joan has just arrived in a small town in Italy. She's writing to her friend Moyra in England. Choose the correct word to put in the gaps.

I arrived about three hours ago. I'm sitting in the living room on the (▶) _third_.......... (three/third) floor of the house. I was (1)................ (excited/exciting), of course, on the way here, but the journey was (2)................ (tired/tiring). It's (3)................ (so/such) a beautiful house! I'm a bit (4)................ (worried/worrying), though. Life here for the next six months is going to be very (5)................ (quietly/quiet). On the (6)................ (sixteen/sixteenth) of June, there's a festival in the village, but that's the only thing this year! I hope you will write to me. I will be (7)................ (disappointed/disappointing) if I don't get a letter now and again. I met my neighbour just after I arrived. She was (8)................ (so/such) helpful! She got married last month, and it's her (9)................ (twenty-one/twenty-first) birthday tomorrow. She speaks English (10)................ (good/well), and she sings (11)................ (beautifully/beautiful) – I can hear her now! Anyway, you know I'm going to try to write a book about my father, so I won't be (12)................ (boring/bored) here. I'm a (13)................ (slowly/slow) writer, but I think it will be an (14)................ (interesting/interested) story in the end.

C Tom, Ingrid, Philip and Hilary are talking about their children. Rewrite the <u>underlined</u> part of the conversation.

Tom: I'm worried, Ingrid. <u>Paul is quicker at schoolwork than Joanna.</u> (▶) _Joanna_........ isn't as _quick at schoolwork as Paul_...................... .

Philip: Kids work too hard at school these days in my view, Tom. <u>Our son Andy didn't watch the football match with me on Saturday. He was too tired!</u>

(1)............................ too tired to ....

Ingrid: But you need to work hard to get a job with good pay. Our oldest boy, Sam, is twenty-five now. <u>He can't buy a house. He hasn't got enough money</u>.

(2)................................. enough money to ....

Hilary: But everything costs so much these days! We took Andy to a cycle shop to see a new bike yesterday. <u>We didn't buy it because it was really expensive</u>.

(3)................................. so expensive that ....

Tom: I know! We looked at a new car. <u>I've never seen a more beautiful machine!</u>

(4) It's the .... I've ever seen!

Ingrid: <u>And you drive wonderfully, Tom!</u>

(5) And you're ....

Tom: Thank you, darling. <u>I'm not as fast as Philip.</u> (6) Philip ....

Hilary: Tom! Don't say things like that! <u>Philip is the worst driver I've ever met!</u>

(7) I've never ....

Philip: How do you know? <u>You don't open your eyes in the car. You're too frightened</u>.

(8)................................. too frightened to ....

Hilary: <u>I'm not going to argue with you. I haven't got enough time.</u>

(9)................................. enough time to .... Boys and their cars! Why don't you spend more time in the garden, Phil?

D Look at this short text about Bath. Put the words in brackets ( ) in the right order.

Bath is (▶) <u>an interesting English city in the South-West.</u> (in the South-West/an/English/interesting/city.) Tourists (1)... (for four or five days/stay/usually/there.) Most people will visit (2).. (the/Roman/old/amazing/Baths), and then they (3).. (probably/will/a bus/up to the Royal Crescent/take.) After that they (4)............................... .... (beautiful/parks/in one of Bath's/green/can either relax) or have tea in (5).. (the/eighteenth-century/elegant/very/Pump Rooms). There's a festival once a year, and (6).. (to get/tickets/difficult/always/it's) because it's so popular. Outside Bath, you can visit (7).. (American/unusual/the/really/Museum), or the lions at Longleat, or you (8).. (can/peacefully in the countryside/drive around/just).

E Esther is leaving a telephone message. Put the correct words in the gaps.

as far as	garden	on the left	~~at home~~	upstairs	away
bags	fairly	sideways	address	table	outside

'Hi there Helen! I thought you'd be (▶) <u>at home</u>..... . Oh dear. Anyway, I'm going (1)............... for a few days. I'm leaving the car (2)............... , though. It's (3)............... old, like me, and the garage is full of rubbish (4)............... . I've lost my (5)............... book, but I think I know the way to The Grange. You take the train (6)............... Little Hollow, and then it's (7)............... when you leave the station. Anyway, the weather looks good, so if you want to borrow my (8)............... chairs while I'm away, go (9)............... , turn left and they're in that little cupboard. You'll have to go into the cupboard (10)............... , I'm afraid, because it's full of old (11)............... legs and things like that! Anyway, I'd better go. Bye for now!'

78 Prepositions of place and movement

1 **In, on** and **at** are used to talk about places:

▶ We use **in** with enclosed spaces (e.g. rooms, buildings) and limited areas (e.g. towns, parks, countries, continents):
in my pocket   *in her car*   *in Germany*

▶ We use **on** with surfaces (e.g. walls, floors, shelves) and lines (e.g. paths, coasts, the equator):
on the grass   *on the sea*
on the line   *on the third floor*

▶ We use **at** with a point (e.g. **at** the bus stop), and **at** with a building, when we mean either inside or outside:
A: *Let's meet at the cinema.*
B: *OK. Shall we meet in the cinema itself or on the pavement outside?*

2 Look at the illustration and read the sentences:

There is a woman in the phone box.
There are people outside the cinema.
The people are on the pavement.
There is a clock above the cinema entrance.
The cinema entrance is under the clock.
The bank is next to/beside the cinema.
The phone box is opposite the cinema.
The bank is between the cinema and the café.
There is a hill behind the town.
The car is in front of the bank.

3 **Into, onto** and **to** are used to talk about movement:
We moved the chairs into my bedroom.
The actor ran onto the stage.
They walked to the next town.

The opposites are **out of, off** and **from:**
We moved the chairs out of my bedroom.
The actor ran off the stage.
We drove from London to Edinburgh.

Here are other prepositions of movement:
They ran across the field to the road.
Jim cycled along the road to the next town.
I walked up the hill and ran down the other side.
The bus went past the bus stop without stopping.
The train goes through three tunnels.

Practice

A The sentences below describe the picture. Look at the picture and change the underlined words which are wrong. Tick (✓) the underlined words which are correct.

▶ There is a TV <u>under</u> on............. the table.
▶ There is a dog <u>on</u> ✓............. the floor.
1 The dog is <u>behind</u> .... the table.
2 The cat is <u>next to</u> .... the flowers.
3 The keys are <u>next to</u> .... the flowers.
4 The flowers are <u>in</u> .... the vase.
5 There is a big book <u>in front of</u> .... the flowers.
6 There is a picture <u>under</u> .... the table.
7 The cat is <u>above</u> .... the table.
8 There is a bird <u>on</u> .... a cage.

3 Put *in*, *on* or *at* in the gaps.

▶ Peter lives .in..... Turkey.
1 There were some beautiful pictures .... the walls of their sitting room.
2 The children are playing .... the grass .... the park.
3 Does this bus stop .... the railway station?
4 I live in a flat .... the fifth floor.
5 Ecuador is .... South America; it lies .... the equator.
6 There is a queue of people .... the bus stop.

C Put the words in the box in the gaps.

| into (x3) onto (x2) ~~to~~ out of off |

▶ The march started in the park. From there we marched .to............ the Town Hall.
1 The tiger escaped from its cage and jumped .... the lake. It took a long time to get it .... the lake and back .... its cage.
2 Stupidly, Simon drove his car .... the beach and then he couldn't move it, because the wheels sank .... the sand. In the end he needed eight people to push it .... the beach and back .... the road.

D Look at this picture of a town showing the route for a race.

Now fill the gaps using the words in the box.

| across along ~~at~~ down in front of past from under through up |

The race starts (▶) .at............ at the Town Hall. The runners go (1)............... the Town Hall and they run (2)............... the main square, to the river. Then they run over New Bridge and they go (3)............... the road beside the river for about 200 yards. They go (4)............... the theatre and (5)............... Castle Hill. They turn right (6)............... the castle, and they go (7)............... Steep Hill. Then they go (8)............... the tunnel (9)............... the river, and they finish at the station.

79 Prepositions of time

1 When we talk about time we often use the prepositions **in**, **on** or **at**.

> ► We use **in** with parts of the day, and with months, seasons and years:
> **in** the morning, **in** the afternoon, **in** the evening
> **in** January, **in** February, **in** March
> **in** the spring, **in** the summer, **in** the autumn, **in** the winter
> **in** 1542, **in** 1868, **in** 1995

> ► We use **on** with days and dates:
> **on** Wednesday, **on** Thursday evening, **on** Christmas Day, **on** her birthday
> **on** April 9th (We say **On** April the ninth or **On** the ninth of April.)

> ► We use **at** for times of the day, and with meals and mealtimes:
> **at** 11 a.m., **at** three o'clock
> **at** breakfast, **at** lunchtime, **at** teatime, **at** dinner

> We also say:
> **at** night, **at** the weekend
> **at** Christmas, **at** Easter

2 The following words can replace **in**, **on** and **at**:

this	next	last	every

I'm going home	**in** April.
	this April.
I'm playing tennis	**on** Wednesday.
	next Wednesday.
She left	**at** the weekend.
	last weekend.
He visits Jane	**on** Saturdays.
	every Saturday.

3 We can use **from ... to** to talk about time:

> **The Frick Collection**
> OPENING HOURS
> 10.00 – 6.00

The museum is open **from** 10 a.m. **to** 6 p.m. Here are some more examples:
> She's staying here **from** Sunday **to** Tuesday.
> We have a tea-break **from** three-thirty **to** four o'clock.

Sometimes, we use **from** on its own:
> I will be in Paris **from** Wednesday.

Monday	Tuesday	Wednesday
		in Paris

Practice

A Fill the gaps in the following sentences with *in*, *on* or *at*.

> ► I went to Turkey *in*...... July.

1 We must leave .... five o'clock.
2 We'll have a break .... the afternoon.
3 She's arriving .... Monday.
4 It's very cold here .... night.
5 I was born .... 1970.
6 I never work .... the weekend.
7 We can play tennis .... the summer.
8 School starts .... September 5th.
9 I'll see you .... lunchtime.

B Fill in the gaps in this conversation using words from the box.

two o'clock	~~summer~~	1990	winter	weekend	Saturday	birthday

Anne: Are you going on holiday in the (►) *summer*...... ?

Tom: No, but I went skiing in Italy in the (1)............... , and I'm going to America at the (2)............... . I'll be in New York on (3)............... ; then I'm travelling south to Texas. What about you? Are you going away this year?

Anne: Yes. In fact, I'm flying to Morocco at (4)............... tomorrow.

Tom: Really? It's a wonderful country. I was there in (5)............... .

Anne: Just think! I'll be on a Moroccan beach on my (6)............... !

C In these sentences there are some mistakes. Sometimes the underlined prepositions are wrong. Sometimes the prepositions are not necessary. Cross out the prepositions which are wrong and replace them if necessary. Put a tick (✓) if the preposition is correct.

▶ I normally go to the south of France ~~on~~ in.............. the winter. I usually go in ✔............. December, but ~~in~~ –............. last December I couldn't go because my wife was ill.

1 We'll leave at .... eleven o'clock in .... Saturday morning.

2 Shall we visit George in .... Spain in .... next April?

3 I always drink two cups of coffee on .... breakfast. In .... the afternoon I drink tea. I drink hot milk in .... night before I go to bed.

4 They play golf on .... every Tuesday in .... the summer.

5 I gave her a painting on .... her birthday at .... June this year.

D Here are your arrangements for the next few days (*today, this week*), and for the next few months (*in December, next year*).

▶ (play/golf) → the afternoon
1 (meet/Steve) → Wednesday morning
2 (go/to the bank) → 10 a.m. on Friday
3 (go/sailing) → the weekend
4 (start/a new job) → next Monday
5 (visit/Egypt) → December
6 (sell/my house) → January 10th

Write sentences using the table above. Use the Present Continuous (*I'm doing*), and a preposition (*in*, *on*, etc.) if necessary.

▶ *I'm playing golf in the afternoon.*..

1 I ....

2 I ....

3 ....

4 ....

5 ....

6 ....

E Use the information in brackets ( ) to finish the sentences.

▶ (2–3) The shop is closed *from 2 to 3.*..

▶ (Friday →) She will be on holiday *from Friday.*..

1 (June → August) The beach is busy ....

2 (10 o'clock) I'll be at the sports centre ....

3 (March →) The new motorway will be open ....

4 (Monday → Friday) We work ....

5 (1991 → 1994) He lived in Kenya ....

6 (January →) She will be in Hong Kong ....

80 As/like; as if/as though

1 We use **as + noun**:

- ▶ to talk about someone's job or role:
  *She works **as an assistant** in a laboratory.*
  *He came to fame **as the main character** in a successful film.*
- ▶ to talk about the function or use of something:
  *I lent him some money **as a favour**.*
  *You can use this sofa **as a bed**.*

2 We use **as** in phrases that refer to something that has already been stated or is already known:
  ***As I told you last week**, I'm going away tomorrow.*
  ***As you know**, some friends are staying with me at the moment.*

3 We use **as** after certain verbs for giving descriptions or talking about attitudes:
  *She **described** her boss **as** a very unpleasant person.*
  *I **regard** her **as** my best friend.*

4 We use **as** in the phrases **such as, the same as** and **as usual**:
  *Some sports, **such as** golf, don't interest me. (= for example)*
  *I really like buildings **such as** this. (= of the same type)*
  *His income is about **the same as** mine.*
  ***As usual**, she gave me some very good advice.*

5 We use **like + noun/pronoun** for comparing, with the meaning 'similar to':
  *He doesn't behave **like other people**.*
  ***Like most boys of his age**, he's keen on sports.*
  *I wish I could sing **like you**.*

6 We use **like + noun/pronoun** with the meaning 'in a similar way to':
  *If you cook it **like this**, it always tastes better.*

7 We use **like + noun/pronoun** with the meaning 'such as':
  *Some people, **like my brother**, really love their jobs.*
  *I really enjoy music **like this**.*

8 We use **look, sound, taste, feel + like + noun/pronoun** to talk about the appearance of someone/something or the impression something gives us:
  *She doesn't **look like her sister** at all.*
  *He **sounds like his father** when he speaks.*
  *This **tastes like coffee**.*
  (See also Unit 33.)

9 We use **as if/as though + subject, verb**, etc. with the meaning 'in a way that suggests ...'.

  We use **as if/as though + subject** to describe how something seems:
  *He talks **as if** he's an expert on the subject.*
  (= he isn't or may not really be an expert)
  *She acted **as though** we had never met before.*
  (= but we had met before)

Practice

A **Complete these sentences taken from reviews of new CDs, using *as* or *like*.**

- ▶ This record sounds exactly like............ the band's previous one.
- 1 At the moment, there is no one quite .... this singer on the music scene.
- 2 Many people regard her .... one of the best singers in the country at the moment.
- 3 Although she looks .... a small and delicate girl, she has a very big voice.
- 4 .... everyone knows, this band shot to fame last year.
- 5 He describes this new CD .... an experiment in a new style of music.
- 6 Bands .... this tend to be popular for only a short time.

3 Complete the dialogues using *as* or *like*.

▶ A: What did you do before this job?
    B: I spent seven years _as_ a teacher at a university.

1 A: Are you coming to the party tonight?
    B: No, ... I told you before, I'm going somewhere else.

2 A: Do you like this programme?
    B: No, it's .... all those 'reality TV' shows, it's really boring.

3 A: I'm having trouble doing this job on the computer.
    B: That's because you shouldn't try to do it .... that. Look, I'll show you.

4 A: Let's stay at this hotel for the whole trip.
    B: Yes, we can use it .... a base for travelling around the region.

5 A: Did you enjoy the book I lent you?
    B: Yes, I don't usually enjoy novels .... that, but it was excellent.

6 A: Did you discuss the problem with William?
    B: Yes, and .... I thought, it was an easy one to solve.

7 A: What's your opinion of Ann?
    B: I get on well with her most of the time, but sometimes she acts .... a child.

8 A: That was a horrible thing to say.
    B: Don't get upset. I only said it .... a joke.

C Complete these sentences describing people, using *as*, *like* or *as if/as though*.

▶ Felicity behaves _as if/as though_ she's more important than everyone else.

1 Sarah doesn't think .... other people, she has her own ideas.

2 .... most people know, Colin has not had an easy life.

3 Helen dresses .... the girls she sees in magazines.

4 Graham talks .... money is the only thing in life that matters.

5 .... all his friends, James is extremely interested in football.

6 When he talks, Simon sounds .... someone who is not from this area.

7 .... a student, Ruth works very hard and is very serious.

D Complete these sentences, using *as*, *like* or *as if/as though*.

▶ He's a very good guitarist and he sounds _like_ a professional when he plays.

1 People .... him really make me angry.

2 This doesn't taste .... anything I've eaten before.

3 He has been described .... the best player in the world.

4 .... usual, she arrived late for work.

5 Older people such .... my parents have different attitudes from mine.

6 Most people were shocked but she acted .... nothing important had happened.

7 You sound .... you've got a bad throat.

8 What you're telling me now is not the same .... what you told me yesterday.

81 In; with; preposition + -ing

1 We can use **in** to describe what somebody is wearing:

> *Jane is the woman **in** the red dress.*
> *I went to the interview **in** my new suit.*
> *It was a sunny day, and everyone was **in** summer clothes.*
> *Are you allowed to go to work **in** jeans?*
> *We saw some soldiers **in** uniform.*

2 We can use **with** to describe a part of somebody's body:

> *A small boy **with** red hair came into the shop.*
> *Our teacher is a tall man **with** a beard.*
> *Lisa is a pretty girl **with** blue eyes.*
> *Jack was talking to a man **with** a big nose.*

We can also use **with** to describe animals:

> *A rabbit is an animal **with** big ears and a small tail.*

3 We can use **with** to talk about a part of something:

> *They live in a white house **with** a flat roof.*
> *I bought a shirt **with** red stripes.*
> *I used the pot **with** the wooden handle.*
> *He has a hi-fi **with** very big speakers.*

4 We can use **with** before something, for example a tool, that we use in order to do something:

> *You clean your teeth **with** a toothbrush.*
> *You open a tin **with** a tin opener.*
> *I cleaned the table **with** a cloth.*
> *Please eat **with** your knife and fork.*

5 We use **by** + **-ing** (e.g. **by doing**) to describe how we do or did something:

> *She learnt French **by listening** to tapes.*
> *You start a car **by turning** the key.*
> *She became successful in business **by working** very hard.*
> *The prisoners escaped **by climbing** over a wall.*

We use **without** + **-ing** (e.g. **without doing**) to say that a particular action is not done or was not done:

> *She passed the exam **without doing** a lot of work.*
> *They left **without waiting** for me.*
> *He did the work **without making** any mistakes.*

Practice

A Put in the correct prepositions. Use *in* or *with*.

> ▶ A young man with.......... a moustache was driving the car.

1 He showed me a photograph of a woman .... blue eyes.
2 We live in a house .... a green door.
3 A lot of businessmen .... suits were on the train.
4 There was a plant .... big green leaves in the corner of the room.
5 John was walking down the street with a woman .... a black coat.
6 Look at that bull .... those enormous horns!
7 One of the children was a girl .... long, dark hair.
8 A man .... a hat came into the cafe.
9 Soldiers .... uniform were standing at the entrance to the building.
10 She wanted to buy a computer .... a screen, a keyboard and a mouse.
11 We booked a hotel room .... a bathroom.
12 It was cold, so I went out .... a coat and scarf.
13 We've bought a television .... a big screen.
14 He arrived for the meeting .... a grey jacket.

3 Match each phrase in the first column with a phrase from the second column and add the appropriate preposition.

▶ You must speak to the woman

1 A giraffe is an animal
2 I want a shirt
3 She cleans her teeth
4 They live in a house
5 I like my coffee
6 He's digging the garden
7 She painted the kitchen
8 You should always cut meat
9 They got into the house
10 The soldiers do all their exercises
11 She has a car
12 He dried his hair
13 You can't make an omelette
14 Some women prefer men

a a sharp knife.
b sitting in the sun.
c a spade.
d lots of sugar.
e beards.
f a brush.
g the green skirt.
h breaking a window.
i four chimneys.
j uniform.
k toothpaste.
l a very long neck.
m a round collar.
n breaking eggs.
o four-wheel drive.

▶ _in (g)_ 1 .... 2 .... 3 .... 4 ....
5 .... 6 .... 7 .... 8 .... 9 ....
10 .... 11 .... 12 .... 13 .... 14 ....

C Rewrite each of the following using *by* or *without*.

▶ She sat in the corner. She didn't say anything.
  She sat in the corner without saying anything.

▶ He opened the door. He turned the key.
  He opened the door by turning the key.

1 He repaired the car. He changed some of the parts.
  ....

2 She answered the question but she didn't read it carefully.
  ....

3 He left. He didn't say thank you.
  ....

4 She got the money because she sold her car.
  ....

5 I threw the letter away. I didn't open it.
  ....

6 We worked all day and we didn't eat anything.
  ....

7 He lost weight. He went on a strict diet.
  ....

8 I went out, but I didn't lock the door.
  ....

82 Other uses of prepositions

There are many common phrases that have prepositions in them.

1 We use **at** in these phrases:

> **at the beginning/end of, at first, at last,
> at the moment, at the weekend, at once**
> (= 'immediately' or 'at the same time')

> *She'll be back **at the beginning of** next week.*
> ***At first**, I didn't believe what he was saying.*
> *I waited for weeks and **at last** the letter
> arrived.*
> *Are you busy **at the moment**?*
> *You don't have to do everything **at once**.*

We also use **at** for speeds:
> *He was driving **at** over 150 kms an hour.*

2 We use **by** with means of transport:

> **by car/bike/bus/plane/boat/ship/train**, etc.

*Do you go to work **by train** or **by car**?*
But we say **on foot** (= walking):
> *I came here **on foot** because I wanted to get
> some exercise.*

We use **in my, our**, etc./**the car** to talk about someone's car:
> *It was only a short journey but we went **in
> my/our/the car**.*

We use **on my, our**, etc. with **bike**:
> *He came **on his bike**.*

We use **on the** before other means of transport:
> *They went to London **on the train**.*

We use **by** in phrases describing processes (e.g. sending something, ordering something, paying for something, making something):
> *I'll send the information **by post/email/fax**.*
> *Can you book tickets **by phone**?*
> *You can pay **by credit card** or **by cheque**.*
> *All these products were made **by hand**.*

But we say **in cash**:
> *I paid for the holiday **in cash**.*

We also use **by** in these phrases:
> **by chance, by accident, by mistake**

3 We use **for** in these phrases:

> **for example, for sale, for ever**

> *Their house is **for sale**.*
> *I'd like to live here **for ever**.*

4 We use **in** in these phrases:

> **in advance, in danger, in future, in a hurry, in
> charge (of), in control, in fashion, in general,
> in love, in my opinion, in the past**

> *You are advised to book a table **in advance**.*
> *I can't talk to you now, I'm **in a hurry**.*
> ***In general**, she has a good life.*

Notice also: **in writing/pen/pencil/capitals**
> *Please write your name **in capitals** in this
> box.*
> *Put your complaint **in writing**.*
> (= write a formal letter)

5 We use **on** in these phrases:

> **on business/on holiday/on a trip, on (the)
> TV/televison, on the radio, on the internet,
> on (a/the) computer, on the phone**
> (= speaking, using it), **on strike, on fire, on
> the floor**

> *I'm going away **on holiday/on business** next
> week.*
> *All this work is done **on computer** these
> days.*
> *There are no trains because the drivers are
> **on strike**.*
> *I found a lot of useful information **on the
> internet**.*
> *She was **on the phone** when I went into the
> room.*

6 Notice also the common prepositions **except
(for)** and **instead of**:
> *Everyone was happy **except (for)** Elaine.*
> (= Elaine was the only person who wasn't
> happy.)
> *I'd prefer a cold drink **instead of** a coffee at
> the moment.*
We use an **-ing** form after **instead of**:
> *I walked to work **instead of going** by car.*

Practice

A Match the first and second halves of the sentences.

▶ I waited for ages until the parcel arrived at ——
1 You should buy your tickets well in
2 As part of her job she has to travel a lot on
3 I didn't plan to meet him, it happened by
4 I won't make the same mistake in
5 There were no trains because the drivers were on
6 This kind of music is currently in

a fashion
b strike
c advance
d last
e business
f chance
g future

▶ d...... 1 .... 2 .... 3 .... 4 .... 5 .... 6 ....

B Complete these official instructions by putting in the correct prepositions.

▶ We can be contacted _by_............ phone at the number below.
1 Complaints must be put .... writing and sent to the address below.
2 Please complete your personal details .... capitals.
3 Applications sent .... post will be dealt with as soon as possible.
4 Payment can be made .... credit card or .... cheque but not .... cash.
5 Feel free to contact me .... email at any time.

C Complete this extract from an email to a friend by using these words and the correct prepositions in the gaps.

| first | holiday | once | ~~hurry~~ | charge | ever | example | mistake |

Dear Pete,
I've been living in this city for a couple of months now. It's a very crowded and
busy place and everyone seems to be (▶) _in a hurry_............ all the time. Nobody is willing
to wait for anything, they want to have it (1)....................... . I see this all the time.
(2)....................... , I was in a restaurant the other day and the man at the next table
demanded to speak to the person (3)....................... because he'd been waiting five
minutes for his meal! When the waiter then brought the wrong meal (4)....................... ,
he went completely mad! (5)....................... I thought I'd like living here, but now
I've decided it's a good place to visit (6)....................... . I wouldn't want to live
here (7)....................... .
Rick

D Complete these sentences with the correct prepositions.

▶ Did you have a good time _at_............ the weekend?
1 .... my opinion, you're wasting your time.
2 A few minutes later, the whole building was .... fire.
3 They've been .... love ever since they first met.
4 They've won every game .... one, which they lost badly.
5 She does most of her work .... a computer.

83 Verb + preposition

1 After some verbs we use a particular preposition* (e.g. **for, to, on**):

VERB + PREPOSITION	
wait for:	*I was **waiting for** a bus.*
listen to:	*She **listens to** the radio a lot.*
belong to:	*Does that book **belong to** you?*
ask for:	*Have you **asked for** the bill?*
apply for:	*He has **applied for** another job.*
depend on:	*The salary **depends on** your age.*
agree with:	*I don't **agree with** you.*

2 Now look at these examples:

▶ **arrive at/in:**
   *We **arrived at** the airport.* (You **arrive at** a place, for example a building.)
   *We **arrived in** Portugal.* (You **arrive in** a town or country.)

▶ **look at/for:**
   Look at that strange man over there! (You **look at** something you can see.)
   *I'm **looking for** my diary.* (You **look for** something that you are trying to find.)

▶ **talk to/about:**
   *She was **talking to** some friends.* (You **talk to** somebody.)
   *They were **talking about** politics.* (You **talk about** something.)

3 In questions that begin with a question word like **What, Who** or **How many,** we usually put the preposition at the end:
   Who are you waiting for?
   Who does this jacket belong to?

4 We do not usually use a preposition after these verbs:

> **phone/ring:** *He **phoned/rang** me last night.* (NOT ~~He phoned/rang to me~~ …)
> **discuss:** *We often **discuss** sport.* (NOT … ~~discuss about sport.~~)
> **answer:** *She didn't **answer** me.* (NOT … ~~answer to me.~~)
> **reach** (= arrive): *I **reached** the office at nine o'clock.* (NOT … ~~reached to the office~~ …)

5 Note that we **pay someone,** but we **pay for something:**
   She paid him yesterday. (You **pay** a person.)
   I paid for the books. (You **pay for** something that you receive.)

But note that we **pay a bill:** *I'll pay the bill.*

*Another term for **verb + preposition** is **prepositional verb.**

Practice

A Complete these sentences with the correct prepositions (*to, for,* etc.). In some sentences no preposition is required.

▶ I'm waiting _for_ a telephone call.
▶ We reached _–_ the airport after eleven o'clock.
1 I'll ask .... some information.
2 Let's listen .... some music.
3 Where do I pay .... this shirt?
4 Let's discuss .... the arrangements for tomorrow.
5 Who's going to pay .... the taxi driver?
6 We paid .... the bill and left the restaurant.
7 I'll phone .... the theatre and book two tickets.
8 The price of the holiday depends .... when you want to travel.
9 He walked out of the room without answering .... me.
10 A lot of people don't agree .... you.
11 I've applied .... a visa.
12 Who does this pen belong .... ?

3 Complete the story by putting a preposition into the gaps if one is necessary. For some gaps no preposition is required.

When Jack arrived (▶) at............ the theatre, Alice was waiting (1)............... him. 'Where have you been?' she asked (2)............... him. 'We can talk (3)............... that later,' said Jack. 'I tried to phone (4)............... you to say that I was going to be late, but you were out. Let's go into the concert.' 'OK,' said Alice, 'but as you were late, you have to pay (5)............... the tickets!' 'What?' said Jack. 'I don't want to argue (6)............... it, but I don't agree (7)............... you. It's not fair!'

C Complete the questions using the words in brackets ( ). Add the correct preposition.

Tim: What are you doing here, Pam?
Pam: I'm just waiting.
Tim: (who/you/wait) (▶) Who are you waiting for? ....
Pam: Sara. She's talking to the boss.
Tim: (what/they/talk) (1)..
Pam: She wants more money.
Tim: (how much/she/ask) (2)..
Pam: I don't know, but she's thinking about looking for a new job.
Tim: (how many jobs/have/she/apply) (3)..
Pam: Five or six, I think. By the way, is that a new walkman that you've got?
Tim: It's new but it's not mine.
Pam: And (what/you/listen) (4)..
Tim: The new Ricky Martin album. It's great!

D Complete the postcard by putting in the prepositions that are necessary. Sometimes, no preposition is required.

Dear Sam,
We arrived (▶) in............ Greece at about 11 o'clock. We got a taxi from the airport to the port, and then we took a lovely little boat to the island. I enjoyed looking (1)............... the scenery on the way. When we reached (2)............... the island, we looked (3)............... our villa but we couldn't find it. I talked (4)............... a local man, and I asked (5)............... directions. He offered to take me there. When we arrived (6)............... the villa, I offered to pay (7)............... him, but he didn't want any money. The weather's lovely. I'll ring (8)............... you when we get back from our holiday.
Love,
Tina

84 Adjective + preposition

1 Some adjectives can be followed by a preposition + noun:

ADJECTIVE	+ PREPOSITION	+ NOUN
I'm *afraid*	*of*	*dogs.*
She's *good*	*at*	*maths.*

Here are some more examples:

afraid of: *I'm afraid of my teacher.*
angry with: *John is very angry with me.*
annoyed with: *I was annoyed with my sister.*
brilliant at: *Jenny is brilliant at maths.*
busy with: *Tom was busy with his work.*
careless with: *Bill is careless with his money.*
cruel to: *Ann's mother was cruel to her.*
famous for: *France is famous for its cheese.*
fond of: *Peter is very fond of children.*
frightened of: *Our cat is frightened of your dog.*
full of: *The rooms were full of old furniture.*
good at: *Are you good at sport?*
grateful for: *They were grateful for our help.*
interested in: *She's interested in old coins.*
keen on: *He's very keen on chess.*
kind to: *Your sister was very kind to us.*
lucky at: *I'm often lucky at games.*
pleased with: *Ian was pleased with the result.*
proud of: *They're proud of their children.*
sure about: *Are you sure about her name?*
surprised by: *I was surprised by her anger.*

2 Some adjectives are followed by a preposition + -ing form:

ADJECTIVE	+ PREPOSITION	+ -ing FORM
He was	*sick of washing*	*dishes.*

*I'm not very **good at running**.*
*Robert is very **fond of talking**.*
*Anne is **used to working** at night.*
  (= She often works at night, and she
  doesn't mind it.)

3 A few adjectives can have an -ing form without a preposition:

busy	no good	not worth

ADJECTIVE + -ing FORM	
They were	*busy getting*	*things ready.*

*It's **no good worrying** about the weather.*
*It's **not worth taking** the car, we can walk.*

Practice

A Put in the missing prepositions (e.g. *with*, *of*).

► Mary was pleased <u>with</u> her exam results. She had got good marks in most subjects.

1 Thank you very much. I am very grateful .... your help.
2 I'm not sure .... the price, but I think they cost about £5.
3 It was the day of the concert, and everyone was busy .... the preparations.
4 I didn't expect to win the match. I was quite surprised .... the result.
5 Sandra was very brave. We are very proud .... her.
6 I like geography and I'm very interested .... history as well.
7 We've got plenty of food. The fridge is full .... things to eat.
8 Mary didn't like the director. She was annoyed .... him.
9 John is very clever. He's brilliant .... physics and chemistry.
10 Jane doesn't like small animals, but she's very fond .... horses.
11 Jeff should look after his disks. He's very careless .... them.

12 Susan and Jane like sports. They are particularly keen .... hockey.

13 Colin must be good .... French. He got top marks in the exams.

14 Mike has never learnt to swim because he's afraid .... water.

3 Write these short dialogues in the Present Simple. Use the words in brackets ( ) and any prepositions (e.g. *with*, *of*, *at*) that you need.

▶ A: (Jane, why/be/you/angry/Peter?)   ~ B: (Because he/be/very careless/his money)

A: *Jane, why are you angry with Peter?* ....

B: *Because he is very careless with his money.* ....

1 A: (be/their daughter/good/school work?)   ~ B: (Yes, in fact she/be/brilliant/everything)

A: ....

B: ....

2 A: (Why/be/Mr Bell's dog/afraid/him?)   ~ B: (Because he/be/often/cruel/it)

A: ....

B: ....

3 A: (be/Jenny/fond/classical music?)   ~ B: (Yes, she/be/very keen/Bach, for example)

A: ....

B: ....

4 A: (be/you/pleased/Peter's exam results?)   ~ B: (Yes, we/be/very proud/him)

A: ....

B: ....

C Complete the dialogue using the words in the box, and put in a preposition if it is necessary.

busy	famous	full	good	interested	~~kind~~
no good	sick	used	worried	worth	

Terry: How did your job interview go?

Penny: All right, I think. The company director was quite (▶) *kind to* .... me.

Terry: What does the company make?

Penny: Clothes. It's (1)........................ its sports clothes, in fact. I had to wait for a while because the director was (2)........................ talking to some clients. The corridor where I waited was (3)........................ boxes with clothes in them.

Terry : And what did he ask you?

Penny: She. The director's a woman. She asked me if I was (4)........................ maths. I said yes. She asked me if I was (5)........................ working under pressure, and I told her that I prefer to be busy at work so that it was no problem. Then she asked me why I was (6)........................ changing jobs, and I told her that I was (7)........................ working hard for so little pay. I'm a bit (8)........................ that answer now; perhaps it wasn't the best thing to say.

Terry : It's (9)........................ thinking about it now. What do you think your chances are?

Penny: I'm not sure. I'm not really sure that I want to change jobs just now, but I think it's (10)........................ going to an interview from time to time because it gives you practice and makes you more confident.

Test H: Prepositions

A This is a weather forecast on a local radio station. Complete the missing words.

Good morning. This is the weather (▶) at............... six in the morning (1) o................
Thursday 7 February. It's cold (2) o................ , and there's ice (3) o................ the
roads, so don't drive too close to the car (4) i................ f................ of you! There
should be forty metres (5) b................ you and that car! If you're driving (6) i................
the city (7) t................ morning, pay attention to schoolchildren walking (8) a................
the road. Remember, you might be (9) n................ t................ a school! Traffic is
moving very slowly (10) t................ the city centre at the moment. There was an accident
(11) l................ night – if you're driving (12) p................ Central Library, the Police may
stop you and ask you a few questions. That's all for now. More weather news
(13) e................ hour, (14) f................ six (15) i................ the morning
(16) t................ six at night, this is the KC News Network making sure you're up to date
with the news on the road!

B Tony is talking to Michelle. Write in the following missing words in the correct place.

| at   by (x2)   in   good   of   with (x3)   without   ~~without~~   worth. |

Tony: Jack says he can learn a new language (▶) /without working.

Michelle: Who's Jack?

Tony: He's that new boy the bright blue jumper. The one long hair. He's bought a book a
              CD, and he says he learns listening to the CD while he's asleep.

Michelle: I think that's silly.

Tony: But you're good learning new words, aren't you? I might try Jack's CD. I'm sick
              making mistakes all the time.

Michelle: It's no use worrying about mistakes. We learn making mistakes.

Tony: It's easy for you. You can pass French exams doing much work. How do you do it?

Michelle: I just sit down a dictionary and a French newspaper. It's not buying an expensive
              CD, in my view.

C Melanie is sending an email to Sheila. Cross out the wrong words.

I want to be (▶) on/in holiday! It's too hot to work. The office is (1) as/like an oven (2) on/at
the moment. It looks (3) as/like if my boss will be in Germany (4) on/in business next week
so I'll be (5) at/in charge. Are you enjoying yourself in Cancun? Is Mexico cheap (6) like/as
a place to stay? (7) Like/As usual, I haven't booked my holiday yet, but I think I'll go to Spain
(8) by/in car and visit my old friend Pilar in Madrid. You really sounded (9) as/like though you
were (10) on/in love when I spoke to you (11) by/on the phone last week. (12) As/Like you
know, I think your new boyfriend is a really nice guy. I'm sure you'll be happy together.

A tour guide is showing tourists a Roman camp near Hadrian's Wall in the north of England. Put words from the box in the spaces.

reach	busy	interested	waiting	talk	sure
proud	~~Listen~~	depended	grateful	surprised	brilliant

▶ Listen................. to me now, please. Can you hear me? I'm going to (1).......................
to you today about daily life for Romans living in the camp. I think you will be
(2)....................... by some of the things that you see. This part of the camp was the
kitchen. Imagine fifteen cooks (3)........................ with the meals for the soldiers and their
families! The cooks (4)........................ on local farms for the food, and they were
(5)........................ at keeping food for a long time, using salt for example. If you're
(6)........................ in cooking, please ask for more information at the tourist centre. Shall
we continue? Who are we (7)........................ for? We're not (8)........................ about
this part of the camp, but we think it was a bathing area, and we know that the Romans were
(9)........................ of their bathrooms. I expect that the people living here were
(10)........................ for hot water in winter. Let's move on. In a moment we'll
(11)........................ the family part of the camp, and I'll let you look around by yourselves.'

Paula and Nigel are talking to each other on the phone. In numbers 1–7, circle the correct preposition. In the rest, put in the correct preposition.

Paula: Hi! Is that you, Nigel? I'm glad you haven't left yet. When you come to the
conference tonight, could you bring the green file? It's (▶) onto/on my desk,
(1) behind/between the telephone. Can you see it? That's right. It's (2) across/under
the address book. Great! Now, do you know how to get to the hotel?

Nigel: I think so. After I've driven out (3) from/of London, I go north (4) in/up the A54,
through Watford, (5) as/like though I was going to Milton Keynes. But in fact I take
the B254 (6) on/to Halton before I reach Milton Keynes. I think I should get there
about nine o'clock, shouldn't I?

Paula: That's right, unless you get lost (7) as/like me!

Nigel: Isn't there a big house (8)................ sale, just before the Halton road?

Paula: Yes. It's (9)................ the left. I didn't see it, so I had to ask (10)................
directions.

Nigel: Is the boss there already? I plan to arrive at the hotel (11)................ jeans instead
(12)................ my suit and tie. I hope that's OK. By the way, did you apply
(13)................ Phil's job?

Paula: I wasn't sure about it, but yes, I did apply. I was a bit annoyed (14)................ the
advertisement on the website, though. There was a sentence (15)................ the
end of it, saying 'You must be good (16)................ talking to people.'

Nigel: What's wrong with that?

Paula: Well, Phil was very good at talking to people, but he wasn't fond (17)................
doing any work, was he?

Nigel: You sound (18)................ you didn't really like Phil.

Paula: Well, I thought he was a bit cruel (19)................ his secretary.

Nigel: Yes, I think she was frightened (20)................ him, wasn't she? Look, I'd better go.
See you later!

85 Have and have got

1 Look at this example with **have**:
*They always **have** breakfast at seven o'clock.*

POSITIVE		
I/you/we/they	have	
He/she/it	has	

NEGATIVE	FULL FORM	SHORT FORM
I/you/we/they	do not have	don't have
He/she/it	does not have	doesn't have

QUESTIONS		
Do	I/you/we/they	
Does	he/she/it	have ...?

2 Look at this example with **have got**:
I've got three brothers.

POSITIVE	FULL FORM	SHORT FORM
I/you/we/they	have got	've got
He/she/it	has got	's got

NEGATIVE		
I/you/we/they	have not got	haven't got
He/she/it	has not got	hasn't got

QUESTIONS		
Have	I/you/we/they	
Has	he/she/it	got ...?

3 We can use **have** or **have got**:

▶ to talk about the things we possess:
*We **have** a house in Spain.*
*We**'ve got** a house in Spain.*
*Paul **doesn't have** a car.*
*Paul **hasn't got** a car.*
*Do you **have** any money?*
*Have you **got** any money?*

▶ to talk about our families:
*Jane **has** a brother and a sister.*
*Jane**'s got** a brother and a sister.*

▶ to describe people:
*She **has** blue eyes.*
*She**'s got** blue eyes.*
*Does your brother **have** long hair or short hair?*
*Has your brother **got** long hair or short hair?*

▶ to say that we are not feeling well:
*I **have** a headache.*
*I**'ve got** a headache.*

4 We use **have** (NOT ~~have got~~) to talk about meals and holidays, and with a bath, a shower, or a wash:
*Do you normally **have** a big **breakfast**?*
*Have a good **holiday**!*
*She's **having a shower** at the moment.*
*I always **have a wash** before I go out.*

Practice

A Write positive or negative sentences or questions, using *have got* and the words in brackets ( ).

▶ (she/not/brown eyes) *She hasn't got brown eyes.*

1 (he/a flat/in the town centre) ....

2 (you/a car?) ....

3 (I/not/a brother) ....

4 (she/a headache) ....

5 (Steve/brown hair?) ....

Now write sentences or questions using *have* in the Present Simple (*have, has, don't have*, etc.).

▶ (we/always/eggs/for breakfast) *We always have eggs for breakfast.*

6 (John/always/a holiday in August) ....

7 (she/a bath/every Friday) ....

8   (you/a shower/in the morning?) ....

9   (I/always/lunch/in the park) ....

10 (They/not/a swimming pool) ....

3 Put the words in brackets ( ) in the correct order to complete the dialogues.

▶   (got – I've – two brothers)   A: Have you got any brothers or sisters?
                                                 B: Yes, *I've got two brothers.*...............

1   (in Edinburgh – a flat – she's got)   A: Does your sister live in Scotland?
                                                 B: Yes, ...

2   (you – got – have – a headache?)   A: What's the matter? ....
                                                 ....
                                                 B: No, but I feel tired.

3   (blonde hair – she – got – hasn't)   A: Jane's tall and blonde.
                                                 B: No, you're wrong. ....
                                                 ....

4   (have – you – do – a holiday every year?) A: ....
                                                 B: No, I don't.

5   (he's – a shower – having)   A: Where's Michael? Is he ready?
                                                 B: No, ...

6   (a car – I – got – haven't)   A: Are you going to drive to Scotland?
                                                 B: No, ...

7   (you – dinner at seven? – have – do)   A: ....
                                                 B: No, we always eat at seven-thirty.

C Some of the sentences are wrong. Rewrite the wrong sentences and tick (✓) the correct sentences.

▶   We've got a holiday in Mexico every year. *We have a holiday in Mexico every year.*.......
▶   Paul's got a sister in Scotland. ✓...
1   She is tired, but she doesn't have a cold. ....
2   I haven't got lunch every day. ....
3   Have you got a shower every day? ....
4   Have you got an English dictionary? ....
5   Do you have a headache? ....
6   I have got a holiday in Spain every year. ....
7   We've got a large garden. ....
8   I've got a bath at ten and I go to bed at eleven. ....
9   They're having got dinner at the moment. ....
10 They've got two dogs. ....
11 Have got a good weekend! ....
12 Have you got a motorbike? ....

86 Make, do, have, get

1 There are many phrases in which a particular verb is used together with a particular noun, for example:

> make a cup of coffee
> do some work
> have breakfast

2 We often use **make** in sentences about producing or creating something:

> They *made a fire* in the woods.
> Shall I *make some coffee*?
> He *made some sandwiches* for lunch.

3 We also use **make** in these phrases:

> Excuse me. I have to *make a phone call*.
> He *makes a lot of mistakes* in his work.
> I couldn't sleep because the neighbours were *making a lot of noise*.

4 We often use **do** in sentences about working, or about doing particular jobs:

> Have you *done your homework*?
> He offered to *do the washing-up*.
> We're going to *do some shopping*.
> I haven't *done much work* today.

5 We use **have + noun** to describe activities:

> I'm going to *have a shower* in the morning.
> We usually *have lunch* at about 1 o'clock.
> I'm *having fish* for dinner tonight.
> I *had a swim* in the sea this morning.

6 We use **get** with adjectives that describe feelings, to say that we begin to have the feeling:

> I'm *getting tired* now. I need a rest.
> They're late and I'm *getting worried*.
> I *got angry* and shouted at them.

7 We use **get** in some phrases that describe a change of situation:

> We *got lost* in Paris. (= We became lost …)
> It's *getting cold*. (= It's becoming cold.)
> Jane was very ill, but she's *getting better*.
> They *got married* three years ago.
> It rained heavily and I *got very wet*.

8 We use **make + someone + adjective** to talk about the cause of a feeling:

> He *made us very angry*.
> The news *made him happy*.

Practice

A Complete the sentences, using the correct forms of *make*, *do*, *have* or *get*. Be careful that you use the correct tense.

▶ He was making....... a cup of coffee in the kitchen.

▶ We had.......... lunch in a very pleasant little restaurant yesterday.

1 She always .... excited before her birthday.

2 A: Helen's ill.

B: Oh dear. I hope she will .... better soon.

3 We have to .... some homework every evening.

4 I think I've .... a terrible mistake.

5 They .... the shopping and then they went home.

6 I was late because I .... lost on my way there.

7 It always .... very hot here during the summer.

8 Could I a .... quick phone call, please?

9 Please don't .... so much noise.

10 It was a lovely surprise and it .... me very happy.

11 Her parents are .... old. They are sixty or seventy.

12 How old were you when you .... married?

3 Look at the notes in the box about what Laura did yesterday. Complete the sentences, using the correct forms of *make*, *do*, *have* or *get*. Sometimes more than one answer is possible.

7.30	Got up. Shower.
8.00	Breakfast (fruit juice and toast).
8.30–9.00	Walk to work. Rain.
9.00–1.00	Work. Very busy.
1.00–2.00	Lunch in office. Sandwiches.
2.00–5.00	Work. Finished everything.
5.30	Shopping. Home.
7.00	Pizza for dinner. Washed up.
8.00–11.00	TV. Tired. Bed.

It was a normal day for Laura yesterday. She got up at 7.30 and she (▶) _had_.......... a shower. Then she (1)............... breakfast. For breakfast she (2)............... fruit juice and toast. While she was walking to work, it rained and she (3)............... wet. She (4)............... angry about this. In the morning she (5)............... a lot of work. She (6)............... lunch at about one o'clock. She (7)............... sandwiches for lunch. When she had (8)............... all her work in the afternoon, she went home. On the way home she (9)............... some shopping. She (10)............... a pizza for dinner. She (11)............... the washing-up and then she watched TV for three hours. By eleven o'clock she felt quite tired, and so she went to bed.

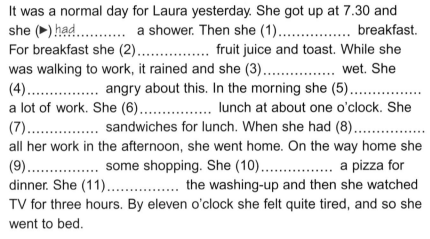

C Complete the dialogues, using the correct form of *make*, *do*, *have* or *get*.

▶ A: Was the film good?
   B: No, I _got_........... bored in the middle of it.

1 A: Could you .... some shopping for me?
   B: Yes, what do you want me to buy?

2 A: Were you pleased by the news?
   B: No, it .... me very unhappy.

3 A: Was it a warm day?
   B: Yes, but it .... rather cold in the evening.

4 A: Are you hungry at the moment?
   B: No, I .... a big meal a couple of hours ago.

5 A: Did he pass the test?
   B: No, he .... a lot of mistakes.

6 A: Are you ready to go out?
   B: No, I'm not. I want to .... a wash first.

7 A: Could you repair this for me?
   B: Yes, but I can't .... the job until tomorrow.

87 Phrasal verbs (1): meanings and types

1 We can use many verbs together with another word to form 'phrasal verbs', e.g. **put on, get up.**

The same verb can go with several different words to form phrasal verbs with different meanings, e.g. **put away, put on, put through.**

The meaning of a phrasal verb is not always clear from the two parts. For example, **put through** means connect (= make a telephone connection). You should check the meaning of phrasal verbs in a dictionary.

2 Grammatically, there are three types of phrasal verb.

▶ One type consists of **verb + adverb** and they have an object, e.g.:
*She **put on** the hat.*
*She **put** the hat **on**.*

Some common verbs of this type are:

> **bring up, calm down, cross out, fill in, find out, give in, give out, look up, pick up, point out, pull off, put away, put through, take off, try on, turn off, work out**

▶ The second type of phrasal verb consists of **verb + adverb** but there is no object, e.g.:
*I usually **get up** at seven o'clock.*

Some common verbs of this type are:

> **break down, check in, get off, get up, go on, go out, hang about, look out, set off, show up, stay up, take off, turn out, turn up**

▶ The third type consists of **verb + adverb + preposition** and they have an object, e.g.:
*We're **looking forward to** your news.*

Some common verbs of this type are:

> **do away with, face up to, run out of, look up to**

(See also Unit 88.)

Practice

A Complete these dialogues with the phrasal verb and a pronoun.

▶ A: Has Mary put her hat on? B: Yes, she's <u>put it on</u> .
1 A: Who brought up the children? B: Their uncle ....
2 A: Did you cross out the wrong words? B: No, the teacher ....
3 A: When do we have to give in the homework? B: We have to .... tomorrow.
4 A: Can you pick Sally up after school? B: OK, I'll .... on my way home.
5 A: Children, can you put your toys away now please. B: Can't we .... later?

B Rewrite each sentence replacing the <u>expression underlined</u> with the correct form of one of the phrasal verbs from the box.

> break down, give out, go on, keep off, ~~look out~~, look up to, put through

▶ <u>Be careful!</u> Don't step into the hole!
<u>Look out</u> .... ! Don't step into the hole!

1 The young boys really <u>admire</u> the first team players.

The young boys really .... the first team players.

2 The teacher <u>distributed</u> the exam papers.

The teacher .... the exam papers.

3 Hold the line. I'll try to <u>connect</u> you.

Hold the line. I'll try to .... you ....

4 What's <u>happening</u> here? What are you doing?

What's .... here? What are you doing?

5 Jim's old car <u>stopped working</u> completely last weekend.

Jim's old car .... completely last weekend.

C **Sally and Jane are staying in Barcelona and are planning to do some shopping. Complete the dialogue with the correct form of one of the verbs in the box. Use a dictionary to check the meanings.**

find out, get off, look up, put on, run out of, set off, take off, try on, ~~work out~~

Sally: Have you (▶) <u>worked out</u> .... where the best shopping centre is?

Jane: Yes, I (1)........................ it .... in the guidebook. We can take the metro right across the street and we (2)........................ at the fourth station.

Sally: By the way, I've (3)........................ euros so we'll have to call at a bank.

Jane: We can go to the hotel reception and (4)........................ if there's a cash machine near here. What are you going to wear?

Sally: If we're going to (5)........................ clothes, I think I'll wear a skirt. It's more difficult to (6)........................ jeans and (7)........................ them .... all the time.

Jane: OK, as soon as you've changed we can (8)........................ .

D **Complete the following story by choosing the second word of each phrasal verb. Use a dictionary to check the meanings**

We were looking forward (▶) to/~~on~~ our holiday but the night before we were going to leave we stayed (1) down/up talking until about three o'clock. We didn't hear the alarm clock so we got (2) up/in late and we were late getting to the airport. When we went to check (3) in/up, we were lucky because some passengers hadn't shown (4) up/out so there were still some seats left. When we got on the plane, Tim was a bit nervous because he hadn't flown before but I gave him a pill and that calmed him (5) down/out. The cabin crew told us to turn (6) in/off our mobiles. Then the lights went (7) up/off and Tim thought something was wrong but I pointed (8) out/up that they always do that before the plane takes (9) out/off. When we got to Rome we went to pick (10) up/off our cases. Mine was one of the first to come out, but Tim's didn't appear. We hung (11) about/up for a long time but it didn't turn (12) out/up. We went to an office to report it and Tim had to fill (13) in/on all his details on a form. After several phone calls it turned (14) out/up that Tim's case was in Athens. Luckily we got it back that same evening. As soon as it arrived, Tim pulled (15) out/off his sweaty clothes, had a cold shower and put (16) in/on a clean shirt and trousers. We were just in time to go and have dinner.

88 Phrasal verbs (2): separability

1 Grammatically, phrasal verbs fall into three* groups. Some phrasal verbs can belong to different groups (see Unit 87), sometimes with different meanings. For example, **clear up**:

> Who's going to **clear up** the mess?
> (= remove)
> The weather soon **cleared up**.
> (= improved)

2 Verbs in the first group consist of **verb + adverb** and they have an object. When the object is a noun, there are two possible positions, e.g.:

> Tim **cleared up** the mess.
> Tim **cleared** the mess **up**.

However, when the object is a pronoun, it goes between the two parts of the verb, e.g.:

> Tim **cleared** it **up**. (NOT: ~~Tim cleared up it.~~)

Some common verbs in this group are:

> **break off, carry on, draw out, get off, give up, knock down, lay off, let out, make up, pay in, put on, rub out, set up, shut down, sort out**

3 Verbs in the second group consist of **verb + adverb** but there is no object, e.g.:

> Where did you **grow up**?

Some common verbs in this group are:

> **call in, come about, cut down, drop in, go on, hang on, look out, stay in**

4 Verbs in the third group consist of **verb + adverb + preposition** and they have an object, e.g.:

> I can't **put up with** all this noise.

Some common verbs in this group are:

> **do away with, face up to, get away with, put up with**

* Some people also classify prepositional verbs (Unit 83) as phrasal verbs.

Practice

A Complete these dialogues with the phrasal verb and a pronoun.

▶ A: Has somebody put the lights on?
  B: I think Joe's <u>put them on</u>.

1 A: When did they knock down the cinema?
  B: They .... several months ago.

2 A: Look at this skirt! How can I get the ink off?
  B: I think the only way to .... is to take it to the cleaner's.

3 A: Somebody's rubbed out my name.
  B: Well, I haven't ....

4 A: Sally and Pete have broken off their engagement.
  B: Oh! When did they .... ?

B Replace the <u>expression underlined</u> in each sentence with the correct form of one of the phrasal verbs from the box.

> drop in, get away with, hang on, ~~knock down~~, put up with, sort out

▶ They're going to <u>demolish</u> those old houses.
  They're going to <u>knock down</u> those old houses.

1 The gang <u>escaped taking</u> 5 million pounds.

The gang .... 5 million pounds.

2 I'm going out. I can't <u>stand</u> the smoke in here.

I'm going out. I can't .... the smoke in here.

3 Marjorie says she's going to <u>visit us</u> on Thursday.

Marjorie says she's going to .... on Thursday.

4 <u>Wait!</u> I've just got to get my jacket.

.... ! I've just got to get my jacket.

5 We still haven't <u>arranged</u> who does the different jobs.

We still haven't .... who does the different jobs.

Complete this interview by putting the correct form of one of the phrasal verbs in each space.

carry on, come about, cut down, do away with, draw out, drop in, face up to, give up, go on, ~~grow up~~, lay off, let out, make up, pay in, set up, shut down, stay in

Interviewer: I understand that your early life was not easy. Can you tell us a little about it? Where were you born?

Ruth: In Barnsley, in the north of England and that's where I (▶) *grew up* ....

Interviewer: Were you lonely as a child?

Ruth: I had three sisters and two brothers so it was never quiet. There was always something (1)......................... . The house was never empty because neighbours (2)......................... all the time.

Interviewer: Do you remember any particularly happy moments?

Ruth: Yes, when we went to bed my mother always told us stories. She didn't have a book – she just (3)......................... them .... herself.

Interviewer: And then things went wrong. How did that (4)......................... ?

Ruth: Well, in the first place my father smoked a lot. He always said that he was going to (5)......................... , but he never did. He got very ill and he was in hospital for several weeks. Even when the hospital (6)......................... him .... , he wasn't well. He had to (7)......................... and keep warm so that his bronchitis wouldn't start again. But at least he had the sense to finally (8)......................... smoking.

Interviewer: But things got worse.

Ruth: Yes, while he was recovering we heard that the factory where he worked had (9)......................... a lot of workers. At first he wasn't affected but then we heard that they were going to (10)......................... the factory ....

Interviewer: And then things got better.

Ruth: Yes, my parents had to (11)......................... their new situation. They said that businesses could (12)......................... factory workers but they would always need office staff. Luckily they had a savings account and every week they had (13)......................... something .... Now they decided to (14)......................... their savings and (15)......................... a little business selling office equipment. It did quite well and when they retired I decided to (16)......................... it ....

Interviewer: Well, that is a story with a happy end. Thank you for speaking to me.

89 Passive sentences (1)

1 We form the Present Simple passive like this:

am/is/are	+ PAST PARTICIPLE
Glass **is** **made**	*from sand.*

POSITIVE AND NEGATIVE
> *This programme **is shown** on TV every Thursday.*
> *These computers **aren't produced** any more.*

QUESTIONS
> *When **is** breakfast **served** in this hotel?*

(For information on the forms of regular past participles see Appendix 2 on page 243, and for irregular past participles see Appendix 3 on page 244.)

2 We form the Past Simple passive like this:

was/were	+	PAST PARTICIPLE
Anna **was**		**born** *in Germany.*

POSITIVE AND NEGATIVE
> *'Romeo and Juliet' **was written** by Shakespeare.*
> *The goods **weren't delivered** yesterday.*

QUESTIONS
> *When **was** your camera **stolen**?*

3 Look at these sentences:

		OBJECT	
ACTIVE:	*They sell*	*cold drinks*	*here.*
PASSIVE:	*Cold drinks*	*are sold here.*	
	SUBJECT		

Notice that the object in the active sentence (**cold drinks**) is the same as the subject in the passive sentence. We use the passive when it is not important who does the action, or when we don't know who does it:
> *These cars are made in Japan.* (We don't need to say … ~~by Japanese workers.~~)
> *This castle was built in the twelfth century.* (We don't know who built it.)

4 Now look at these examples:
> (i) **Alfred Hitchcock** *was a great film-maker. He directed this film in 1956.*
> (ii) *This is a wonderful **film**. **It** was directed by Alfred Hitchcock.*

In (ii) we use the passive because we have been talking about something (**the film**), and not the person who did it (**Hitchcock**). We use **by** to say who does, or did, the action:
> *This film was directed **by** Hitchcock.*

Practice

A Complete these sentences using the correct form of the verbs from the box. Use the passive form of the Present Simple or Past Simple.

build	check	found	hold	~~make~~	produce	~~repair~~	sell	speak	write

► Scotch whisky is made .... in Scotland.
► The car was repaired .... last week.
1 The Olympic Games .... every four years.
2 English .... in many countries.
3 'Yesterday' .... by John Lennon and Paul McCartney.
4 Car speeds .... by radar.
5 The Channel Tunnel .... to connect Britain with Europe.
6 Souvenirs .... at all popular tourist places.
7 The first Volkswagen Beetles .... in 1937.
8 The Times newspaper .... in 1785.

3 Now write the questions for the sentences in exercise A, using the passive form.

▶ Where *is Scotch whisky made?* ....

▶ When *was the car repaired?* ....

1 How often ....

2 Where ....

3 Who ....

4 How ....

5 Why ....

6 Where ....

7 When ....

8 When ....

C Change the active sentences into passive sentences. Use the words in brackets ( ).

▶ We sell tickets for all shows at the box office. (Tickets for all shows/sell/at the box office)
  Tickets for all shows are sold at the box office. ....

1 Thomas Edison invented the electric light bulb. (The electric light bulb/invent/by Thomas Edison)

  ....

2 Someone painted the office last week. (The office/paint/last week)

  ....

3 Several people saw the accident. (The accident/see/by several people)

  ....

4 Where do they make these video recorders? (Where/these video recorders/make)

  ....

5 Six countries signed the agreement. (The agreement/sign/by six countries)

  ....

6 A stranger helped me. (I/help/by a stranger)

  ....

7 They don't deliver the post on Sundays. (The post/not/deliver/on Sundays)

  ....

D Put in the correct active or passive form in brackets ( ).

Fiat (▶) *was started* .... (started/was started) by a group of Italian businessmen in 1899. In 1903, Fiat (1)........................ (produced/was produced) 132 cars. Some of these cars (2)........................ (exported/were exported) by the company to the United States and Britain. In 1920, Fiat (3)........................ (started/was started) making cars at a new factory at Lingotto, near Turin. There was a track on the roof where the cars (4)........................ (tested/were tested) by technicians. In 1936, Fiat launched the Fiat 500. This car (5)........................ (called/was called) the Topolino - the Italian name for Mickey Mouse. The company grew, and in 1963 Fiat (6)........................ (exported/was exported) more than 300,000 vehicles. Today, Fiat is based in Turin, and its cars (7)........................ (sold/are sold) all over the world.

90 Passive sentences (2)

1 Here is a summary of passive tenses. Note that we always use a past participle in a passive verb (e.g. **repaired, taken**). For more information on past participles, see Appendices 2 and 3 on pages 243–4.

Present Simple:

	VERB (present) + PARTICIPLE
ACTIVE:	Someone **repairs** the machine.
PASSIVE:	The machine **is repaired.**

Past Simple:

	VERB (past) + PARTICIPLE
ACTIVE:	Someone **took** my camera.
PASSIVE:	My camera **was taken.**

Present Perfect:

	have/has + PARTICIPLE
ACTIVE:	She **has packed** the books.
PASSIVE:	The books **have been packed.**

Past Perfect:

	had + PARTICIPLE
ACTIVE:	Bob **had paid** the bill.
PASSIVE:	The bill **had been paid.**

Present Continuous:

	am/is/are + -ing + PARTICIPLE
ACTIVE:	They **are mending** the car.
PASSIVE:	The car **is being mended.**

Past Continuous:

	was/were + -ing + PARTICIPLE
ACTIVE:	They **were building** it.
PASSIVE:	It **was being built.**

will, can, must, etc.

	+ INFINITIVE + PARTICIPLE
ACTIVE:	We **will finish** the job.
PASSIVE:	The job **will be finished.**
ACTIVE:	We **must do** the work.
PASSIVE:	The work **must be done.**

2 In all passive sentences, the first verb (= auxiliary verb) is singular if the subject is singular, and plural if the subject is plural:

	AUXILIARY VERB	
The house	**is**	being built.
The houses	**are**	being built.

We also use the auxiliary verb to make questions and negatives:
Have the books been packed?
The bill **hadn't** been paid.

Practice

A Make questions from the passive sentences in brackets ( ).

► (That car was made in Germany.) Where was that car made?

1 (Mary was examined by the doctor this morning.) When ....

2 (The food will be prepared on Friday.) When ....

3 (This window has been broken three times.) How many times ....

B Write the negative of the sentences in exercise A.

► That car was not made in Germany. ....

1 Mary ....

2 The food ....

3 This window ....

C　Complete the sentences with a passive form of the verb in brackets ( ).

▶ Bread <u>is made</u>............... (make) from flour.
▶ I was at school when these houses <u>were being built</u>..... (was building).
1　Cakes .... (make) from flour.
2　We lived in a caravan in the garden while our house .... (was building).
3　This work .... (must finish) before five o'clock.
4　All the windows .... (have cleaned) this week.
5　These cups .... (broke) when we arrived.
6　Some money .... (have stolen) from Tom's jacket.

D　Make these active sentences passive. Use a phrase with *by*.

▶ Your manager must write the report.
　 The report <u>must be written by your manager.</u>...............
▶ The children are organizing the Christmas party.
　 The Christmas party <u>is being organized by the children.</u>...............
1　The French team has won the silver medal.
　 The silver medal ....
2　A woman was training the guard dogs.
　 The guard dogs ....
3　People of all ages can play this game.
　 This game ....
4　A large crowd was watching the match.
　 The match ....
5　The headmaster sent a reply.
　 A reply ....
6　Two different teachers have marked the exams.
　 The exams ....
7　A police car is following that green van.
　 That green van ....

E　Complete the sentences with the correct passive form of the verb in brackets ( ).

▶ The castle <u>was built</u>............ (build) in 1546.
▶ These mountains can <u>be seen</u>............... (see) from a great distance.
1　These houses .... (build) in 1946.
2　The repairs must .... (finish) by tomorrow.
3　The town has .... (attack) several times since the beginning of the war.
4　The decision has already .... (take).
5　The emails will .... (send) tomorrow morning.
6　White wine can .... (make) from red grapes.
7　The accident happened while the cars .... (load) onto the lorries.
8　The new models will .... (deliver) next week.

91 Have something done

1 Look at this sentence:

*Mary and Tim **painted** their flat.*

This tells us that Mary and Tim were the painters; they painted their flat.

Now look at this sentence with **have something done:**

*Jenny and John **had** their flat **painted.***

This tells us that Jenny and John wanted their flat painted, and that someone painted it for them.

2 Here are some more examples:

HAVE	+	SOMETHING	+	DONE
I have mended		*my bike.*		
I have had		*my bike*		*mended.*

*Sheila **is going to cut** her hair.*
*Sheila **is going to have** her hair **cut.***
  (= Someone is going to cut it for her.)
*She **washes** her car every Sunday.*
*She **has** her car **washed** every Sunday.*
  (= Someone washes her car for her.)

*I **must clean** my suit this week.*
*I **must have** my suit **cleaned** this week.*
  (= I must pay someone to clean it for me.)
*I'll **mend** that broken window.*
*I'll **have** that broken window **mended.***
  (= Someone will mend that window for me)

3 We sometimes use **get** instead **of have:**
*I must **get** my suit **cleaned.***

4 Now look at this example:

*Susan is very cross. She **had** her bike **stolen.***

Here, we use **have something done** to talk about something that happens to someone, usually something unpleasant. Here is another example:

*The group **had** two concerts **cancelled** because of bad weather.*

Practice

A Make sentences with a form of *have something done* for these situations. Use the correct tense.

▶ Tom's windows were dirty, but he didn't have time to clean them himself.
Last Saturday, Tom had his windows cleaned...

1 The shop delivers Mary's food to her house.
Mary ....

2 At the butcher's Fred said, 'Please cut the meat into small pieces'.
Fred .... into small pieces.

3 The hairdresser cuts Rachel's hair about twice a year.
Rachel .... about twice a year.

4 Last week, the optician checked Mr Stone's eyes.
Last week, Mr Stone ....

5 Mrs Frost's doctor says to her: 'When you come to see me next week, I'll check your blood pressure.'
When Mrs Frost goes to see the doctor next week, she ....

6 Last week, the garage serviced Jane's car.
Last week, Jane ....

7 A builder is going to mend the roof on our house.
We .... on our house.

3 Look at these signs from some shops and a garage. Then write what people think when they see the signs using the words in brackets ( ) and *have* or *had*.

▶ WE REPAIR ALL KINDS OF BOOTS AND SHOES
   (That reminds me. I/must/my brown boots/repair)
   That reminds me. *I must have my brown boots repaired.*

1 LET US CLEAN YOUR CARPETS AND CURTAINS
   (My parents use that company. They/their carpets/clean/there)
   My parents use that company. ....

2 CAN WE CHECK YOUR OIL AND TYRES?
   (That reminds me. I/must/the tyres/check)
   That reminds me. ....

3 WE MAKE KEYS OF ALL TYPES
   (I'd almost forgotten. I/ought to/a new key/make/for the front door)
   I'd almost forgotten. ....

4 OUR SPECIALITY: PAINTING HOUSES AND FLATS
   (I don't think I can afford to/our flat/paint)
   I don't think I can afford to ....

5 WE MEND WATCHES AND CLOCKS
   (That shop isn't expensive. I/my watch/mend/there last week)
   That shop isn't expensive. ....

6 WE TEST YOUR EYES FOR FREE
   (Ah, yes! My husband/his eyes/test/there last winter)
   Ah, yes! ....

7 WE REMOVE ALL KINDS OF STAINS FROM ALL KINDS OF CLOTHES
   (Wonderful! I'll take my suit there and/that coffee stain/remove)
   Wonderful! I'll take my suit there and I'll ....

C Some unpleasant things happened to these people last week. Use the sentence in brackets ( ) to write a sentence with *had something done*.

▶ (Mary's bag was pulled off her shoulder.)
   Mary *had her bag pulled off her shoulder.*

1 (Peter's driving licence was taken away by the police.)
   Peter ....

2 (Paula's bike was stolen from the garage.)
   Paula ....

3 (Fiona's glasses were broken.)
   ....

4 (John's clothes were torn in a fight.)
   ....

5 (Jane's flat was burgled at the weekend.)
   ....

6 (Our electricity was cut off because we had forgotten to pay the bill.)
   ....

92 Infinitive with/without **to**

1 Look at this example:

| **to** + INFINITIVE |
I want | to buy | some stamps.

We use **to do**, **to buy**, **to start**, etc. (**to** + infinitive) after some verbs, e.g.:

want	decide	
agree	promise	
forget	offer	+ **to** + INFINITIVE
hope	plan	
arrange	try	

> She **agreed to lend** him some money.
> He **forgot to book** the tickets.
> I'm **hoping to get** a new bike soon.
> I've **arranged to play** tennis tonight.
> They've **decided to start** a new company.
> You **promised to help** me.
> She **offered to do** the washing-up.
> We're **planning to go** away this weekend.
> He's **trying to learn** French.

2 We can also say **want** + someone + **to**:
> His parents **want him to go** to university.
> Do you **want me to help** you?

3 Now look at this example:

| INFINITIVE |
He **can** | speak | Spanish.

Can is a modal verb. We use **do**, **speak**, **see**, etc. (infinitives) after a modal verb. Some of the most common modal verbs are:

| **will** ('ll) **should may** | |
| **might can could must** | + INFINITIVE |

> I'**ll see** you soon.
> She **won't agree**.
> Where **should I sit**?
> We **may go** by train.
> It **may not cost** much.
> **Can I park** here?
> I **couldn't hear** her.
> We **must pay** now.

4 We can use **make** + someone + infinitive, to mean 'cause' or 'force':
> The film **made me cry**.
> (= It caused me to cry.)
> They **made us leave**.
> (= They forced us to leave.)

5 We can use **let** + someone + infinitive, to mean 'allow':
> She **let me stay**. (= She allowed me to stay.)

Practice

A Put the verbs in brackets ( ) into these sentences. Use an infinitive (*phone*) or *to* + *infinitive* (*to phone*).

▶ You can't smoke......... (smoke) here. Smoking is not allowed in this building.

1 I'm sorry I forgot .... (phone) you yesterday. I was very busy.

2 Don't worry. The exam may not .... (be) very difficult.

3 Her mother makes her .... (clean) her room.

4 It's not a very good film. You won't .... (enjoy) it.

5 She didn't want .... (wait) any longer, so she left.

6 When are you planning .... (eat) tonight?

7 She couldn't .... (reply) because she didn't know what to say.

8 This kind of music makes me .... (feel) good.

9 My friend let me .... (drive) her car.

10 I'm afraid I've forgotten .... (bring) the map.

11 They might not .... (receive) the letter until next week.

3 Complete each sentence so that it has the same meaning as the sentence in brackets ( ).

► (I don't think it's a good idea to argue with him.)
I don't think you should argue with him.

1 (I won't be able to come to the meeting on Friday.)
I can't ....

2 (I'm meeting some friends tonight.)
I've arranged ....

3 (Listen to what I'm telling you.)
I want you ....

4 (It's important that you lock the door when you go out.)
Don't forget ....

5 (Perhaps we'll go out for a meal this evening.)
We may ....

6 (Allow me to pay for the meal.)
Let ....

7 (I'd like to do a course in Art History.)
I want ....

8 (He said, 'I'll pay the bill.')
He offered ....

9 (Should I sit in this chair?)
Do you want me ....

10 (His stories were very funny, and I laughed a lot.)
His funny stories made ....

11 (Perhaps he'll phone you tomorrow.)
He might ....

12 (It's possible that Tom won't be angry with you.)
Tom might not ....

13 (Jane allowed me to drive her new car.)
Jane let ....

C Complete the conversation, using the verbs in brackets ( ) with or without *to*.

Charlie: I want (►) to do .... (do) something interesting this weekend. Can we
(1)...................... (do) something together?

Carol: Well, I've arranged (2)...................... (go) on a trip to the coast with some
friends. Do you want (3)...................... (come) with us?

Charlie: Yes, that sounds good. When are you planning (4)...................... (leave)?

Carol: Well, we've decided (5)...................... (start) early in the morning tomorrow,
and I've promised (6)...................... (take) the others in my car. We're hoping
(7)...................... (reach) the coast by lunchtime. So, you must
(8)...................... (meet) me here at six thirty a.m.

Charlie: OK, good. I won't (9)...................... (be) late.

93 Verb + -ing; like and would like

1 Look at this example:

I like [-ing FORM *listening*] to music.

(For details on -ing forms, see Appendix 2 on page 243.)

We can use certain verbs (e.g. **like**) with an -**ing** form:

| like enjoy love keep finish stop mind hate | + -ing FORM |

*She doesn't **like cooking**.*
*Do you **enjoy driving**?*
*They **love living** in a village.*
*He **keeps saying** the same things.*
  (= He says the same things many times.)
*Have you **finished eating**?*
*Suddenly she **stopped talking**.*
*I don't **mind waiting**.*
*She **hates using** a drill.*

2 Compare this pair of sentences:

*I **like working** here. (= I enjoy my job here.)*
*I'd **like** (= I would like) to get a better job.*
  (= I want to get a better job.)

We use **like** + -**ing** (e.g. **like listening, like working**) to talk about things that we enjoy doing. We use **would like to** to say that we want to do something.:

*She **likes painting** pictures. (= She enjoys painting pictures.)*

*She **would like to be** an artist.*
  (= She wants to be an artist.)
*I **like going** to the theatre.*
  (= I enjoy going to the theatre.)
*I'd **like to go** to the theatre tonight.*
  (= I want to go to the theatre tonight.)
*Do you **like playing** cards?*
  (= Do you enjoy playing cards?)
***Would** you **like to play** cards now?*
  (= Do you want to play now?)

In offers and requests it is more polite to say **would like** than **want**:

***Would** you **like to come** for dinner? (offer)*
*I'd **like to leave** work early, please. (request)*

3 We use **go** + -**ing** for sports and hobbies that we go out to do, and with shopping:

*We often **go skiing** in the winter.*
*Let's **go swimming** this afternoon.*
*She **goes dancing** at weekends.*
*I'm **going shopping** this afternoon.*

4 We can use the -**ing** form of a verb as the subject of a sentence to talk about activities:
***Swimming** is a healthy activity.*

In sentences like this, we can use a noun, adverb or prepositional phrase after the -**ing** form:

***Riding** motorbikes can be dangerous.*
***Exercising** regularly is good for you.*
***Dancing** to this kind of music can be difficult.*

Practice

A **Complete the sentences using a Present Simple form of the first verb in brackets ( ). Study the example first.**

▶ She _likes playing_ (like/play) tennis, but she _doesn't like watching_ (not/like/watch) it.

1 The buses .... (stop/run) at midnight.

2 I .... (not/mind/listen) to his problems.

3 He's not very good at playing chess, so he .... (keep/lose).

4 She .... (enjoy/go) to other countries and she .... (like/meet) new people.

5 I .... (keep/make) the same stupid mistakes!

6 They usually .... (finish/eat) at about 8.30 in the evening.

7 She .... (not/enjoy/drive), but she .... (love/cycle).

3 Complete the sentences using *like/not like* + *-ing* or *would like* + *to* with the words in brackets ( ).

► She doesn't like working .... (work) here. She hates this job and is going to look for a better one.

► Would you like to watch ... (you/watch) a different programme, or do you want to watch this one?

1 I .... (live) here. I have lived here for many years and I think it's a nice town.

2 Sarah .... (be) a journalist when she leaves university. She wants to work on a newspaper or a magazine.

3 I .... (get up) so early every morning, but I have to do it.

4 I .... (go out) for dinner in an Italian restaurant tonight.

5 Clare .... (find) a job in the United States. She wants to work in Boston or in New York.

6 I .... (watch) television all the time; I think it's a waste of time.

7 Mary .... (lie) on the beach when she's on holiday. She doesn't like swimming or going on trips.

C Look at the pictures. They show what John did last week on holiday. Complete the sentences using the correct form of *go* and a verb from the box.

| dance |
| ~~shop~~ |
| sail |
| swim |
| ski |
| cycle |

►

Monday

1

Tuesday

2

Wednesday

3

Thursday

4

Friday

5

Saturday

► On Monday he went shopping. ....

1 On Tuesday ....

2 On Wednesday ....

3 On Thursday ....

4 On Friday ....

5 On Saturday ....

D Put the *-ing* form of one of these verbs in each sentence:

| eat   play   ~~walk~~   drive |

► Walking .... in the countryside is very pleasant at this time of year.

1 .... the guitar is his favourite hobby.

2 .... on motorways can be very tiring.

3 .... unhealthy things all the time is sure to be bad for you.

94 Verb + **to** or verb + **-ing**

1 Look at these sentences:

My sister promised to help me.
John doesn't want to wait.

We use **to** + **infinitive** after some verbs, e.g.:

afford	dare	decide	
deserve	want	hope	
learn	mean	offer	**+ to +**
pretend	promise	refuse	INFINITIVE
seem	plan	agree	
arrange	have (='must')		

2 Look at these sentences:

Have they finished painting the garage?
We enjoy sitting in the garden.

We use an **-ing** form after other verbs, e.g.:

avoid	dislike	enjoy	
finish	give up	imagine	**+ -ing**
keep	practise	stop	

3 Look at these sentences:

Jenny likes to stay at home.
Jenny likes staying at home.

These verbs can usually take an **-ing** form or **to** + **infinitive** with no difference in meaning:

begin	continue	hate	intend
like	love	prefer	start

But after **would hate, would like, would love** or **would prefer**, we use **to** + **infinitive**:

Would you like to go for a walk?
I'd love to visit Australia.

4 We can use an **-ing** form or **to** + **infinitive** after these verbs, but the meaning is different:

try	remember	forget

▶ *I tried to lift that heavy stone.* (= make an attempt: I made an attempt to lift the stone.)
  If you can't read where you are, try sitting nearer the window. (= Test something out: sit nearer the window and see if you can read there.)

▶ *Remember to go to the bank.*
  (= Remember that you must go to the bank.)
  She remembers going to the bank.
  (= She remembers that she went to the bank.)

▶ *Don't forget to phone Mrs Grey.*
  (= Remember that you must phone Mrs Grey.)
  I'll never forget seeing that castle.
  (= I saw that castle, and I'll always remember it.)

Practice

A Put in the correct form of the verb in brackets ( ).

▶ Paul dared to argue............. (argue) with the police.
▶ I can't imagine living................. (live) in the country.
1 We've decided .... (go) to the beach.
2 I stopped .... (play) tennis when I got married.
3 I meant .... (buy) some butter, but I forgot.
4 Did you promise .... (take) the children to the zoo?
5 Have the men finished .... (repair) the roof yet?
6 I'd love .... (visit) China.
7 You shouldn't avoid .... (talk) about your problems.
8 Peter refused .... (help) us.
9 Would you prefer .... (pay) now or later?
10 I couldn't afford .... (live) in London.
11 Why does Peter keep .... (talk) about his mother?

B Complete this conversation between Janet and Sharon with the correct form of the verbs in brackets ( ).

Janet: What do your children (▶) *want to do* .... (want/do) when they leave school?

Sharon: Well, Ann (▶) *enjoys writing* .... (enjoy/write), so she's (▶) *hoping to work* ...... (hope/work) for a newspaper. But I don't know about Paul. He (1) .... (give up/study) months ago. He seems to (2) .... (enjoy/do) nothing now. He doesn't (3) .... (deserve/pass) his exams. And he (4) .... (refuse/listen) to us, when we tell him to (5) .... (keep/study).

Janet: With our children, in the past, if we (6) .... (offer/help) them, they always (7) .... (promise/study) hard. Nowadays if they (8) .... (want/talk) to us, that's fine, but I've learnt to (9) .... (stop/ask) them questions. I suppose they (10) .... (dislike/listen) to my suggestions. They (11) .... (seem/think) that they don't (12) .... (need/study) hard, but one day they'll (13) .... (have/find) a job.

C Use an *-ing* form, or *to + infinitive*, of the word in brackets ( ) to complete each sentence.

▶ You say that I've met Janet, but I can't remember her.
  I can't remember *meeting* ...... (meet) Janet.
1 Please remember that you must buy some stamps.
  Please remember .... (buy) some stamps.
2 We wanted to open the door, but we couldn't.
  We tried .... (open) the door.
3 John met Madonna once. He'll never forget it.
  John will never forget .... (meet) Madonna.
4 Sheila intended to phone Peter, but she forgot.
  Sheila forgot .... (phone) Peter.
5 Jenny had a headache. She took an aspirin, but it didn't help.
  Jenny tried .... (take) an aspirin for her headache.
6 I have a special soap that will probably get your hands clean.
  Try .... (wash) your hands with this special soap.
7 It will not be easy to do all the work today.
  We'll try .... (finish) the work before tonight.
8 I stayed in Jane's flat while she was on holiday. I remembered that I had to feed her cats every day.
  I remembered .... (feed) Jane's cats every day while she was on holiday.
9 Remember that you must invite Mary to the party next week.
  Don't forget .... (invite) Mary to the party next week.

95 Purpose: **for ...ing**

1 Look at this dialogue:
   A: *What's this machine for?*
   B: *It's for cutting cloth.*

The question **What is it for?** asks about the purpose of something (what we use something for). When we describe the purpose of a thing, we use **for + -ing.** Here are some more examples:
   This is an instrument for measuring wind speed.
   This tool is used for making holes.

2 Now look at this dialogue:
   A: *What does he need my camera for?*
     (= Why does he need my camera?)
   B: *He needs it for his work.* (= His work is the reason why he needs the camera.)

The question **What ... for?** asks about purpose. To talk about someone's purpose, we can use **for + noun.** Here are some more examples:
   A: *What did he go to the shops for?*
   B: *He went to the shops for some fruit.*
     (He wanted to buy some fruit.)

*I buy the newspaper **for the sports news.***
(= ... in order to read the sports news.)

3 Now look at this dialogue:
   A: *What does he need my camera for?*
   B: *He needs it to take some photos.*
     (= ... in order to take some photos.)

To talk about someone's purpose, we can also use **to + infinitive** (e.g. **to take**). Here are some more examples:
   *He went to the shops **to buy** some fruit.*
     (= ... in order to buy some fruit.)

*John phoned the police **to tell** them about the burglar.*

Practice

A Make definitions of the things in box A using one of the phrases from box B.

A	B
telescope — instrument	boil water
~~hammer — tool~~	measure temperature
fridge — appliance	~~knock in nails~~
kettle — appliance	clean carpets
thermometer — instrument	see things at a distance
vacuum cleaner — appliance	keep food cold
drill — tool	measure speed
speedometer — instrument	keep food frozen
freezer — appliance	make holes

▶ A hammer *is a tool for knocking in nails.*

1 A kettle ....

2 A thermometer ....

3 A vacuum cleaner ....

4 A fridge ....

5 A telescope ....

6 A speedometer ....

7 A freezer ....

8 A drill ....

3 In the following short dialogues, use *What ... for?* to make questions from the words in brackets ( ). Then write a reply using the words in brackets and *for*.

▶ A: (/did/Tom/go/to the park/?) What did Tom go to the park for?
   B: (He/go/to the park/some fresh air.) He went to the park for some fresh air.

1 A: (/does/Mary/want/the money/?) ....
   B: (She/want/the money/a train ticket.) ....

2 A: (/does/Philip/want/the flour/?) ....
   B: (He/want/the flour/a cake.) ....

3 A: (/did/Bill/go/to the butcher's/?) ....
   B: (He/go/to the butcher's/some sausages.) ....

4 A: (/does/Helen/want/the polish/?) ....
   B: (She/want/it/her shoes.) ....

5 A: (/did/Alison/go/to the library/?) ....
   B: (She/go/to the library/a book on India.) ....

6 A: (/did/Jane/phone/Ann/?) ....
   B: (She/phone/Ann/some advice.) ....

C Now write the answers from exercise B using one of the verbs in the box, as in the example. Use each verb once.

borrow	buy (x2)	clean	get (x2)	make

▶ Tom: He went to the park to get some fresh air.
1 Mary: ....
2 Philip: ....
3 Bill: ....
4 Helen: ....
5 Alison: ....
6 Jane: ....

D Find the errors and rewrite the sentences correctly.

▶ This machine is for make pasta. This machine is for making pasta.
1 For what did he come? ....
2 A bus is for carry passengers. ....
3 She went to the post office for to buy some stamps.

   ....
4 The mayor came for give the prizes. ....
5 The woman jumped into the river to saving the child.

   ....
6 I'm training hard for to get fit. ....
7 This is a computer program for make three-dimensional drawings.

   ....
8 Can I use your pen for signing this letter? ....

96 Verb + object (+ **to**) + infinitive

1 Look at these examples:

> Carol said to Bob:
>   *'Make some coffee, please.'*
> We can say:
>   *Carol **asked Bob to make** some coffee.*

> Ann said to Rose:
>   *'Can you come to my party, Rose?'*
> We can say:
>   *Ann **invited Rose to come** to her party.*

> Tom thinks Chris should see a doctor.
> He can say:
>   *I'll **persuade Chris to go** to the doctor's.*

The structure is:

VERB	+	OBJECT	+ **to** +	INFINITIVE
She asked		*Jill*	*to*	*wait.*
She asked		*her*	*to*	*wait.*

We use these verbs in this structure:

tell	force	teach	
help	allow	would like	
ask	invite	encourage	+ OBJECT + **to**
want	forbid	persuade	
advise	remind		

2 Note that the first verb can change its tense, but the second verb is always **to + infinitive** (**to make**):

> *She **is asking** Bob* ⎫
> *She **will ask** Bob* ⎬ *to make some coffee.*
> *She **has asked** Bob* ⎭

Note that if we use a pronoun, we use **me, him, her, it, us, you, them** (object pronouns) after the verb:

> *Carol asked **him** to make some coffee.*

3 Now look at these two sentences:

> *The teacher **let Jane leave** school early.*
> *I **made him tell** me the truth.*

Let here means 'allow', and **make** means 'force' or 'order'. **Make** and **let** are followed by an infinitive (without **to**):

	VERB	+ OBJECT	+ INFINITIVE
She	*let*	*Jane*	*leave.*

Feel, hear, see and **watch** can also be followed by an infinitive (without **to**):

> *I **heard** your sister **shout** 'Fire!'*
> (NOT ... ~~to shout~~ ...)
> *Tom **saw** a car **come** round the corner.*

Practice

A Write complete sentences from the words in brackets ( ). Be careful to use the correct tense.

▶ (Tomorrow/I/encourage/Janet/enter/the competition.)
  Tomorrow I will encourage Janet to enter the competition.

▶ (I was already tired, but I/force/myself/go on working.)
  I was already tired, but I forced myself to go on working.

1 (Ann/teach/Mary/drive/last year.)

  ....

2 (Don't worry! Tomorrow I/persuade/my father/see/a doctor.)

  ....

3 (The boss has/forbid/his staff/wear/jeans in the office.)

  ....

4 (Last Sunday, John/invite/Sheila/come/for lunch.)

  ....

5 (Next year the teachers/allow/the students/use/calculators in exams.)

  ....

3 Use the words in brackets ( ) to complete the sentences.

▶ (Policewoman: 'Can everyone please stay indoors?')
The policewoman asked everyone to stay indoors.

1 (Jane: 'Remember to come home early, Tim.')
Jane reminded Tim ....

2 (Manager: 'You must work more quickly.')
The boss wants us ....

3 (Captain: 'Let's do our best in the game.')
The captain encouraged us ....

4 (Jo: 'Can you come to my party next Saturday?')
Jo invited me ....

C Answer the questions, changing the nouns (e.g. *Michael*) to pronouns (e.g. *him*). Be careful to use the correct tense.

▶ A: Did Nicola tell Michael to be careful?
B: Yes, she told him to be careful.

1 A: Would Kate like Peter to stay?
B: Yes, ...

2 A: Did Mrs Slater help her son to finish?
B: Yes, ...

3 A: Did the doctor advise Michael to stay in bed?
B: Yes, ...

4 A: Does Susan allow her children to go to late-night parties?
B: Yes, ...

5 A: Did Mary remind Mark to phone?
B: Yes, ...

D Write a sentence with a similar meaning, using the verb in brackets ( ).

▶ The police told everyone to leave the building.
(make) The police made everyone leave the building.

1 The driver allowed the old man to travel on the bus without a ticket.
(let) ....

2 Jack told his younger brother to wash the dishes.
(make) ....

3 I don't allow people to smoke in my house or in my car!
(let) ....

E Combine the two sentences into one.

▶ Your sister shouted 'fire!'. I heard her.
I heard your sister shout 'Fire!'.

1 Tom prepared the sandwiches. Diane watched him.
Diane ....

2 The ground shook. We felt it.
We ....

3 Brian left early. Did you see him?
Did you ....

Test I: Verbs, passives, infinitives, -ing forms

A Chris and Graham are walking in the mountains. If the words in brackets ( ) are wrong, cross them out and rewrite them. If they're right, put a tick (✓).

Graham: (We're getting) (►) ✓............. lost. What shall we do?

Chris: (~~We did~~) (►) We made..... a mistake an hour ago. We took the wrong road.

Graham: (I've got) (1)............... a headache, and (I'm making) (2)............... more and more tired.

Chris: Try not to worry. (I got) (3)............... some aspirin in my bag.

Graham: It's cold! (Do you have) (4)............... an extra jumper?

Chris: I think we'll have to stop for the night. (It's getting) (5)............... dark.

Graham: What do you mean? (We haven't done) (6)............... a tent!

Chris: Try to stay calm. (We'll make) (7)............... a fire and (we'll have got) (8)............... a meal.

Graham: I suppose you're going (to make) (9)............... the shopping!

Chris: We're OK. (I've got) (10)............... some tea and some cheese and pasta in my bag.

Graham: What if it rains?

Chris: Stop worrying! I've got a job for you (to make) (11)............... . Go and find some wood.

Graham: I want (to have got) (12)............... a hot bath!

Chris: Now (you're making) (13)............... me angry. Let's get busy!

B Christine is talking to her doctor. Add the missing words from the box.

it (x3)	~~gets~~	put	ran	out	in	down

                                        gets
'I'm worried about my husband. He ⋀ up very late. He never wants to go. You can't stay all your life, can you, Doctor? If the TV is on when our friends come round, he doesn't turn off. Last Saturday we out of milk. When we reached the supermarket, he said to me: 'I don't like your hat. Take off! Put away!' That's a strange thing to say, Doctor. I'm getting more and more worried. I don't think I can up with the situation much longer. When I try to talk to him he just says: 'Calm! I'm alright.' What shall I do?

C Look at this conversation. Make it more natural by using the passive form in all the sentences with the word 'someone'.

Anne: Well, we watched this TV programme about moving to Spain, and we decided to go. (►) Someone has packed our bags. We're ready to leave!

Celia: We wouldn't leave England, would we, John? (1) Someone decorated our house last month. It looks beautiful. (2) And someone is designing a summer house for the garden.

John: (3) But someone also stole our car last week. Perhaps Spain is a good idea, after all.

Celia: Anyway, I hope you two know what you're doing! Our neighbours went to France, and when they got there, (4) someone hadn't built their new house! So they bought an old chateau instead. (5) After someone repaired the windows, (6) and someone mended the roof, they got bored!

Mick: (7) Well, someone has made our decision. (8) Someone booked our flight yesterday.

(9) Someone is selling our house next month. We're on our way!

▶ Our bags *have been packed.* ....
1 Our house ....
2 And a summerhouse ....
3 But our car ....
4 their new house ....
5 their windows ....
6 and the roof ....
7 Well, our decision ....
8 Our flight ....
9 Our house ....

D Margaret is replying to a letter from a new friend. In the gaps, use the infinitive without changing it, or add *to* or change it to the *-ing* form.

'It was nice to hear from you. You asked me to tell you as much as I could about myself, so I will! To begin with, I don't like (▶) *cooking* .... (cook). And I hate (1) .... (wash) up. I can't (2) .... (drive), but I'm planning (3) .... (learn) one day! I gave up (4) .... (smoke) ten years ago. You don't (5) .... (smoke), do you? What else can I (6) .... (tell) you? Onions and old films make me (7) .... (cry). I go (8) .... (dance) on Sunday afternoons. And I don't mind (9) .... (walk) in the rain. I think that's almost everything about me. Oh yes. I've decided (10) .... (get) fit. (11) .... (Jog) regularly makes me (12) .... (feel) better, but I don't like (13) .... (cycle), and I love (14) .... (eat) chocolate! If you want me (15) .... (continue), you'll have to write back! (But I'd rather hear about you.)'

E Will is talking to his boss. Rewrite the words in brackets ( ), adding *to* if necessary, or changing the infinitive to the *-ing* form.

Will: You promised (give/me) a new job after two years here. (▶) *to give me* ....
Boss: Yes, but you must (finish/do) the job you've got. (1) ....
Will: But I would (prefer/start) something new now. (2) ....
Boss: Try (be/patient)! What did you join the company for? (3) ....
Will: I wanted (do/something) interesting, I suppose. (4) ....
Boss: And I allowed (you/do) lots of different things, didn't I? (5) ....
Will: And now you are asking (me/do) the same thing every day!
      (6) ....
Boss: I've seen (you/improve) so much! Just keep going a little longer.
      (7) ....
Will: You can't make (me/stay) in this job. (8) ....
Boss: No, I can't. But I can encourage (you/think) about the future.
      (9) ....

97 Zero Conditional and First Conditional

1 Look at this:

If + PRESENT SIMPLE	+ PRESENT SIMPLE
If I **eat** too much,	I **feel** bad.

(= Every time I eat too much, I feel bad.)

We use this structure (**if + Present Simple + Present Simple**) for facts that are generally true. This structure is called the Zero Conditional:

> If I **don't get** enough sleep, I **feel** tired.
> (= Every time I don't get enough sleep, I feel tired.)
> If you **want** to become a doctor, you **have to** study hard. (= Anyone who wants to become a doctor has to study hard.)

2 We can say the same thing by reversing the two parts of the sentence:

PRESENT SIMPLE	+ **if**	+ PRESENT SIMPLE
I **feel** bad	if	I **eat** too much.

Note that we do not use a comma (,) before if.

3 Now look at this:

If + PRESENT SIMPLE	+ WILL/WON'T
If I'm late,	she'll be angry.

(= Perhaps I will be late; then she'll be angry.)

We use this structure (**if + Present Simple + will/won't**) to talk about things that may happen in the future. The verb after **if** is Present Simple, but we use it for a possible future action or situation; we use **will/won't** + **verb** for the result. This structure is called the First Conditional:

FUTURE POSSIBILITY	+ RESULT
If we **don't hurry**,	we **won't finish**.

4 We can reverse the order:
> She'll be angry **if** I'm late.
> We won't finish **if** we don't hurry.

5 We do not use **will/won't** after **if**:
> NOT ~~If I will be late, she'll be angry.~~

Practice

A Put these facts about various types of people into sentences with *if + Present Simple + Present Simple*. Make *you* the subject of both parts of the sentence.

▶ Doctors treat people who are ill.
  If you're a doctor, you treat people who are ill. ....

1 Vegetarians don't eat meat.
  If you're a vegetarian, ...

2 People who live in a hot country don't like cold weather.
  If you live ....

3 Teachers have to work very hard.
  If you're a teacher, ...

4 People who do a lot of exercise stay fit and healthy.
  If you ....

5 Mechanics understand engines.
  If you're a ....

6 People who read newspapers know what's happening in the world.
  If you ....

3 Complete these sentences with *if + Present Simple + will/won't*, using the words in brackets ( ). Sometimes you do not need to change the words in brackets.

▶ If <u>it rains</u> (it/rain), <u>we won't go</u> (we/not/go) out.

1 If .... (the weather/be) nice tomorrow, ... (we/drive) to the coast.

2 If .... (she/post) the letter now, ... (they/receive) it tomorrow.

3 .... (Fiona/be) angry if .... (John/arrive) late again.

4 .... (I/go) to their party if .... (I/have) enough time.

5 If .... (she/not/pass) this exam, ... (she/not/get) the job that she wants.

6 .... (you/learn) a lot if .... (you/take) this course.

7 If .... (I/get) a ticket, ... (I/go) to the concert.

8 .... (I/buy) that camera if .... (it/not/cost) too much.

9 If .... (you/run) very fast, ... (you/catch) the bus.

10 .... (I/go) to the doctor's if .... (I/not/feel) better tomorrow.

11 If .... (they/win) this game, ... (they/be) the champions.

C Complete the dialogues with the Present Simple or *will/won't* forms of the words in brackets ( ). Sometimes you do not need to change the words in brackets.

▶ A: We must be at the airport at two o'clock.
  B: Well, if <u>we take</u> (we/take) a taxi at one o'clock, <u>we won't be</u> (we/not/be) late.

1 A: I'd like a newspaper.
  B: Well, ... (I/buy) one for you if .... (I/go) to the shop later.

2 A: Has John phoned yet?
  B: No, and if .... (he/not/phone) this afternoon, ... (I/phone) him this evening.

3 A: Is Fiona there, please?
  B: No, but if .... (you/want) to leave a message, ... (I/give) it to her.

4 A: Is Tim going to pass his exam?
  B: Well, ... (he/fail) if .... (he/not/work) harder.

5 A: Could I have some information about this year's concerts, please?
  B: Yes, if .... (you/fill in) this form, ... (I/send) it to you in the post.

98 Second Conditional

1 Look at this sentence:

*If Charlie Chaplin **was** alive today, he **would be** over 100 years old.*

Of course, Chaplin isn't alive today. The sentence imagines something that is not true. The verb after **if** is Past Simple, but it refers to the present. This structure is called the Second Conditional:

If + PAST SIMPLE	+ **would** (or 'd)
If	*he **worked** harder,*	*he **would do** better.*

Another example is someone who doesn't have enough money to buy a new car and says:

*I'd **buy** a new car if I **had** enough money.*

Note that we do not use a comma (,) before **if**.

2 We can use the same type of sentence to talk about the future:

If + PAST SIMPLE	+ **would** (or'd)
If	*I **won** a lot of money,*	*I'd **buy** a big house.*

This sentence describes an unlikely future situation: it is unlikely that I will win a lot of money.

3 We can use **wish** to say that we want something to be different from how it is now. Note that the verb after **wish** is past (e.g. **could, was, had**):

I wish you could talk

*I **wish** (that) Chaplin **was** still alive.*
*Mary **wishes** she **had** enough money for a new dress.*
*I **wish** I **was** very rich.*

4 After **if** and after **wish**, we sometimes use I/he/she/it with **were**:

*If he **were** (OR was) alive today, …*
*I **wish** Charlie Chaplin **were** (OR was) still alive.*

Notice also the expression **if I were you**, when you give someone advice:

*If I **were** you, I'd go to the police.*
(NOT ~~If I was you,~~ …)

Practice

A Complete these sentences.

▶ If Sally lived in Brighton, she <u>would be</u>............... (she/be) near her parents.

▶ Fred would read more if <u>he didn't work</u>....... (he/not/work) so hard.

1 If Elizabeth didn't have to work in the evenings, ... (she/go) to concerts.

2 Susan wouldn't go to work by car if .... (she/live) near a train station.

3 Alan wouldn't be overweight if .... (he/not/eat) so much.

4 If Peter didn't live in a flat, ... (he/have) a dog.

5 Pam would definitely learn French if .... (she/get) a job in France.

6 If Mark wanted to be healthy, ... (he/not/smoke).

3 In the next few years:

> It is unlikely that astronauts will visit Mars.
> It is unlikely that governments will stop buying guns.
> It is unlikely that doctors will find a cure for cancer.
> It is unlikely that they will discover oil in Ireland.
> It is unlikely that young people will stop buying CDs.

Now use the predictions in the box to complete these sentences.

▶ If *governments stopped buying guns* .... , the world would be safer.

1 If .... , the Irish would be very happy.

2 If .... , this terrible disease would disappear.

3 If .... , the popular music industry would disappear.

4 If .... , we would learn a lot about the planet.

C A manager tells people why they can't have a job. Write their thoughts with *I wish*.

▶ You don't have a driving licence, so you can't have the job.
  I wish *I had a driving licence.* ....

▶ You can't have the job because you can't type.
  I wish *I could type.* ....

1 You can't have the job because you don't have good eyesight.
  I wish ....

2 You can't speak German, so you can't have the job.
  I wish ....

3 You don't have a degree, so you can't have the job.
  I wish ....

4 You can't have the job because you are not eighteen.
  I wish ....

D Imagine how life nowadays could be better. Complete the sentences using the words in brackets ( ), and any other words you need.

▶ People don't do enough exercise, so there is a lot of heart disease.
  (more, less) If people *did more exercise* .... , there *would be less* ....
  heart disease

1 There are too many cars. The city is very polluted.
  (fewer) I wish there .... , then the city wouldn't be very polluted.

2 People drive too fast, so there are a lot of accidents.
  (more slowly) I wish people .... , then there would be fewer
  accidents.

3 People watch too much TV, so they don't have much time for reading.
  (more) If people watched less TV, they ....

4 Children have bad teeth because they eat too many sweets.
  (fewer) Children would have better teeth if they ....

5 Not enough people travel by bus, so the roads are crowded.
  (more) I wish .... , then the roads would be less crowded.

6 People haven't got enough time to cook, so they eat a lot of 'fast food'.
  (more, less) If people .... , they ....

99 Third Conditional

1 Look at this sentence:

*If Charlie Chaplin **had died** in 1989, he **would have been** 100 years old.*

Chaplin did not in fact die in 1989. He died before he was 100 years old. The sentence imagines something that did not happen in the past. This structure is called the Third Conditional:

> If + PAST PERFECT + **would have** (or **'d have**)
> + **past participle**
> *If he **had tried** harder, he **would have** won.*

Here is another example:

*If Jane **had come** on her usual train, I **would have seen** her.* (She didn't come on her usual train, so I didn't see her.)

Notice how we can also use the negative forms **wouldn't have** and **hadn't**:

*John F. Kennedy **wouldn't have died** in 1963 if he **hadn't gone** to Dallas.* (Kennedy died in 1963 because he went to Dallas, but this sentence imagines the opposite.)
*I **would have phoned** you if I **hadn't lost** your phone number.* (I didn't phone you because I lost your phone number.)
*I **wouldn't have gone** to the museum if I had known it was shut.* (I went to the museum because I didn't know it was shut.)

2 We can use **wish + had done** to talk about the past when we are sorry that something didn't happen, and we imagine that it did:

*He **wishes** he **had studied** harder at school.* (He didn't study hard, and now he's sorry about it.)
*I woke up very late this morning. I **wish** I **had gone** to bed earlier last night.*

We can use a negative form (**wish ... hadn't done**) to say that we are sorry that something did happen:

*Many people **wish** that John F. Kennedy **hadn't gone** to Dallas.* (Many people are sorry that John F. Kennedy went to Dallas.)

Practice

A Read this story about Ellen.

> In May 1992 Ellen lost her job in London. She didn't have much money in the bank, so she was very worried. She looked in the newspapers and she saw an advertisement for a job as a translator from German into English. She didn't speak German very well, so she didn't apply for it. In June, she heard about some teaching jobs abroad because a friend phoned to tell her about them. She phoned the company, and they asked her to go for an interview with the director. Ellen thought the interview went badly, but in fact the director was happy with the interview and offered Ellen a job in Spain. However, Ellen couldn't start at once because she didn't know any Spanish. She took a course to learn the language. She was good at languages and she made rapid progress. So, by September she had a new job, and she still had a little money left in the bank.

Now write sentences using the words in brackets ( ).

▶ (If Ellen/have/a lot of money in the bank, she/not/be/so worried.)
  If Ellen had had a lot of money in the bank, she wouldn't have been so worried.

▶ (If she/not/look/in the newspapers, she/not/see/the advertisement.)
  If she hadn't looked in the newspapers, she wouldn't have seen the advertisement.

1 (If she/speak/German very well, she/apply/for the job.)

....

2 (If her friend/not/phone, she/not/hear/about the teaching jobs.)

....

3 (If she/not/contact/the company, they/not/ask/her to go for an interview.)

....

4 (If the interview/go/badly, the director/not/offer/Ellen a job.)

....

5 (If Ellen/know/some Spanish, she/start/at once.)

....

6 (If she/not/be/good at languages, she/not/make/rapid progress.)

....

3 Use the information in brackets ( ) to complete these sentences.

▶ (Sam didn't get the job as a translator because he failed the exam.)
Sam _would have got_ the job as a translator if he _had_ not
failed the exam.

1 (Alan lost our phone number, so he didn't phone us.)
If Alan .... not .... phone number, he .... us.

2 (Sally broke her leg, so she didn't go on holiday.)
If Sally .... not .... her leg, she .... on holiday.

3 (We didn't make a cake because we forgot to buy any eggs.)
We .... a cake if we .... not .... to buy
some eggs.

C Write sentences about these people who are sorry about things they did in the past.
Use *wish* or *wishes*.

▶ Ian wasted his time at school; now he's sorry.
Ian wishes he hadn't wasted his time at school. ....

1 I didn't tell the truth; now I'm sorry.
I wish ....

2 John borrowed some money from his mother; now he's sorry.
John ....

3 Mary didn't get up early; now she's sorry.
Mary ....

4 Peter didn't go to the party; now he's sorry.
Peter ....

5 I didn't send Jill a birthday card; now I'm sorry.
I ....

6 Fiona didn't help her sister; now she's sorry.

....

7 He shouted at the children; now he's sorry.

....

100 Reported speech (1)

1 When we report something that somebody said, we usually change the tense of the verb like this:

ACTUAL WORDS	REPORTED SPEECH
Present Simple →	Past Simple
'I **live** in a small flat,' she said.	She said she **lived** in a small flat.
Present Continuous →	Past Continuous
'**I'm leaving** on Tuesday,' I said.	I said that I **was leaving** on Tuesday.
Past Simple Present Perfect } →	Past Perfect
'I **learnt** a lot,' he said.	He said he **had learnt** a lot.
'Mr Jackson **has left**,' she said.	She said that Mr Jackson **had left**.
will →	would
'**I'll help** you,' she said.	She said she **would help** me.
am/is/are going to →	was/were going to
'**We're going to be** late,' I said.	I said that we **were going to be** late.
can →	could
'I **can't find** my money,' he said.	He said he **couldn't find** his money.

2 Note that it is not necessary to use **that** in reported speech:

*She said (**that**) she knew the answer.*

3 Compare **say** and **tell** in these sentences:
*She **said** (that) she lived in a small flat.*
*She **told me** (that) she lived in a small flat.*

We **say something**. We do not **say someone something**.
She said she was going to be late.
(NOT ~~She said me she was~~ ...)
I said that I disagreed with him.
(NOT ~~I said him that I~~ ...)

We **tell someone something**. We do not **tell something**.
He told me he was happy.
(NOT ~~He told he was happy.~~)
He told me that he would pay me immediately.
(NOT ~~He told that he would pay me immediately.~~)
She told Fred she was going to meet someone.
(NOT ~~She told that she was going to meet someone.~~)

Practice

A Look at these pictures of people coming through passport control at an airport. Change the things they said into reported speech.

▶ He said _that he was visiting friends._

1 She said ....

2 He said ....

3 They said ....

4 She said ....

B Read this conversation and then report what Claudia and Nicole said.

Nicole: How long have you been in France?
Claudia: Six weeks.
Nicole: Are you enjoying your stay?
Claudia: Yes, I'm enjoying it a lot.
Nicole: Have you been here before?
Claudia: Yes. I've been to France many times.
Nicole: What are you doing here?
Claudia: I'm on holiday.
Nicole: Are you staying in a hotel?
Claudia: No, I'm staying with some friends.
Nicole: Where do they live?
Claudia: They have a flat in the city centre.
Nicole: How long are you staying?
Claudia: I'm leaving in March.
Nicole: Can you speak French very well?
Claudia: No, I can't. I'm going to have some lessons.
Nicole: I'll teach you.

▶ Claudia said _(that) she had been_ .... in France for six weeks.
1 Claudia said .... her stay a lot.
2 Claudia said .... to France many times.
3 Claudia said .... on holiday.
4 She said .... with some friends.
5 She said .... a flat in the city centre.
6 She said .... in March.
7 She said .... French very well.
8 She said .... some lessons.
9 Nicole said .... Claudia.

C Complete the sentences with *said* or *told*.

▶ She _said_ .... she wasn't feeling very well.
1 Alex .... me that he would buy the tickets.
2 They .... that the train was going to be late.
3 She .... him that she was very angry with him.
4 She .... him that she couldn't help him.
5 Who .... you that I was leaving? It's not true!
6 They .... us that they were leaving in the morning.
7 He .... that he didn't know what was wrong with the car.
8 She .... she had four sisters.
9 She .... me that Tom worked in a factory.
10 He .... me that he was a doctor, but he .... Anna that he was
   a dentist.

101 Reported speech (2)

1 REQUESTS

There are different ways to make a request, e.g.:

Sarah: '*Please wait a minute, Tom.*'
Sarah: '*Will you wait a minute, please?*'
Sarah: '*Tom, could you wait a minute, please?*'

We can report all of these requests in the same way, using **asked**:

*Sarah **asked** Tom to wait a minute.*

We do not usually use **please** in a reported question.

2 ORDERS

There are different ways to give an order:

'*Stand up, John.*'
'*You must work harder.*'

We can report orders like this, using **told**:

*He **told** John to stand up.*
*He **told** me to work harder.*

3 ADVICE

We can give advice like this:

'*You should get married, Peter.*'
'*You should stop smoking, Jane.*'

We can report advice like this, using **advised**:

*He **advised** Peter to get married.*
*He **advised** Jane to stop smoking.*

4 In reported speech, we use **ask**, **tell** and **advise** like this:

VERB	+ OBJECT	+ to +	INFINITIVE
Sarah	*asked*	*Tom*	*to wait.*
She	*told*	*him*	*to stand.*
He	*advised*	*Jane*	*to stop smoking.*

Here is a list of common verbs that we use in this structure:

advise	ask	tell	order
persuade	remind	forbid	warn

Examples:

I'll remind them to come early.
I advised them to go to the police.

We cannot use **say** in this structure:

She said (that) he should wait.
(NOT ~~She said him to wait.~~)

5 To report a negative request, order, etc. (e.g. '*Don't laugh*'), we use **not + to + infinitive**:

VERB +	OBJECT +	not + to + INFINITIVE
Sara told	*Tom*	*not to laugh.*
They warned	*Ian*	*not to borrow money.*
I reminded	*John*	*not to be late.*

Practice

A Rewrite the sentences using an *object* + *to* + *infinitive*, as in the example.

▶ 'Make some coffee please, Bob.'
Carol asked *Bob to make some coffee.* ....

1 'You must do the homework soon, Jane.'
She told ....

2 'Remember to buy a map, Ann.'
He reminded ....

3 'You should see a doctor, Mrs Clark.'
He advised ....

4 'Keep all the windows closed, Bill.'
They warned ....

5 'Go home, Paul.'
Francis told ....

3 Report what these people said using the words in brackets ( ). Use the Past Simple.

▶ Fred said, 'Anne, would you lend me five pounds, please?'
(ask) *Fred asked Anne to lend him five pounds.* ....

1 I said to John, 'Remember to phone Sally.'
(remind) ....

2 'You must wash your hands, children,' the teacher said.
(tell) ....

3 'Mary, please lend me your bicycle pump,' said Paul.
(ask) ....

4 She said, 'Children, stay away from the water.'
(warn) ....

5 'You should see a lawyer,' the policeman said to Mark.
(advise) ....

C Complete the conversations using the words in brackets ( ). You will also need a pronoun (e.g. *me, him, them*) and the word *not.* Use the Past Simple.

▶ A: Did you tell the children to clean the car?   B: (Yes, but I/tell/to use too much water.)
B: *Yes, but I told them not to use too much water.* ....

1 A: Did you ask Bill to come to the meeting?   B: (Yes, and I/tell/to be late.)
B: ....

2 A: Did the doctor tell Sue to keep warm?   B: (Yes, and she/warn/to go outside the house.)

B: ....

3 A: Did you ask Michael to post the letters?   B: (Yes, and I/tell/to forget the stamps.)
B: ....

4 A: Did the policeman advise everyone to stay indoors?   B: (Yes, and he/tell/to go near the windows.)

B: ....

5 A: Did the dentist advise you to eat carefully?   B: (Yes, and she particularly/warn/to eat nuts.)

B: ....

D Complete the sentences using the words in the box. Use each word once.

| advise | ask | order | remind | ~~tell~~ | warn |

▶ The official said to Gerry, 'Go to Room 23.' The official *told him to go* .... to Room 23.

1 'Girls, you mustn't touch these wires. It can be dangerous,' said the guide.
The guide .... the wires.

2 'The bus is all right, Anne, but it's better for you to take the train,' we said.
We .... the train.

3 'Bring the money, Simon. Don't forget,' Mrs Walters said.
Mrs Walters .... the money.

4 'This is the police,' the voice said. 'Spectators must leave at once.'
The police .... at once.

5 I said, 'Please come in, Mr Tufnell.' I .... in.

102 Reported questions

1 'Yes/no' questions have a form of **be** (e.g. **is**, **are**) or an auxiliary verb (e.g. **can**, **do**, **have**) that goes before the subject:

	SUBJECT	
'*Are*	*they*	*English?*'
'*Can*	*John*	*type?*'

We report these questions with **ask if/ whether**:

	SUBJECT	
She asked if	*they*	*were English.*
She asked if	*John*	*could type.*

or:

*She asked **whether** they **were** English.*
*She asked **whether** John **could** type.*

Note that in a reported question we do not put **be** or an auxiliary before the subject (NOT *She asked were they English.*)

2 Many questions begin with a question word (**Who, What, Where**, etc.):

	SUBJECT	
'*Where does*	*Ann*	*live?*'
'*Why has*	*Jane*	*gone ?*'

We report these questions with **ask**:

	SUBJECT	
*They asked **where***	*Ann*	*lived.*
*She asked **why***	*Jane*	*had gone.*

3 We can also **ask someone something**:
*The manager asked **me** if I could type.*
*They asked **him** where Sarah lived.*

4 Note that when we report a question that somebody asked, we usually change the tense of the verb:
'*Can John swim?*'
*He asked if John **could** swim.*

The most common tense changes are:

▶ Present → Past:
am/is → was	are → were
is living → was living	live → lived

▶ Present Perfect → Past Perfect:
has gone → had gone

▶ Past Simple → Past Perfect:
arrived → had arrived

▶ Modals:
will → would   can → could

We often also change other words, for example:
'*Have **you** finished, Mike?*'
*She asked Mike if **he** had finished.*

5 We can use **wanted to know** and **wondered** instead of **asked**:
*She **wanted to know** if they were English.*
(OR *She wanted to know **whether** they were English.*)
*She **wondered** why Jane had gone.*

Practice

A **Change each sentence into reported speech or a direct question by filling in the gaps. End each sentence with a full stop (.) or a question mark (?).**

▶ (Did they come?) She asked *if*............. they had come ....

▶ (I asked him where he worked.) *Where*........ do you work *?*......

1 (Do you speak English?) They asked me .... I spoke English ....

2 (I wanted to know why he had taken my key.) .... did you take my key........

3 (How many people came to the party?) I asked .... people had come to the party........

4 (Does Ann work on Saturdays?) I asked .... Ann worked on Saturdays........

5 (Can we meet tomorrow?) I asked .... we could meet tomorrow........

6 (I asked what he had done.) .... has he done........

7 (Was Tom born in 1965 or 1966?) I asked them .... Tom was born........
8 (Why has Jane gone home?) I asked .... Jane had gone home........
9 (Where do you go for your holidays?) I wanted to know .... they went for their holidays........
10 (Is Bill coming to the party, Jane?) I asked Jane .... Bill was coming to the party........

B Use the words in brackets ( ) to write a question, and then complete the reported question.

▶ (Where/have/Maria/go/?) Question: Where has Maria gone? ....
Reported question: I asked where Maria had gone. ....
1 (Do/Jim/often/play/football/?) Question: ....
Reported question: I wondered if ....
2 (What/have/the children/eat/?) Question: ....
Reported question: She wanted to know ....
3 (Where/be/Mark/going/?) Question: ....
Reported question: I asked ....
4 (When/be/the next bus/?) Question: ....
Reported question: We wanted to know ....
5 (Have/Ann/see/this film/?) Question: ....
Reported question: Tom asked ....

C Steven Ellis robbed a bank. The police believe that Alan Reeves helped him. A policeman asked Reeves these questions:

> ▶ How long have you been out of prison?
> 1 Have you worked since then?
> 2 Does your sister give you money?
> 3 Who else gives you money?
> 4 Do you know Steven Ellis?
> 5 How long have you known Steven?
> 6 Have you seen Steven recently?

Later the policeman talked about the interview. Complete what he said, using the questions in the box.

▶ I asked him how long he had been out of prison ...., and he replied that he had left prison six months ago.
1 Then I asked him .... He told me that he hadn't found a job.
2 I asked him ...., and he said she did give him some money, but not very much.
3 Then I asked him .... He replied that nobody else did.
4 I asked him ...., and he said that he and Steven were friends.
5 So I asked him .... and he said that he had known him for six years.
6 Then I asked him ...., and he said that he couldn't remember.

Test J: Conditionals and reported speech

A Antonio and Sally are having a break at work. Put the verbs in brackets ( ) in the right tenses. Use contracted forms, if they sound more natural.

Antonio: I feel old and useless.

Sally: You're OK. Don't worry so much.

Antonio: If I (▶) was................... (be) in a different job, I might be happier.

Sally: You always talk like this if you (1)........................ (be) tired.

Antonio: Yes, but if I had applied for other jobs, I (2)........................ (get) something more interesting by now. I wouldn't be so tired.

Sally: If I (3)........................ (be) you, I'd take a holiday.

Antonio: I wish I (4)........................ (have) enough money.

Sally: If you saved up, you (5)........................ (be) able to have holidays. We've had this conversation before, haven't we?

Antonio: But if I (6)........................ (not talk) to you, I won't find an answer.

Sally: I wish I (7)........................ (can) help you more.

Antonio: But I would have stopped work completely if I (8)........................ (not met) you, Sally!

Sally: If people (9)........................ (not speak) to each other, they lose hope. That's my opinion. What makes you happy, anyway?

Antonio: I wish I (10)........................ (know). The only thing I know is that I (11)........................ (sing) badly if I'm happy. Does that help?

Sally: Perhaps. Where do you sing?

Antonio: In the bath, I think, and in the shower.

Sally: Perhaps you (12)........................ (be) happier if you got a job at the swimming pool?

Antonio: Shall we go back to work?

B Peter is making a political speech in the town centre. Improve his speech by using Second and Third Conditionals instead of the underlined text.

'Please listen to me. (▶) We don't work together, so we don't succeed. (1) You didn't vote for me at the last election, so your lives have not improved. Don't go away. I know it's raining! (2) Churchill isn't alive today. (3) Life isn't better, and he isn't our Prime Minister. Come back, sir! I haven't finished. (4) We don't feel good about ourselves, because we don't win all our football matches. (5) I won't become Prime Minister, so I won't give every child a new pair of football boots. (6) I didn't bring my wife with me today. (7) She isn't here, so she doesn't listen to me.'

▶ If we worked together, we would succeed. ....

1 If you ....

2 I wish Churchill ....

3 Life would ....

4 We would ....

5 If I ....

6 I wish I ....

7 If she ....

Luke's parents got divorced ten years ago. Luke has just met his father, Bill, for the first time in five years. In this conversation, he is telling his girlfriend what his father said. Report it.

> *What Bill said:*
> (▶) 'Are you living on your own?'
> (1) 'Please get enough sleep.' (4) 'Why did Paul leave the flat?'
> (2) 'You should get some qualifications.' (5) 'Where do you work?'
> (3) 'Don't take any drugs.' (6) 'Please give me your new address in New York.'

Shelly: What did he say?
Luke: ▶ (ask) *He asked me if I was living on my own.* ....
Shelly: None of his business! What else?
Luke: 1 (advise) ....
Shelly: What does he think you've been doing for five years? What about college?
Luke: 2 (tell) ....
Shelly: Did he get any himself? Anything else?
Luke: 3 (warn) ....
Shelly: I suppose that's sensible. What about Paul?
Luke: 4 (ask) ....
Shelly: Did you talk about work?
Luke: 5 (ask) ....
Shelly: So you told him about the job in America?
Luke   6 (persuade) ....

D Now use Bill's report to his second wife to write what Luke actually said.

> *Bill's report:*
> ▶ He said I didn't look very well.
> 1 He said he would give me the name of his doctor.
> 2 He told me to eat more fruit.
> 3 He told me he was living in a flat on his own.
> 4 He said he had tried sharing with his friend, Paul, but Paul had left.
> 5 He said he was going to live in America.

Luke: ▶ *You don't look very well.* ....
Bill: I'm alright actually.
Luke: 1 ....
Bill: But I'm never ill.
Luke: 2 ....
Bill: Perhaps. Anyway, what are you doing these days?
Luke: 3 ....
Bill: Don't you get lonely?
Luke: 4 ....
Bill: Really? What are you going to do next, anyway?
Luke: 5 ....

1 We use **and** and **both … and** to link two similar ideas in one sentence:

> She is tired.   She is hungry.
>> *She is tired **and** hungry.*
>> *She is **both** tired **and** hungry.*

> *We found **both** our tickets **and** our money.*

2 We use **but** to contrast two different ideas:
> *He swims. He doesn't play tennis.*
> *He swims, **but** he doesn't play tennis.*
> *I live in Bristol, **but** I work in London.*

3 We use **so** to talk about the result of something (see Unit 104); it links two actions (= and therefore …)

> SITUATION: RESULT:
> *I'm tired.*   *I'm going to bed.*
>> *I'm tired, **so** I'm going to bed.*
>> *They were late, **so** they missed the train.*

4 We use **or** and **either … or** to talk about two possibilities:

> POSSIBILITY A: POSSIBILITY B:
> *She's French.*   *She's Swiss.*
>> *She's French **or** Swiss.*
>> *She's **either** French **or** Swiss.*

*That man is **either** a footballer **or** an actor.*
*I never work all day. I work **either** in the morning **or** in the afternoon.*

5 We use **neither … nor** to put two negative statements together:

> *Peter didn't come.   Joan didn't come.*
>> ***Neither** Peter **nor** Joan came.*

The verb form (**came**) is positive, because **neither … nor** makes the sentence negative: NOT *Neither Peter nor Joan didn't come.*

6 We can also use **both**, **either** and **neither** like this:

> both
> either } of { the
> neither }   my
>   his
>   these } PLURAL NOUN

> PLURAL VERB
> *Both of these suitcases* |are| *heavy.*
> *I haven't seen **either of the films**.*

> SINGULAR OR PLURAL VERB
> *Neither of his sisters* |was/were| *there.*

We can also say:

> **both/either/neither + of + them/us**

> *He has two cars, but **neither of them** works.*

A Put *but* or *so* in the gaps.

▶ The film was very long,   but.... it was interesting.
          so..... we got home late.

1 The restaurant is very expensive, ... the food is terrible.
          .... only rich people go there.

2 I'm studying hard, ... I don't have much free time.
          .... I'm not making much progress.

3 I've got her address, ... I can write to her.
          .... I haven't got her phone number.

4 We wanted to swim, ... we went to the seaside.
          .... the sea was too cold.

5 They didn't have any money, ... they wanted to eat in a restaurant.
          .... they couldn't go to a restaurant.

6 I lost my bag, ... I went to the police station.
          .... I found £10 in my pocket.

3 Combine these sentences with *both … and*.

▶ Jane owns a shop. She owns a restaurant.　Jane owns both a shop and a restaurant.
1 This restaurant is cheap. It is nice.　...
2 Jo bought a dress. She bought a jumper.　...
3 They play golf. They play tennis.　...
4 The film was funny. It was exciting.　...

C Now combine these sentences with *either … or*.

▶ POSSIBILITY A: She's at the office.　　POSSIBILITY B: She's at the airport.
　She's either at the office or at the airport...
1 POSSIBILITY A: Paul's at home.　　　　POSSIBILITY B: Paul's at the gym.
　...
2 POSSIBILITY A: The shop is in East Street. POSSIBILITY B: The shop is in Fox Street.
　...
3 POSSIBILITY A: Her father is a doctor.　　POSSIBILITY B: Her father is a dentist.
　...
4 POSSIBILITY A: The museum is in Oxford.　POSSIBILITY B: The museum is in Bath.
　...

D Now combine these sentences with *neither … nor*.

▶ Chris didn't have time to take a holiday. Sheila didn't have time to take a holiday.
　Neither Chris nor Sheila had time to take a holiday...
1 The bus didn't arrive on time. The train didn't arrive on time.
　...
2 David doesn't play tennis. Mike doesn't play tennis.
　...
3 The restaurants aren't good. The hotels aren't good.
　...
4 The English team didn't play well. The Scottish team didn't play well.
　...

E Complete the sentences with *both/either/neither + of + us/them* (e.g. *neither of us*).

▶ I went to the concert with Mary, but neither of us........ enjoyed it very much because it was very boring.
1 There are two flights we can catch to New York. Both flights cost the same amount, so we can choose ....
2 I played two games against Harry, and I lost .... because he is a much better player than me.
3 I saw Jane and Alison walking down the street and I waved at them, but .... saw me because they were talking.
4 I looked at George, and George looked at me. Then .... started to laugh because it was such a funny situation.
5 A man spoke to us but .... could understand him, so we didn't answer.
6 Tim and I wanted to go to the game, but .... could get tickets, so we watched it on TV.

104 Because, in case, so, so that

1 We use **because** to give the reason for something:

> REASON
> *Jack is in bed* **because** *he's got the flu.*
> *We couldn't go out* **because** *the weather was terrible.*
> *I took a taxi* **because** *I was in a hurry.*

We use **because of** with a noun (e.g. **flu, weather, noise**):

> REASON
> *Jack's in bed* **because of** *his flu.*
> *We couldn't go out* **because of** *the storm.*
> *I couldn't sleep* **because of** *the noise.*

2 We use **in case** when the reason is something that might happen:

> REASON
> *I'm taking an umbrella* **in case** *it rains.*
> (= I'm taking an umbrella because it might rain.)
> *I'll phone John now,* **in case** *he wants to come with us.*
> (= … because he might want to come with us.)

3 We use **so** to talk about the result of something:

> RESULT
> *I was in a hurry* **so** *I took a taxi.*
> *Jack has got the flu* **so** *he's in bed.*
> *The weather was terrible* **so** *we couldn't go out.*
> *My neighbours were having a party and making a lot of noise* **so** *I couldn't sleep.*

4 We use **so that** to talk about the purpose of an action:

> PURPOSE
> *I took a taxi* **so that** *I would arrive on time.*
> *I listen to the news in the morning* **so that** *I know what's happening in the world.*
> *Tom goes jogging every day* **so that** *he'll stay fit.*
> *I took a taxi* **so that** *my friends would not have to wait for me.*

(We can also use **to** + **infinitive** to talk about purpose; see Unit 95.)

Practice

A Write each sentence in a different way using the words given.

▶ Tom didn't want to go out because he had a cold.
Tom didn't want to go out because of _his cold_____ .

▶ Take some money because you might need to take a taxi.
_Take some money_____ in case _you need to take a taxi___ .

▶ John and I asked for a drink because we were thirsty.
_John and I were thirsty___ so _we asked for a drink_____ .

1 Mary went to bed because she was tired.
.... so ....

2 I couldn't sleep because it was so hot.
.... the heat.

3 Jill doesn't like apples so she doesn't eat them.
.... because ....

4 The streets were crowded because of the football match.
.... there was a football match.

5 I'll give Jane a key to the house because she might get home before me.
.... in case ....

3 Complete the sentences with *because*, *in case* or *so*, and a phrase from the box. Use each phrase once.

I'll take a book to read	his passport was out of date
I want to lose weight	his wife was ill
she's at home	there is a power cut this weekend
~~they had to wait for the next one~~	

▶ They missed one bus *so they had to wait for the next one.*.................

1 I don't know where my sister is, but I'll try phoning her ....

2 I'm eating less these days ....

3 Peter had trouble at the airport ....

4 It's a long journey ....

5 We've bought some candles ....

6 Mr Smith didn't go to the meeting ....

C Write out complete sentences from the words in brackets ( ), making any necessary changes and including *so that*.

▶ (Mark/go/swimming every day/he can stay healthy.)
  Mark goes swimming every day so that he can stay healthy...................

1 (Last week, my brother/lend/me £20/I could buy some new shoes.)
  ....

2 (Last month, the Government/pass/new traffic laws/fewer people will have accidents.)
  ....

3 (Our school has/open/a new library/we can have more books.)
  ....

4 (Ann always/write/everything in her diary/she doesn't forget her appointments.)
  ....

5 (Last Friday, we/leave/home early/we could avoid the morning traffic.)
  ....

D If the sentence is correct, put a tick (✓). If it is incorrect cross out any incorrect words and, if necessary, write in the correct word.

▶ A: Why are they tired? ✓..............
   B: Because ~~that~~ their long journey. *of*.............

1 I can't come tomorrow, so that I came today. ....

2 Take a sandwich with you in case you get hungry. ....

3 Julie had to go to the shops so she needed something for lunch. ....

4 A: Why are you here? ....
   B: I'm here for have a medical examination. ....
   A: Well, since you're here, so we can check your teeth as well. ....

105 Since, as, for

1 We can use **because**, **since** and **as** to express a reason for something. Normally we use **because** when the reason has not been mentioned previously; the reason usually comes in second place:

> *We stayed at home **because** Tom was ill.*

If the conversation has already mentioned that Tom was ill, we normally express the reason with **since** or **as**; the reason usually comes in first place:

> *Tom wasn't feeling well. **Since / As** Tom was ill, we stayed at home.*

2 We can use **for** to express purpose or reason with different structures. We can use it with a noun to express a purpose:

> *I went to the shops **for some cheese**.*
> *We stopped **for a drink**.*

3 When the action and the purpose involve different people, we express this with **for** and a noun or pronoun followed by the infinitive with **to**:

> *We stopped **for the children** to have a drink.*
> *I waited **for him** to finish his homework.*

4 We can use **for** with a noun or an **-ing** form to give the reason for a reaction:

> *The teacher sent Jill home **for cheating**.*
> *My cousin was arrested **for robbery**.*

*Johnson is in prison **for dangerous driving**.*
*Sam won a medal **for saving a young boy**.*

Here the reason happens before the reaction.

5 You will sometimes see **for** used in a way similar to **because**:

> *Diane was pleased to receive the books, **for** she was fond of reading.*

However, this is not common and you can always use **because** in these cases.

6 We can also use prepositions **due to** and **owing to** with a noun to express a reason:

> *Many people arrived late **due to / owing to** the heavy rain.*
> ***Due to / Owing to** the road repairs, we had to take a different route.*

If we use these prepositions with a clause, we have to include **the fact that**:

> *The concert was cancelled **due to/owing to the fact that** the pianist had appendicitis.*

Note that we can use **noun + be + due to + noun**:

> *The delay **was due to fog**.*

We cannot use **owing to** in this way:

> NOT ~~The delay was owing to fog.~~

Here the reason happens before the action or fact.

Practice

A Complete the sentences with an expression from the box.

due to a problem with the brakes	~~for a cup of coffee~~	for some bottled water
for the best drawing	for the children	owing to the underground strike
since Carolyn's a vegetarian		

▶ The workers had a break *for a cup of coffee* .

1 She kept a box of toys .... to play with.

2 Sandra won a prize ....

3 ... and .... , we can't take her to our usual restaurant.

4 Jane's accident was ....

5 Jack has gone to the shops ....

6 Many people were late for work ....

3 In each question, complete the second sentence so that it means the same as the first. In some cases there is more than one possibility.

▶ Sue went to the kitchen to get some ice cubes.
Sue went to the kitchen for *some ice cubes*............ .

1 Mother sent Timmy to bed because he insulted her.
Mother sent Timmy to bed for ....

2 The ferry was late due to the heavy winds.
The ferry was late due to .... it was very windy.

3 Ken hit his sister and his father punished him.
Ken's father punished him for ....

4 We had the meeting in the annex because they were repairing the main building.
We had the meeting in the annex owing to .... the main building.

5 The boss gave Terry a bonus because he worked at the weekend.
The boss gave Terry a bonus for .... at the weekend.

6 I can't get into the bathroom because Debbie's there.
Since .... , I can't get in there.

7 The road is blocked because some trees have fallen.
The blocked road is due to ....

8 They waited while the sheep crossed the road.
They waited for .... cross the road.

C Here is a story about a day out for the Long family. Complete the story by choosing the correct option in each case.

Mr Long is a careless driver. In fact he has a reputation as a dangerous driver
(▶) because/owing to the police have fined him three times (1) because/for speeding.
(2) Due to/Since he drives carelessly, his wife usually drives the family car, especially
when the children are with them. The children often feel sick in the car (3) due to the
fact that/owing to they are not good travellers, and when this happens Mrs Long has
to stop the car (4) for/as them to have a break. Some people take pills for travel
sickness, of course, but Mrs Long doesn't like the idea (5) because/due to she thinks
the children will get addicted. One hot summer's day the family were on their way to
visit Mrs Long's mother (6) owing to the fact that/owing to it was her birthday.
(7) Since/For it was a special day the children were wearing their best clothes, so it
was obviously a bad day (8) for/because them to get dirty. Very soon the children were
feeling sick, probably due (9) to/for the heat, so Mrs Long stopped the car several
times (10) for/since them to get out and have a drink. When they finally arrived,
grandmother said, 'You're a bit late but I suppose that's (11) due to/owing to the
traffic.' 'Not really,' said Mrs Green. 'The journey took longer than usual
(12) because/owing to the heat and we had to stop several times (13) to/for a break.'
At their grandmother's the children soon felt better and they had a great afternoon.
After lunch they went for long walk with Grandma's dog, Queenie. On the way home
they were tired and fell asleep straightaway in the car.

106 Although, while, however, despite, etc

1 We can contrast two ideas or situations within a sentence with **although**:

Although the weather was very cold, we decided to go for a walk.
The government passed the new law although many people opposed it.

Informally we can use **though** in the same way:

Though the weather was very cold, we decided to go for a walk.
The government passed the new law though many people opposed it.

While is not possible here.

2 We can use **while** to contrast two aspects of the same thing or two similar things within a sentence:

While I agree with the idea, I don't think it's very practical.
Some of my friends have found work while others are still unemployed.

(**Al**)**though** is also possible here.

3 When the contrast is expressed in a separate sentence, we use **however**:

The government passed the new law.
However, many people were against it.

I agree with the idea. I don't think it's very practical, however.

We use a comma to separate **however** from the rest of the sentence.

Though can also go at the end of a separate sentence:

I agree with the idea. I don't think it's very practical, though.

Although is not possible here.

4 We can use prepositions **in spite of** and **despite** with a noun (but not usually a personal pronoun) to express concession or contrast:

In spite of / Despite the cold weather, we decided to go for a walk.
The government passed the new law in spite of / despite the opposition.

If we use these prepositions with a clause, we have to include **the fact that**, e.g.:

The government passed the new law in spite of / despite the fact that many people were against it.

Practice

A In each question, complete the second sentence (or pair of sentences) so that the meaning is the same as the first sentence (or pair of sentences).

▶ Larry is older than Meg but she is taller than he is.
  Although Larry is older than Meg, she is taller than he is .

1 In spite of the fact that it was dangerous, many people helped in the rescue.
  Many people helped in the rescue although ....

2 Many people continue to smoke cigarettes although there is a serious warning on every packet.
  .... the warning on every packet, many people continue to smoke cigarettes.

3 There were several stronger teams but it was Greece that won the cup.
  There were several stronger teams. It was Greece that won the cup, ...

4 Although London is more expensive than the rest of Britain, many people prefer to live there.
  Many people prefer to live in London despite .... it is more expensive than the rest of Britain.

5 My work is interesting but it is not very well paid.

   While .... , it is not very well paid.

6 Although Amy complained about the exams, she got very good marks.

   Amy complained about the exams. .... , she got very good marks.

3 Complete this speech about drugs by putting in *although*, *despite*, *however* or *while*. In some cases there is more than one possibility.

Ladies and gentlemen. Today I want to explain why I think drugs should be legalized. Many people think that all drugs are illegal. (▶) <u>However</u> .... , the legal situation is different in different countries. For example, (1)........................ coca leaves are legal in some parts of South America, they are banned in the USA and many other countries. But even in the USA and Europe, it is not true that all drugs are illegal. (2)........................ tobacco and alcohol are seriously addictive, they are a regular aspect of most social gatherings in our countries. Not everybody who smokes tobacco or drinks alcohol is an addict, of course. Many regular smokers would like to cut down or stop, (3)........................ , and in fact many have tried several times. (4)........................ their many attempts, they continue smoking, precisely because nicotine is so addictive. Anyway, what are the disadvantages of the illegal drugs remaining illegal? In the first place, illegality means that there is no quality control to protect the consumer. People think they are buying cocaine, for example, (5)........................ the substance is perhaps mixed with dust or even poisonous powders. Also drugs on the street are fairly expensive so (6)........................ consumers might not have a job, they need their drugs and this quickly leads to stealing and prostitution in order to pay for them. Second, the drug industry generates enormous quantities of money, enough money to corrupt many police officers and politicians. We like to think that our authorities control crime. The reality, (7)........................ , is that in some countries crime controls the authorities. Ladies and gentleman, (8)........................ you may not like drugs, as long as drugs are illegal, they are outside democratic control.

C Later two people discuss the talk about drugs. Use each expression from the box once only to complete the dialogue.

~~although~~   although   despite   however   in spite of the fact that   though

Tony: What did you think of the talk?

Pam: I don't agree with her (▶) <u>although</u> .... I have to accept that her talk was clever. It's true that the present situation isn't perfect. (1)........................ , if they legalize drugs, things will be much worse.

Tony: Oh, I don't know. Society seems to manage all right with tobacco and alcohol (2)........................ they're perfectly legal.

Pam: You make it sound as if they're harmless. I think it's truer to say that society functions (3)........................ they're legal because they cause problems for a lot of people.

Tony: A few people misuse them. Most people use them sensibly, (4)........................ .

Pam: It doesn't make sense to say that you can smoke sensibly. That's why there are health warnings on the packets. People are stupid enough to smoke (5)........................ all the warnings.

107 Relative clauses (1)

1 If we use a sentence like:
The police have found the boy.

it may not be clear which boy.
We can make it clear like this:
*The police have found the boy who
disappeared last week.*

Who links the relative clause (**who
disappeared last week**) to the main clause
(**The police have found the boy**).

2 When we talk about people, we use **that** or
who:
*I talked to the girl **that** (OR **who**) won the
race.*

When we talk about things or animals, we
use **that** or **which**:
*I like the car **that** (OR **which**) won the race.*

3 **That, who** or **which** can be the subject of the
relative clause, like this:

	SUBJECT	
I talked to the girl	**who**	**won.**
	The girl	*won.*
That is the dog	**that**	**attacked me.**
	The dog	*attacked me.*

There is no other pronoun (e.g. **it, they**):
NOT *That is the dog that it attacked me.*

4 **That, who** or **which** can be the object of the
relative clause, like this:

	OBJECT	
The card	**which**	**Ken sent** *was nice.*
Ken sent	the card.	
The man	**that**	*I saw was very rude.*
I saw	the man.	

There is no other pronoun (e.g. **him, them**):
NOT *The man I saw him was very rude.*

When **that, who** or **which** is the object of the
relative clause (e.g. *The card **which** Ken sent*),
we can leave them out:
*The card **Ken sent** was nice.*
*The man **I saw** was very rude.*

5 Now look at this sentence with **whose**:
*Susan is the woman **whose husband is an
actor**.* (= Susan's husband is an actor.)

We use **whose** in place of **his, her, their**, etc.
We only use it with people, countries and
organizations, not things. It has a possessive
meaning. Here is another example:
*The man **whose** dog bit me didn't apologize.*
(= The man didn't apologize. **His** dog bit
me.)

Practice

A Complete the sentences using the information in brackets ( ) and *who* or *which*.

▶ (I went to see a doctor. She had helped my mother.)
I went to see the doctor *who had helped* .... my mother.

1 (A dog bit me. It belonged to Mrs Jones.)
The dog .... belonged to Mrs Jones.

2 (A woman wrote to me. She wanted my advice.)
The woman .... wanted my advice.

3 (A bus crashed. It was twenty-three years old.)
The bus .... was twenty-three years old.

4 (Ann talked to a man. He had won a lot of money.)
Ann talked to the man ....

5 (Mary was wearing the red dress. She wears it for parties.)
Mary was wearing the red dress ....

6 (He's an architect. He designed the new city library.)
He's the architect ....

B Complete the sentences using the information in brackets ( ) and *that*.

▶ (Jack made a table. It's not very strong.)
The table <u>that Jack made</u> is not very strong.

1 (I read about a new computer. I had seen it on TV.)
I read about the new computer ....

2 (Jane made a cake. Nobody liked it.)
Nobody liked the cake ....

3 (Mary sent me a letter. It was very funny.)
The letter .... was very funny.

4 (My sister wrote an article. The newspaper is going to publish it.)
The newspaper is going to publish the article ....

5 (I met an old lady. She was one hundred and three years old.)
The old lady .... was one hundred and three years old.

6 (I saw a house. My brother wants to buy it.)
I saw the house ....

C Complete the sentences with one of the phrases in the box and *who* or *whose*.

interviewed me had	has visited so many different countries
~~had saved their son~~	wives have just had babies
book won a prize last week	~~divorce was in all the papers~~
car had broken down	complain all the time

▶ The parents thanked the woman <u>who had saved their son</u> .

▶ The couple <u>whose divorce was in the newspapers</u> have got married again.

1 It is very interesting to meet somebody ....

2 The person .... asked me some very difficult questions.

3 In my office there are two men ....

4 What's the name of that writer .... ?

5 I don't like people ....

6 We helped a woman ....

D Put in *who* or *that* only if necessary.

▶ The match <u>–</u> we saw was boring.

▶ Did I tell you about the people <u>who</u> live next door?

▶ The horse <u>that</u> won the race belongs to an Irish woman.

1 I love the ice cream .... they sell in that shop.

2 The book .... I'm reading is about jazz.

3 The woman .... came to see us was selling magazines.

4 We'll go to a restaurant .... has a children's menu.

5 The factory .... closed last week had been there for seventy years.

6 Have you read about the schoolgirl .... started her own business and is now a millionaire?

7 Ethel says that the house .... Tom has just bought has a beautiful garden.

108 Relative clauses (2)

1 In informal English, in defining relative clauses, when **who**, **that** or **which** is the object of the verb, it can be omitted:

> *The name of the woman I interviewed was Mrs Norris.*
> *The car they bought was quite expensive.*

Notice that there is no pronoun in the relative clause:

> *The name of the woman I interviewed ~~her~~ was Mrs Norris.*
> *The car they bought ~~it~~ was quite expensive.*

2 When the verb has a preposition, in formal English the preposition goes with **whom** or **which**:

> *That is the young man **to whom** I spoke.*
> *The job **for which** she's applied is in Paris.*

Informally, we can omit the relative word and then the preposition goes at the end of the relative clause:

> *That is the young man I spoke **to**.*
> *The job she's applied **for** is in Paris.*

3 Informally, we often omit the relative word **when** after **day**, **year**, etc.:

> *That was the **year** I finished university.*

We often omit the relative word **where** after **place**, **somewhere**, etc.:

> *Do you know **a place / somewhere** we can get a good sandwich?*

We often omit the relative word **why** after **reason**:

> *The real **reason** she came was to speak to my father.*

We often omit a relative expression after **way**:

> *That's the **way** they make beer in Germany.*

Practice

A In the following sentences cross out the words that are not possible or not necessary. If there are no such words, mark the sentence with a tick (✓).

▶ The first book ~~which~~ she wrote ~~it~~ was *Lost Steps*. ....

▶ This is the boy who broke the window. ✓......

Do you know the woman that my father's talking to? ....

They're going to close the factories that they make too much smoke. ....

People who live in flats shouldn't have dogs. ....

An animal that comes out at night must have good eyes. ....

The boat that my cousins sailed in it was hit by a bomb. ....

An amphibian is an animal which can live on land or in water. ....

People who are from Manchester are called Mancunians. ....

B In the following, if a sentence is incomplete, indicate where a word is necessary and write the word at the end. If the sentence is correct, mark it with a tick (✓).

▶ Is there a shop near here sells stamps?
Is there a shop near here⁄sells stamps? that..................

▶ Mrs Thomas is the teacher my sister likes best. ✓.....................

1 The referee is the person takes the decisions. ....

2 The bus they were waiting for never came. ....

3 The old lady we saw was wearing a pink dress. ....

4 Is this the train goes to Nottingham? ....

5 There's a place near here you can get a good hamburger. ....

6 It took a long time to find the doctor we wanted to see. ....

7 Do you know anybody plays the piano really well? ....

C In each case combine the two sentences into one. Put in *who*, *that*, *which* or *where* only if it is necessary.

▶ I lent you a book. Have you read it?
   Have you read *the book I lent you* ....?

▶ My mother works in a factory. It makes parts for cars.
   The factory *where my mother works* .... makes parts for cars.

1 Sharon's got a new mobile. It takes photos.
   Sharon's got a new mobile ....

2 They lived in a block of flats. It was struck by lightning.
   The block of flats .... was struck by lightning.

3 The hotel had a magician. He was very clever.
   The hotel had a magician ....

4 The porters are paid a salary. They can't live on it.
   The porters can't live on the salary ....

5 Nobody else wanted the food. My father ate it.
   My father ate the food ....

6 We ran out of petrol in a little village. It didn't have a petrol station.
   The village .... didn't have a petrol station.

D Freda and Len are packing to go on holiday. Complete the conversation with the expressions from the box and include *that* if it is necessary.

you can take onto the plane	go with my green dress	~~has a lock~~
have just been mended	I knitted myself	needs a film
you can walk all day in	covers all the Mediterranean islands	
we bought in that second-hand bookshop		

Len: We'd better take two cases. The one (▶) *that has a lock* ....
      and that smaller one ....

Freda: Which camera do you want to take? The digital one or the one
        .... ?

Len: Let's take the digital one. How about the travel guide? There's that big one
      .... and that smaller one – the one just
      about Corsica ....

Freda: Perhaps the small one will be enough.

Len: I think I'll take my shoes .... How many
      pairs of shoes are you taking?

Freda: Well, we'll need some comfortable ones ....
        and perhaps for the evenings I'll take the new green ones, the ones
        ....

Len: It might be cool in the evenings. I suppose you're taking a sweater.

Freda: Yes, the white one. You know, the one ....
        Anyway, let's have a break. I feel like a drink.

109 Relative clauses (3)

1 Look at these two sentences:

London has over 6 million inhabitants.
*London, **which is the capital of Britain**, has over 6 million inhabitants.*

The clause **which is the capital of Britain** gives us more information about London, but we do not need this information to define **London**. We can understand the first sentence without this extra information. **which is the capital of Britain** is a non-defining relative clause. It has commas (,) to separate it from the rest of the sentence.

2 For things or animals, we use **which** (BUT NOT **that**) in non-defining relative clauses:

*Fred sold his computer, **which he no longer needed**, to his cousin.* (NOT … *that he no longer needed* …)
*In the summer we stay in my uncle's house, **which is near the sea**.*

3 For people, we use **who** (but not **that**) in non-defining relative clauses. We use **who** when it is the subject of the relative clause:

Elvis Presley, | SUBJECT **who** | *died in 1977, earned millions of dollars.* (**Presley** died in 1977.)

We use **who** (or sometimes **whom**) when it is the object of the relative clause:

My boss, | OBJECT **who** (or **whom**) | *I last saw before Christmas, is very ill.* (I last saw **my boss** before Christmas.)

4 We use **whose** to mean 'his', 'her', or 'their':

*Marilyn Monroe, **whose real name was Norma Jean**, was born in Los Angeles.* (**Her** real name was Norma Jean.)

5 We can also use **which** (BUT NOT **that**) to refer to a whole fact:

| Ann did not want to marry Tom | *, which surprised everybody.*

Here, **which** refers to the fact that Ann did not want to marry Tom.

Practice

A Make one sentence from the two that are given. Use *who* or *which* with the underlined words.

▶ Mont Blanc is between France and Italy. It is the highest mountain in the Alps.
  Mont Blanc, which is between France and Italy, is the highest mountain in the Alps.

▶ Alfred Hitchcock was born in Britain. He worked for many years in Hollywood.
  Alfred Hitchcock, who was born in Britain, worked for many years in Hollywood.

1 The sun is really a star. It is 93 million miles from the earth.

  ....

2 John F. Kennedy died in 1963. He was a very famous American President.

  ....

3 Charlie Chaplin was from a poor family. He became a very rich man.

  ....

4 The 1992 Olympics were held in Barcelona. It is in the north-east of Spain.

  ....

5 We went to see the Crown Jewels. They are kept in the Tower of London.

   ....

B **From the notes, make one sentence. Use *who*, *whose* or *which* with the words in brackets ( ).**

▶ Greta Garbo. (She was born in Sweden.) She moved to America in 1925.
   Greta Garbo, who was born in Sweden, moved to America in 1925. ....

▶ Darwin. (His ideas changed our view of the world.) He travelled a lot when he was young.
   Darwin, whose ideas changed our view of the world, travelled a lot when he was young. ....

1 Football. (It first started in Britain.) It is now popular in many countries.
   Football, ...

2 Margaret Thatcher. (She was the Prime Minister of Britain for 11 years.) She studied science at university.

   ....

3 Michelangelo. (He lived until he was 90.) He is one of Italy's greatest artists.

   ....

4 Bill Clinton. (His wife is a brilliant lawyer.) He became President of the USA in 1993.

   ....

5 The Nile. (It runs through several countries.) It is the longest river in Africa.

   ....

6 Madonna. (Her parents were born in Italy.) She is a famous American singer.

   ....

7 Gandhi. (He was born in 1869). He was assassinated in 1948.

   ....

8 Elephants. (They are found in Africa and India). They are hunted for their ivory.

   ....

9 The Beatles. (Their music is still popular.) They were probably the most famous pop group in the world.

   ....

10 Brands Hatch. (It is not far from London.) It is famous for its motor races.

   ....

C **Complete this text about Lewis Carroll by putting *who*, *which* or *whose* in the gaps.**

Alice in Wonderland, (▶) which .... is one of the most popular children's books in the world, was written by Lewis Carroll, (1)............... real name was Charles Dodgson. Carroll, (2)............... had a natural talent as a story-teller, loved to entertain children, including Alice Liddell, (3)............... father was a colleague of Carroll's at Oxford University. One day Carroll took Alice and her sisters for a trip on the River Thames, (4)............... flows through Oxford. After the trip, Carroll wrote in his diary that he had told the children a wonderful story, (5)............... he had promised to write down for them. He wrote the story, illustrated it with his own drawings, and gave it to the children. By chance, it was seen by Henry Kingsley, (6)............... was a famous novelist, and he persuaded Dodgson to publish it.

Test K: Building sentences

A Carlo is working on the busy reception desk of a large hotel in Bristol. Put in the correct words from the box.

either in case nor both so (x2) and ~~Neither~~ because or

Carlo: Can I help you, sir?

First man: I hope so. (►) <u>Neither</u>............... the shower (1)....................... the bath works in my room.

Carlo: I'm sorry, sir. We'll have them repaired this afternoon.

***

First woman: I've got an early flight, (2)....................... I need an alarm call at five o'clock in the morning.

Carlo: No problem, Madam. I'll arrange that for you.

***

Second man: Can I borrow an umbrella (3)....................... it rains? I don't want to get my suit wet.

Carlo: Of course you can, sir. Here you are.

***

Second woman: I'm unhappy (4)....................... my room doesn't have a view. I'd like to see (5)....................... the park (6)....................... the river.

Carlo: I'll see what I can do, Madam.

***

Third man: Can you book me a taxi (7)....................... that I can get to the airport by ten o'clock tonight?

Carlo: Certainly sir. I'll book it for half past nine.

***

Third woman: (8)....................... the bed (9)....................... the bath are too small for my husband and me.

Carlo: I'm sorry, Madam, but that's all we have at the moment.

B This is the first of two articles from a holiday magazine. Cross out the wrong words.

Beach, City or Lake?

(►) Although/~~Since~~ most British holidaymakers traditionally go to the seaside for their holidays, lakes and mountains are also popular places (1) as/for people to relax and enjoy themselves. (2) While/However, a lake holiday usually costs more than a beach holiday because the local hotels and restaurants are more expensive.

   (3) Since/Although most people think very carefully about prices, the beach is still the top location (4) for/as a one-week or two-week holiday. (5) While/However you may not think of a city as a place for relaxing, many people enjoy a short break or a long weekend in Paris or Beijing or Rio De Janeiro.

   (6) Although/In spite of the noise and the traffic, tourists love going to big cities and seeing the art galleries, museums, shops and nightlife. (7) However/Although they are expensive, big cities all over the world welcome millions of visitors every year.

C Joe and Miriam have been invited to a neighbour's wedding. Cross out the underlined words if it is possible.

Joe: What would you like to drink?

Miriam: Something (▶) ~~that~~ I can drink slowly, I think. Joe, can you see the man (▶) ~~who~~ is drinking orange juice? Is he the man (1) who repaired our roof in the summer?

Miriam: I think so. The day (2) when he came to our house was your birthday, wasn't it?

Joe: That's right. But the work (3) that he did wasn't very good, was it?

Miriam: No, it wasn't. Do you know the woman (4) who is eating a piece of cake by the window?

Joe: Yes. I'm sure she's the woman (5) whose dog bit my leg a month ago.

Miriam: Oh dear. Is there anyone here (6) that you want to talk to?

Joe: I'd like to find the man (7) that turns on the radio in his garden at six in the morning!

Miriam: Joe! Try to be friendly. The young housewife (8) that I met in the street yesterday was really nice.

Joe: Yes, but did you think about the reason (9) why she was nice? She wanted to borrow two of our chairs.

D This is the second holiday article. Write the correct words in the spaces.

| that has | that thousands | which means | you see | which has | that visit | ~~which has~~ |

Beautiful Eire

Eire, (▶) <u>which has</u>................... a population of less than four million people, is a country with some of the world's most beautiful mountains and valleys. The first things (1)................................ as you drive south from Dublin are the green grass and the hills of Wicklow. Further south, on the way to County Wexford, there are many small hotels, (2)................................ you can find somewhere to stay without booking in advance. The place (3)................................ of tourists visit every year, however, is the west coast. This is the coast (4)................................ fantastic views of the Atlantic Ocean, and pretty seaside towns. Galway, for example, (5)................................ a wonderful bay, is well worth a visit. Or two visits! It is a fact that tourists (6)................................ Eire always come back soon for a second or third holiday!

E This is an announcement on a train from London to Lyon. Put one of the following words in each gap.

| case | but | ~~Although~~ | nor | who | which | however | neither | due |

'(▶) <u>Although</u>.... we will arrive late in Paris, we still expect to reach Lyon by 19.00 this evening. Passengers (1)................ would like tea, coffee or cold drinks should visit the café between coaches C and D. Please remember, (2)................ , that the café will close in twenty minutes (3)................ to a problem with the refrigerator. Remember also to keep your ticket with you at all times in (4)................ you pass the Ticket Inspector as he walks through the train. We are sorry to say that (5)................ Coach F (6)................ Coach K has air-conditioning at the moment, (7)................ if you are in one of these coaches we would like to offer you a free bottle of water. Finally, please remember that Coach B, (8)................ is at the front of the train, is a quiet coach – the use of mobile phones is not allowed. Thank you. Enjoy your trip!'

Appendix 1: Nouns

1 Plural nouns

1 We usually add -s to a noun to form the plural:

a book → some **books**	one kilo → ten **kilos**
radio → **radios**	shop → **shops**
tyre → **tyres**	

2 After -s, -ss, -sh, -ch and -x we add -es:

bus → **buses**	dress → **dresses**
glass → **glasses**	dish → **dishes**
wish → **wishes**	beach → **beaches**
watch → **watches**	box → **boxes**

3 When a noun ends in a consonant* + -y, the y changes to -ies:

city → **cities**	family → **families**
lorry → **lorries**	story → **stories**

We do not change y after a vowel*:

day → **days**	journey → **journeys**

4 Nouns ending in -f or -fe have the plural -ves:

leaf → **leaves**	life → **lives**
shelf → **shelves**	thief → **thieves**

5 A few nouns ending in -o have -es:

potato → **potatoes**
tomato → **tomatoes**
hero → **heroes**

But most have -s:

discos	kilos	photos	pianos
radios	stereos	studios	zoos

6 Some nouns have irregular plurals:

man → **men**	woman → **women**
child → **children**	foot → **feet**
mouse → **mice**	sheep → **sheep**
fish → **fish**	person → **people**
tooth → **teeth**	

2 Uncountable nouns

1 Here is a list of common uncountable nouns:

ice	water	rain	snow
heat	noise	cotton	glass
petrol	money	luggage	information
work	homework	advice	news
milk	butter	bread	cheese
tea	coffee	sugar	meat
marmalade		toast	

2 Uncountable nouns do not have a plural form:

petrol (NOT ~~petrols~~)   bread (NOT ~~breads~~)

3 We do not use **a/an** with uncountable nouns, but we can use **some/any, the, much** (NOT ~~many~~), **such** and **my/your/his**, etc.:

I always have **toast** and **marmalade** for breakfast.
I'd like **some tea**, please.
Look at **the snow** outside.
How **much luggage** have you got?
We've had **such** wonderful **news.**

4 Some nouns can be countable or uncountable:

I heard a **noise** from downstairs. (countable)
I can't sleep. The neighbours are making **so much noise**. (uncountable)

---

* Consonants: b c d f g h j k l m n p q r s t v w x y z
  Vowels: a e i o u
  Syllables: |hit| = 1 syllable, |vi|sit| = 2 syllables,
  |re|mem|ber| = 3 syllables

Appendix 2: Regular verbs

1 Present Simple

1 Add an -s to make the **he/she/it** form of most Present Simple verbs:

I/you/we/they	he/she/it
leave	*leaves*
make	*makes*
say	*says*
work	*works*

2 After -ss, -sh, -ch, -o or -x (e.g. *finish, go*), we add -es:

I/you/we/they	he/she/it
catch	*catches*
finish	*finishes*
pass	*passes*
teach	*teaches*
do	*does*
go	*goes*
mix	*mixes*

3 When a verb ends in a consonant* + -y, the y changes to -ies:

I/you/we/they	he/she/it
fly	*flies*
try	*tries*
carry	*carries*
study	*studies*

2 The -ing form

1 For most verbs we add -ing:
   ask → *asking*   *go* → *going*

2 For verbs ending with a consonant* + -e, we normally leave out **e** when we add -ing:
   hope → *hoping*   *live* → *living*
   take → *taking*
But we keep a double e before -ing:
   see → *seeing*   *agree* → *agreeing*

3 When a verb ends in -ie, it changes to y when we add -ing:
   die → *dying*   *lie* → *lying*
But y does not change:
   hurry → *hurrying*

4 When a word ends with one vowel* and one consonant (e.g. *run, swim, jog*), we double the final consonant:

get → *getting*   *jog* → *jogging*
run → *running*   *swim* → *swimming*
But note that we do not double the consonant:
• when it is **y, w** or **x** (e.g. *stay*)
   buy → *buying*   *draw* → *drawing*
   fax → *faxing*   *stay* → *staying*
• when the final syllable* is not stressed
   listen → *listening*   *visit* → *visiting*
   wonder → *wondering*
Note however that in British English l is usually doubled, even if the syllable is unstressed (e.g. *travel*):
   cancel → *cancelling*   *travel* → *travelling*

3 The past tense and past participles

1 Most verbs have **-ed** in the past tense; most past participles also end in **-ed**:

INFINITIVE	PAST TENSE	PAST/PASSIVE PARTICIPLE
happen	*happened*	*happened*
work	*worked*	*worked*

2 If the verb ends in -e, we add **d**:
   live → *lived*   *phone* → *phoned*

3 When a verb ends in a consonant + -y, the y changes to -ied:
   study → *studied*   *try* → *tried*

4 When a word ends with one vowel and one consonant (e.g. *stop*), we double the final consonant:
   grab → *grabbed*   *plan* → *planned*
   stop → *stopped*
But note that we do not double the consonant:
• when it is **y, w** or **x** (e.g. *enjoy*)
   allow → *allowed*   *enjoy* → *enjoyed*
• when the final syllable is not stressed
   open → *opened*   *listen* → *listened*
   discover → *discovered*
Note however that in British English l is usually doubled, even if the syllable is unstressed (e.g. *travel*):
   cancel → *cancelled*   *travel* → *travelled*

* Consonants: b c d f g h j k l m n p q r s t v w x y z
  Vowels: a e i o u
  Syllables: |*hit*| = 1 syllable, |*vi*|*sit*| = 2 syllables,
  |*re*|*mem*|*ber*| = 3 syllables

Appendix 3: Irregular verbs

INFINITIVE	PAST TENSE	PAST/PASSIVE PARTICIPLE	INFINITIVE	PAST TENSE	PAST/PASSIVE PARTICIPLE
be	was/were	been	learn	learnt/learned	learnt/learned
beat	beat	beaten	leave	left	left
become	became	become	lend	lent	lent
begin	began	begun	let	let	let
break	broke	broken	lose	lost	lost
bring	brought	brought			
build	built	built	make	made	made
burn	burnt	burnt	mean	meant	meant
buy	bought	bought	meet	met	met
catch	caught	caught	pay	paid	paid
choose	chose	chosen	put	put	put
come	came	come			
cost	cost	cost	read	read	read
cut	cut	cut	ring	rang	rung
			run	ran	run
do	did	done			
draw	drew	drawn	say	said	said
drink	drank	drunk	see	saw	seen
drive	drove	driven	sell	sold	sold
			send	sent	sent
eat	ate	eaten	show	showed	shown/showed
			shut	shut	shut
fall	fell	fallen	sing	sang	sung
feel	felt	felt	sit	sat	sat
find	found	found	sleep	slept	slept
fly	flew	flown	speak	spoke	spoken
forget	forgot	forgotten	spend	spent	spent
			stand	stood	stood
get	got	got	steal	stole	stolen
give	gave	given	sweep	swept	swept
go	went	gone/been	swim	swam	swum
grow	grew	grown			
			take	took	taken
have	had	had	teach	taught	taught
hear	heard	heard	tell	told	told
hide	hid	hidden	think	thought	thought
hit	hit	hit	throw	threw	thrown
hold	held	held			
hurt	hurt	hurt	understand	understood	understood
keep	kept	kept	wake	woke	woken
know	knew	known	wear	wore	worn
			win	won	won
			write	wrote	written

Appendix 4: Adjectives and adverbs

1 Comparatives and superlatives

1 We form the comparative and superlative of short adjectives (adjectives with one syllable*) with -**er** and -**est**:

cheap	→	cheap**er**, the cheap**est**
long	→	long**er**, the long**est**
warm	→	warm**er**, the warm**est**

2 If the adjective ends in -**e**, we add **r** and **st**:

late	→	late**r**, the late**st**
nice	→	nice**r**, the nice**st**

3 When a one-syllable adjective ends with one vowel* and one consonant* (e.g. *big*), we double the final consonant:

big	→	big**ger**, the big**gest**
hot	→	hot**ter**, the hot**test**
wet	→	wet**ter**, the wet**test**

Note that we do not double **w**:

few	→	few**er**, the few**est**

4 We put **more/the most** before adjectives of two or more syllables:

beautiful	→	**more** beautiful, **the most** beautiful
expensive	→	**more** expensive, **the most** expensive
polluted	→	**more** polluted, **the most** polluted

5 When an adjective ends in a consonant + -**y** (e.g. *happy*), the **y** changes to -**ier** or -**iest**:

dirty	→	dirt**ier**, the dirt**iest**
easy	→	eas**ier**, the eas**iest**
happy	→	happ**ier**, the happ**iest**
lucky	→	luck**ier**, the luck**iest**

6 Some adjectives have irregular comparative and superlative forms:

good	→	better, the best
bad	→	worse, the worst
far	→	farther, the farthest
little	→	less, the least

7 Be careful to use **fewer** with plural nouns (e.g. *shops*), and **less** with uncountable nouns (e.g. *money*):

> There are **fewer shops** in the centre of town than there used to be.
> John earns **less money** than Mary.

2 Adverbs

1 We form most adjectives by adding **ly** to an adjective:

polite	→	polite**ly**	quick	→	quick**ly**
slow	→	slow**ly**			

2 When an adjective ends in a consonant + -**y**, the **y** changes to -**ily**:

easy	→	eas**ily**	happy	→	happ**ily**
lucky	→	luck**ily**			

3 When an adjective ends in a consonant + -**le**, the **e** changes to -**y**:

probable	→	probabl**y**
remarkable	→	remarkabl**y**

4 Some adverbs are irregular:

good	→	well	fast	→	fast
hard	→	hard	late	→	late

---

* Consonants: b c d f g h j k l m n p q r s t v w x y z
Vowels: a e i o u
Syllables: |*hit*| = 1 syllable, |*vi*|*sit*| = 2 syllables, |*re*|*mem*|*ber*| = 3 syllables

Appendix 4 Adjective
and adverb

Exit test

Choose the right answer (a, b, c, d) and write a, b, c, or d, as in the example.

▶ Russia is the .....*a*..... country in the world.
   a largest   b larger   c most large   d most largest

Tenses: present

1 My sister and I .... from Scotland.
    a we are   b am   c are   d is
2 How old .... ?
    a are you   b you are   c you have   d have you
3 They .... in London.
    a no live   b don't live   c live not   d doesn't live
4 Where .... Mary live?
    a does   b do   c are   d is
5 Where are Geoff and Anne? .... in the garden.
    a They're siting   b They sitting   c There sitting   d They're sitting
6 What .... , Sally?
    a you are   b are you   c do you   d are you doing
7 It's very cold today and ....
    a it's snowing   b it snows   c its snowing   d it snowing
8 .... close the window please.
    a No   b Not   c Don't   d You don't

Tenses: past

9 Where .... yesterday?
    a was you   b you were   c were you   d did you be
10 They .... last week.
    a didn't come   b came not   c don't came   d didn't came
11 What .... doing at nine o'clock yesterday evening?
    a Peter were   b Peter was   c did Peter   d was Peter
12 I didn't hear the phone because when it rang, I .... a shower.
    a had   b was having   c have had   d having
13 My cousins .... seen a kangaroo.
    a have never   b never have   c has never   d haven't never
14 Have you .... to Canada?
    a ever been   b ever gone   c been ever   d gone ever
15 I'm sorry. Mrs Johnson hasn't ....
    a arrived just   b already arrived   c arrived already   d arrived yet
16 My husband and I .... to Edinburgh in 2001.
    a have moved   b moved   c did moved   d has moved
17 I .... to London five times already this week.
    a went   b have gone   c have been   d was going

18 Margaret has .... here since February.
   a being worked   b working   c been working   d been worked
19 I'm a vegetarian. I .... meat since I was a child.
   a haven't eaten   b don't eat   c haven't been eating   d am not eating
20 When we arrived, the train .... the station.
   a already left   b had already left   c had left already   d has left already
21 When Carol was younger, she .... in a jazz band.
   a use to sing   b sang usually   c was singing   d used to sing

Tenses: future

22 What .... do tomorrow?
   a you are going to   b are you going   c you are going   d are you going to
23 Are you thirsty? .... make you a drink?
   a Will I   b Shall I   c Do I   d I'll
24 My cousins .... visit us next weekend.
   a will to   b going to   c are going to   d are going
25 I can't see you tomorrow. .... lunch with Paul.
   a I'm having   b I'll have   c I'm going have   d I will to have
26 We can start as soon as they ....
   a arrive   b are arriving   c will arrive   d are going to arrive
27 Can somebody come and help me? ~ Yes, ... you.
   a I'll help   b I'm helping   c I will to help   d I help

Sentences and questions

28 They bought ....
   a in the country a big old house   b a big old house in the country
   c an old big house in the country   d in the country an old big house
29 Joe was thirsty so I made ....
   a a cup of tea to him   b him a cup of tea
   c for him a cup of tea   d to him a cup of tea
30 Are you hungry? ~ ....
   a Yes, I am   b Yes, I'm   c No, I aren't   d No, I no
31 .... did you get to Brighton? By train?
   a When   b Where   c Why   d How
32 Do you know that girl? .... is her name?
   a How   b Which   c What   d Who
33 How .... will the journey take? Two hours or more?
   a often   b far   c much   d long
34 Julie .... her mother: very tall.
   a is like   b is liking   c likes   d like
35 How do you know? .... you?
   a Who did tell   b Who have told   c Who has told   d Who did told
36 Whose is that bike? ~ ....
   a It's Tom's   b It's Toms'   c Its Tom's   d Its Toms'
37 Marc lives in Paris, ...
   a isn't it?   b isn't he?   c don't he?   d doesn't he?

38 Did they go to Canada? ~ Yes, they ....
   a went   b did   c did go   d gone

39 Jack doesn't speak French and ....
   a Jill doesn't neither   b Jill neither   c neither Jill   d neither does Jill

Modal verbs

40 When Philip was at school, he .... speak French quite well.
   a was able   b could   c able to   d can

41 Excuse me. .... you help me?
   a Could   b May   c Shall   d Do

42 You .... buy a ticket before boarding the bus.
   a might   b must   c might to   d must to

43 .... go to the supermarket after work.
   a I've got to   b I've get to   c I was getting to   d I have got

44 It's a present so you .... pay anything.
   a don't get to   b haven't to   c mustn't to   d don't have to

45 Who's the woman in that car? ~ .... be Carol. She's in Germany.
   a It mustn't   b She mustn't   c It can't   d She can't

46 In my opinion, you .... smoke so much.
   a shouldn't to   b shouldn't   c needn't   d don't have to

47 If you have stomach pains, you .... to go to the doctor's.
   a had better   b should   c ought   d must

48 We've got enough blue paint. Your sister .... to buy any more.
   a don't need   b doesn't need   c needn't   d hasn't need

49 .... wear a uniform when you were at school?
   a Must you have worn   b Must you wear
   c Had you to wear   d Did you have to

Articles, nouns, pronouns, etc:

50 What's her job? ~ She's .... lecturer.
   a an university   b a university   c one university   d university

51 Are you a vegetarian? ~ Yes, I never eat ....
   a meat   b the meat   c some meat   d a meat

52 .... is my favourite art.
   a A music   b The music   c Music   d Some music

53 .... is your favourite – the White Horse or the Golden Hart?
   a Which one   b What one   c Which ones   d What ones

54 I'd like .... , please.
   a four loaves of bread and two boxes of tomatoes
   b four loafs of bread and two boxs of tomatoes
   c four loave of bread and two boxes of tomatos
   d four loaves of bread and two boxes of tomato

55 Look at .... cows in the field over there.
   a these   b that   c those   d this

56 Her eyes are blue and her .... dark.
   a hair are   b hair is   c hairs are   d hairs is

57 We don't need to buy .... milk.

    a a   **b** some   **c** any   **d** no

58 We saw Mary, but ....

    a him didn't see us **b** she didn't see we

    c her didn't see us **d** she didn't see us

59 How many cinemas .... near here?

    a are they   **b** is there   **c** are there   **d** is it

60 My bike is red but .... blue.

    a she's   **b** her is   **c** hers is   **d** her one is

61 Your children are very good. They always help .... a lot.

    a each other   **b** themselves   **c** them   **d** each the other

62 I want to check the meaning of these words. Can you .... ?

    a get the dictionary for me   **b** give to me the dictionary

    c get the dictionary to me   **d** give the dictionary for me

63 Have you got .... ?

    a many luggages   **b** many luggage   **c** much luggages   **d** much luggage

64 Have you got any money? ~ I've only got ....

    a little   **b** a little   **c** few   **d** a few

65 I don't know .... near here to have lunch.

    a anything   **b** something   **c** anywhere   **d** something

66 They've got two cars. One is a Rover and .... is a Mini.

    a the other   **b** another   **c** other   **d** one other

67 I didn't speak to all the people but I spoke to ....

    a most them   **b** most of it   **c** them most   **d** most of them

Adjectives and adverbs

68 Mrs Pearson had everything in a .... bag.

    a plastic green large   **b** large green plastic **c** green large plastic   **d** green plastic large

69 We thought the film was ....

    a very bored   **b** much boring   **c** very boring   **d** much bored

70 My birthday is the .... of May.

    a twenty-eighth   **b** twentyeth   **c** twenty-nineth   **d** twenty-forth

71 Paris isn't .... London.

    a big as   **b** as big as   **c** as big that   **d** so big that

72 Sara is only 15. She isn't .... drive a car.

    a enough old to   **b** enough old for   **c** old enough for   **d** old enough to

73 It was .... night that we didn't see the animals.

    a a so dark   **b** so a dark   **c** such a dark   **d** a such dark

74 In the photo Tom looks .... his friends.

    a happier that   **b** happier than   **c** more happy than   **d** more happy

75 Which is the .... the world?

    a longer river in   **b** longer river of   **c** longest river of   **d** longest river in

76 Jane drives carefully but her sister drives ....

    a fastly   **b** very fast   **c** more quick   **d** very quick

77 I take the bus but Tim .... to work.

    a hardly ever walks   **b** walks hardly ever **c** often walks   **d** walks often

78 Turn left at the garage then go .... until you get to the school.
    a ahead   b straight on   c on ahead   d on straight

79 The way she said that made me ....
    a extreme angrily   b angrily extreme   c extremely angry   d angry extremely

80 He doesn't talk much and he doesn't listen much ....
    a too   b neither   c either   d as well

81 After 25 minutes take the meat .... the oven.
    a out from   b out of   c from of   d from out

Prepositions

82 I think we can meet .... the bus stop.
    a on   b at   c in   d behind

83 The train has to go .... three tunnels.
    a across   b along   c through   d under

84 It happened .... Friday.
    a at lunch-time in   b at lunch-time on
    c in lunch-time on   d on lunch-time at

85 She described the thief .... a tall, bearded man.
    a like   b such as   c as   d as though

86 That student over there – the one ....
    a in the blonde hair b with the blonde hair
    c in blonde hair   d blonde haired

87 It was very late but .... last we reached the hotel.
    a in the   b at the   c in   d at

88 What time did they arrive .... the airport?
    a at   b in   c on   d to

89 She learnt French .... listening to tapes.
    a by   b for   c on   d with

90 The rooms were full .... old furniture.
    a of   b with   c from   d off

Verbs

91 Peter .... a car.
    a hasn't got   b hasn't   c haven't got   d doesn't have got

92 We're going to .... some shopping.
    a make   b get   c do   d have

93 The plane .... in bad weather.
    a pulled off   b put up   c got up   d took off

94 There was no truth to his story. He simply ....
    a made up it   b made it up   c drew it out   d drew out it

The passive

95 Fiat .... a group of Italian businessmen.
   a is started for   b is started by   c was started by   d was started for

96 Oh, no! My camera isn't here. It .... stolen!
   a has been   b is   c is being   d has

97 His hair is too long. He should .... cut.
   a let it be   b get it be   c make it   d have it

Infinitives and -ing forms

98 The film was very sad. It .... cry.
   a made us to   b made us   c let us   d let us to

99 The teacher .... go home early.
   a wanted that we   b made us to   c decided us to   d let us

100 When you've .... , I'll tell you what I think.
   a stopped talking   b stopped to talk
   c been stopping talking   d been stopped to talk

101 Would you .... to the cinema?
   a to like go   b like to go   c like going   d to like to going

102 I'm going to India next year. .... Kerala, Goa and Mumbai.
   a I'm going to plan visiting   b I plan visiting
   c I'm going to plan to visit   d I plan to visit

103 This is a machine .... boxes.
   a for make   b for to make   c for making   d to making

104 We invited .... come to the party.
   a them to   b to them   c that they   d that they

Conditionals

105 Tomorrow we can go for a picnic if the weather .... fine.
   a is being   b will be   c would be   d is

106 If I .... you, I'd go to the police.
   a would be   b should be   c were   d am

107 I wish I .... to bed earlier last night.
   a went   b had gone   c was going   d have gone

Reported speech

108 Your cousin .... she lived in a small flat.
   a said me   b said to me   c told   d told me

109 Jane had a lot of work and so she asked .... help her.
   a me to   b to me   c that I   d that I should

110 Do you know where .... ?
   a lives Joe   b do Joe lives   c does Joe live   d Joe lives

111 Mr and Mrs Simpson neither came .... sent a message.
   a or   b neither   c nor   d either

112 Take your umbrella .... it rains.
   a because   b because of   c for   d in case

113 His mother told him off ....
    a for laughing   b because laughing
    c for he laughed   d because of laughing
114 Most people go by train. The bus, ... , is cheaper and faster.
    a although   b despite   c while   d however
115 .... the fact that nobody thought he should do it, he did it.
    a However   b While   c In spite of   d Because
116 The team .... scored the most goals won the competition.
    a , which   b , that   c that   d which it
117 Do you know those boys .... are talking to Yvonne?
    a which   b that they   c who   d who's
118 We saw that woman .... was on TV.
    a the son of her   b whose son   c that the son   d that the son
119 I received your letter of 22 March, ... I'm very grateful.
    a which   b that   c for which   d to which
120 Philip went to see the film Robocop 4, ... had already seen three times.
    a which   b which he   c that   d that he

Index

The numbers in this index are unit numbers unless they have the letter 'p' for 'page.'

a 49–50, 54, Test F pp140–1
  or **an** 49
  or no article 50
  or **the** 49, 50
a few 61
a little 61
a lot of 61
  such a lot of 70
ability: **can, can't, could, couldn't** 39
above 78
abroad 75
across 78
adjectives 27, Test G pp168–9, p245
  + adjective 76
  adverb + adjective 76
  and adverbs 73
  as ... as 68
  comparative 71, p245
  -ed or **-ing** 66
  order 65
  possessive 57
  + preposition 84
  'size' 76
  superlative 72, p245
adverbs 27, 73–7, Test G pp168–9, p245
  + adjective 76
  and adjectives 73
  as ... as 68
  comparative 73
  -ly ending 73, p245
  of certainty 77
  of completeness 77
  of direction 75
  of emphasis 77
  of frequency 74
  of manner 77
  of place 75, 77
  of sequence 75
  of time 77
  position in sentence 77
  superlative 73
advice 45, 101
advise 101
after
  after that 75
  for the future 25

afterwards 75
all 64
almost 77
along 78
already 15, 19
also 77
although 106
always 74
am 1, 2
an 49–50, Test F pp140–1
and 103
another 63
answers, short 37, 43, Test D p84
any 54, Test F pp140–1
any more 60
anybody 62
anyone 62
anything 62
anywhere 62
apostrophe (') 35, 57
are 1, 2
arrive at/in 83
articles 49–50, Test F pp140–1
as 80
  as ... as 68
  reason 105
  the same as 80
  such as 80
as if 80
as soon as: for the future 25
as though 80
as usual 80
ask 101
at
  place 78
  speed 82
  time 79, 82
auxiliary verbs 27
away 75

be
  Past Simple 9
  Present Simple 1–2
  questions 2
  there + be 2, 56
be going to 21, Test C pp58–9
  or **will** 23, 26

because 104
because of 104
been to and gone to 14
before: for the future 25
behind 78
beside 78
best 73
better 73
between 78
both ... and 103
but 103
by
   by car/bike/bus 82
   by chance/accident/mistake 82
   + -ing 81
   by post/email/phone 82

can Test E pp106–7
   ability 39
   permission 40
   questions 40
   requests 40
cannot 39
can't
   ability 39
   impossibility 44
cardinal numbers 67
case: in case 104
certainly 77
certainty
   adverbs 77
   must 44
comparative Test G pp168–9
   adjectives 71, p245
   adverbs 73
   (not) as ... as 68
conditionals 97–9, Test J p224
could Test E pp106–7
   ability 39
   possibility 44
   questions 40
couldn't: ability 39
countable nouns 53

dates 55, 67
definitely 77
despite 106
did: in questions 29
direct objects 59
do 86
   in negative forms 3
   in the Present Simple 3, 4
   in question tags 36

in questions 4, 29, 30
   in short answers 43
does
   in negative forms 3
   in the Present Simple 3, 4
   in question tags 36
   in questions 4, 29, 30
   in short answers 43
don't have to 43
down 78
due to 105

each 63
each other 58
either 77, 103
   I'm not either 38
either ... or 103
else 62
enough 69
even 77
ever 13
   hardly ever 74
every 63, 74, 79
everybody 62
everyone 62
everything 62
everywhere 62
except (for) 82
extremely 76

fact: the fact that 105
fairly 76
fast 73
few 61
fewer p245
First Conditional 97
first(ly) 75
for
   for example/sale/ever 82
   purpose 95, 105
   reason 105
   and since 14, 17
forbid 101
forget 94
from
   place 78
   time 32, 79
front: in front of 78
future 26, Test C pp58–9
   be going to 21, 23, 26
   Present Continuous 24, 26
   when/before/after/until + Present Simple 25
   will 22, 23, 26

get 86
    get something done 91
go + -ing 93
going to *see* be going to
gone to and been to 14
got 85

had: in Past Perfect 19
had better 46, Test E pp106–7
had to do/go 42, 48
hard 73
hardly ever 74
have 85
    and have got 85
    + noun 86
    Present Continuous 6
    will have to 42
have got 85
have got to 42
have something done 91
have to 42, 43, Test E pp106–7
    don't have to 42
he 55, 58
her 55, 57, 58
here 75
hers 57
herself 58
him 55, 57, 58
himself 58
his 57
how 30, 33, Test D p85
How far? 32
How long? 17, 18, 32
How many? 18, 32, 60, Test F p141
How much? 18, 32, 60, Test F p141
How often? 32
How old? 32
however 106

I 55, 58
I am too 38
if: as if 80
I'm not either 38
imperative 8
impossibility 44
in 82
    clothing 81
    phrases 82
    place 78
    time 79
    transport 82
in case 104
in cash 82

in spite of 106
indirect objects 59
infinitive Test I p211
    to + infinitive 94
    with/without to 92
-ing forms Test I p 211, p243
    adjectives 66
    after a preposition 81
    after a verb 93, 94
    Past Continuous 11
    Present Continuous 5
    Present Perfect Continuous 17
    spelling 5, p243
instead of 82
into 78
is 1, 2
it 55, 56, 57, 58
its 57
itself 58

just
    = simply 77
    + past participle 15

last 79
least
    the least + adjective 72
    the least + adverb 73
left 75
less 73
let + someone + infinitive 92
like 80
    + -ing 93
    What ... like? 33
    would like 93, 94
little 61
look at/for 83
lots of 61 *see also* a lot of

make 86
    make + someone + infinitive 92
many 60
    as many ... as 68
    so many 70
may Test E pp106–7
    permission 40
    possibility 44
    questions 40
    requests 40
me 55, 57, 58
might 44
mine 57
modal verbs 39–48, Test E pp106–7

more
    comparative adjective 71, p245
    more + adverb 73
    quantity 60
most 64
    the most + adverb 73
    superlative adjective 72, p245
much 60
    as much ... as 68
    so much 70
must Test E pp106–7
    certainty 44
    for the future 41
    necessity 41, 43
    recommendation 41
mustn't 41, 43
my 57
myself 58

nearly 77
necessity 41, 43
need 47, Test E pp106–7
needn't 47
needn't have 47
negative forms 1, 3
neither 103
neither ... nor 103
Neither am I 38, Test D p85
never 13, 19, 74
next
    sequence 75
    time 79
next to 78
no 54
no one 62
nobody 62
none 64
normally 74
not ... any 54
nothing 62
nouns 27, Test F pp140–1
    countable 53
    + noun 76
    plural 51, Test F pp140–1, p242
    uncountable 32, 53, p242
nowhere 62
numbers 67

object pronouns 55, 57, 58, Test F p141
off 78
often 74

on
    on business/holiday/a trip 82
    place 78, 82
    time 79
    transport 82
    on TV/the radio/the internet 82
once a ... 74
one 51, Test F pp140–1
    one + singular noun/verb 63
    one of the/possessive + plural 63
    and **ones** 51
ones 51
only 77
onto 78
opinion 45
opposite 78
or 103
orders 101
ordinal numbers 67
other
    each other 58
    the/possessive + **other** + singular 63
    the/possessive/quantifier + **other** + plural
       noun 63
others 63
    the others 63
ought to 46, Test E pp106–7
our 57
ours 57
ourselves 58
out 75
out of 78
outside 78
owing to 105

passive sentences 89–90, Test I pp210–11
passive tenses 90
past 78
Past Continuous 11, Test B pp44–5
    or Past Simple 12
    passive 90
past participles 13, p243
    irregular verbs p244
    in passive 90
Past Perfect 19, Test B pp44–5
    passive 90
Past Simple 9–10, Test B pp44–5, p243
    be 9
    irregular verbs p244
    or Past Continuous 12
    or Present Perfect 16
    passive 89, 90
    and **used to** 20

pay 83
permission 40
persuade 101
phrasal verbs 87–8 see also prepositional verbs
place
    adverbs 75, 77
    prepositions 78, 82
    relative clauses 108
possessive forms Test F p141
    adjectives 57
    pronouns 57
    's, s' 35, 57
possibility 44, 103
prepositional verbs 83
prepositions 27, Test H pp184–5
    after adjectives 84
    after verbs 83
    + -ing 81
    of movement 78
    of place 78, 82
    of time 32, 79, 82
    phrases 82
Present Continuous 5–6, Test A p19
    for the future 24, 26, Test C pp58–9
    -ing form 5
    or Present Simple 7
    passive 90
    questions 6
Present Perfect 13–16, Test B pp44–5
    for the future 25
    or Past Simple 16
    or Present Perfect Continuous 18
    passive 90
Present Perfect Continuous 17, Test B pp44–5
    or Present Perfect Simple 18
Present Simple 1–4, Test A pp18–19
    be 1–2
    for the future 25, 26
    negative 3
    or Present Continuous 7
    passive 89, 90
    questions 2, 4
    regular verbs p243
present tense: when, before, after, until, etc. 25
probably 77
pronouns 27, Test F pp140–1
    object 55, 57, 58
    possessive 57
    reflexive 58
    subject 55, 58
purpose 95, 104, 105

question tags 36, Test D p85
questions 29–33, Test D pp84–5
    be 2
    Can? May? Could? 40
    How long/far/often ...? 32
    Present Continuous 6
    Present Simple 2, 4
    reported questions 102
    short answers 37, 43
    What ... like? 33
    where, when, why, how 30
    who, what, which 31
    'yes/no' questions 29
quite 76

rarely 74
rather 76
really 76
reason 104, 105
reason 108
reflexive pronouns 58, Test F p141
relative clauses 107–9
remember 94
remind 101
reported speech 19, 100–2, Test J p225
    advice 101
    orders 101
    questions 102
    requests 101
    say and tell 100, 101
requests 40, 101
result 103, 104
right 75

's, s' 35, 57
same: the same as 80
say 100
Second Conditional 98
shall 22, Test C pp58–9
she 55, 58
short answers, 37, 43, Test D pp84
short forms: be 1
should 45, 46, Test E pp106–7
    do you think I should ...? 45
    I think we should 45
    should I? 45
should have done/gone 48
shouldn't 45
since
    and for 14, 17
    reason 105
so

or **such** 70
result 103, 104
so am I 38, Test D p85
so many 70
so much 70
so that 104
some 54, 64, Test F pp140–1
some more 60
somebody 62
someone 62
something 62
sometimes 74
somewhere 62, 108
soon: as soon as 25
straight on 75
subject pronouns 55, 58
such a lot of 70
such a/an 70
such as 80
such or so 70
superlative Test G pp168–9
   adjectives 72, p245
   adverbs 73

talk to/about 83
tell 100, 101
tests
   adjectives Test G pp168–9
   adverbs Test G pp168–9
   articles Test F pp140–1
   building sentences Test K pp240–1
   conditionals Test J p224
   infinitives Test I p 211
   -ing forms Test I p 211
   modal verbs Test E pp106–7
   nouns Test F pp140–1
   passive Test I pp210–11
   prepositions Test H pp184–5
   pronouns Test F pp140–1
   questions and answers Test D pp84–5
   reported speech Test J p225
   sentences Test D pp84–5
   tenses – future Test C pp58–9
   tenses – past Test B pp44–5
   tenses – present Test A pp18–19
   verbs Test I pp210–11
that 52
   relative pronoun 107, 108
   in reported speech 100
   so that 104
the Test F pp140–1
   or a/an 49
   or no article 50

their 57
theirs 57
them 55, 57, 58
themselves 58
then 75
there 75
there is/are 2, 56, Test F p141
these 52
they 55, 56, 58
think: Present Continuous 6
Third Conditional 99
this 52, 79
those 52
though 106
   as though 80
through 78
time
   adverbial phrases 77
   it 55, 56
   prepositions 32, 79, 82
to
   with infinitive 92, 94
   movement 78
too 69, 77
try 94
twice a ... 74

uncountable nouns 32, 53, p242
under 78
until 25, 32
up 78
us 55, 57, 58
used to 20
usual: as usual 80
usually 74

verbs 27, Test I pp210–11
   + **to** 94
   auxiliary verbs 27
   + -ing 93, 94
   irregular verbs p244
   + object (+ **to**) + infinitive 96
   phrasal verbs 87–8
   + preposition 83
   regular verbs p243
very 76

warn 101
was 9
way 108
we 55, 58
weather 55, 56
well 73

were 9
what
  what 31
  what: subject and object 34
What ... like? 33
when
  for the future 25
  in past tenses 11, 19
  relative adverb 108
  when 30
where
  relative adverb 108
  where 30
which
  relative pronoun 107, 108, 109
  which 31
Which one/ones? 51
while
  contrast 106
  in past tenses 11
who
  relative pronoun 107, 108, 109
  who 31
  who: subject and object 34
whom 108, 109
who's 35
whose 107, 109
Whose is this? 35

why
  after reason 108
  why 30
will 22, Test C pp58–9
  or be going to 23, 26
will be able to 39, Test E pp106–7
with 81
without + -ing 81
word order
  adjectives 65
  adverbs 77
  subject, verb, object 28
worst 73
would like 93, 94
Would you? 40

'yes/no' questions 29
yet 15
you 55, 57, 58
your 57
yours 57
yourself 58
yourselves 58

Zero Conditional 97